Walking Camino de Santiago

Bethan Davies
& Ben Cole

Pili Pala Press
www.pilipalapress.com

Walking the Camino de Santiago

2nd edition

Published by Pili Pala Press, 2934 Woodland Drive, Vancouver, BC V5N 3R1 Canada

www.pilipalapress.com

ISBN-10: 0-9731698-2-6
ISBN-13: 978-0-9731698-2-9

© Bethan Davies and Ben Cole, 2006

Editor: Lucy Kenward

cover photo: statue of pilgrim, Alto de San Roque, Galicia
back cover photo: pilgrim crossing, Arzúa, Galicia

Printed in Canada on 100% post-consumer recycled paper

Library and Archives Canada Cataloguing in Publication

Davies, Bethan, 1970-
    Walking the Camino de Santiago / Bethan Davies & Ben Cole.

Includes index.
Previous edition published 2003.
ISBN 0-9731698-2-6

    1. Christian pilgrims and pilgrimages--Spain--Santiago de Compostela--Guidebooks. 2. Santiago de Compostela (Spain)--Guidebooks. 3. Spain, Northern--Guidebooks. 4. Hiking--Spain, Northern--Guidebooks. I. Cole, Ben, 1970- II. Title.

DP285.D38 2006   914.6'11   C2005-906653-9

About the Authors

Bethan Davies has been dreaming of Spain ever since her first glass of Rioja, and is now marked out as a rabid supporter of the Spanish national football team (especially Raúl) in bars along the camino. A librarian and former editor, she co-authored Pili Pala Press' *Walking in Portugal* and *Walking the Via de la Plata* with Ben Cole.

Ben Cole has worked in travel bookshops for longer than he cares to remember, after gaining a degree in archaeology and ancient history. Ben fell in love with Iberia in 1993 while exploring the mountains of Portugal, and a chance encounter with the camino a few years later led to a fascination with the *camino francés*. He finds it hard to start the day without a *café solo, grande*.

Walking the Camino de Santiago

Thank you

Thanks to everyone who helped put *Walking the Camino de Santiago* together.

Our fellow pilgrims, especially Marie, Katy, Dwight, Barbara, Walter, Norbert, Regina, Luis, Linda, Carlos, Marisa, Chisaki, Carlo, Maria, Robert, Esther and Ursula. The *hospitaleros* along the camino who staff the *albergues* with grace and patience, and the people along the camino for incredible generosity to strangers.

Bar Fonda, still the best bar in the world. And we're still not telling you where it is.

Lucy Kenward for editing and Daphne Hnatiuk for proofreading and fact-checking.

Ed Luciano for mighty behind-the-scenes contributions.

Tony McCurdy for encouragement, enthusiasm and generous leave-granting.

To our parents, for continued love, support and storage.

But most of all to Albert Idris Xaxo, who learnt to walk in Castrojeriz.

About Pili Pala Press

Pili Pala Press was founded in 1993 to publish walking guides to the Iberian Peninsula. Pili Pala, for the uninitiated, is Welsh for butterfly (the clue's in the logo). We could say that we chose the name to reflect our love of nature and our restless desire for travel, but really we just like the way it sounds. We donate 4% of the cover price of each book to environmental organizations in Iberia. For updates, photos and more on the camino, see our web site at www.pilipalapress.com. Look out for *Walking the Via de la Plata*, our comprehensive guide to the alternative camino from Sevilla to Santiago, and *Walking in Portugal*, our invaluable guide to this forgotten walking destination.

Trails become overgrown, quiet lanes become main roads, and *albergues* open up and close down. Drop us a line if you find something new or different, and check out our web site at www.pilipalapress.com for updates.

Contents

Meseta · 86

Cordillera Cantábrica · · · · · · · · · · · · · · · · · · · 116

Galicia · 136

Reference · 167

Index · 174

Keys · 182

How This Guide Works

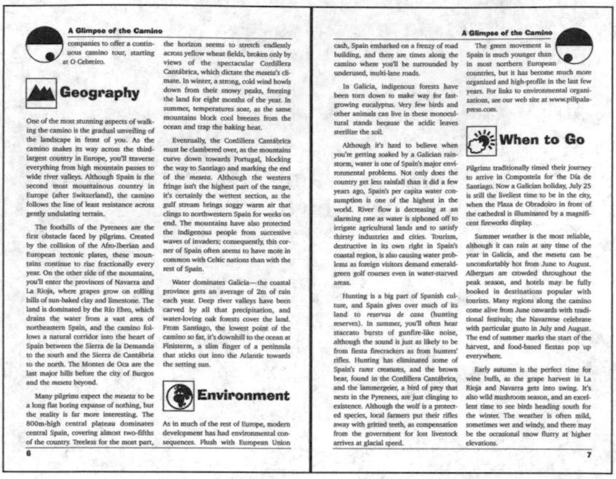

A Glimpse of the Camino

Geography

One of the most stunning aspects of walking the camino is the gradual unveiling of the landscape in front of you. As the camino makes its way across the third-largest country in Europe, you'll traverse everything from high mountain passes to wide river valleys. Although Spain is the second most mountainous country in Europe (after Switzerland), the camino follows the line of least resistance across gently undulating terrain.

The foothills of the Pyrenees are the first obstacle faced by pilgrims. Created by the collision of the Afro-Iberian and European tectonic plates, these mountains continue to rise fractionally every year. On the other side of the mountains, you'll enter the provinces of Navarra and La Rioja, where grapes grow on rolling hills of sun-baked clay and limestone. The land is dominated by the Rio Ebro, which drains the water from a vast area of northeastern Spain, and the camino follows a natural corridor into the heart of Spain between the Sierra de la Demanda to the south and the Sierra de Cantabria to the north. The Montes de Oca are the last major hills before the city of Burgos and the meseta beyond.

Many pilgrims expect the meseta to be a long flat boring expanse of nothing, but the reality is far more interesting. The 800m-high central plateau dominates central Spain, covering almost two-fifths of the country. Treeless for the most part,

the horizon seems to stretch endlessly across yellow wheat fields, broken only by views of the spectacular Cordillera Cantábrica, which dictate the meseta's climate. In winter, a strong, cold wind howls down from their snowy peaks, freezing the land for eight months of the year. In summer, temperatures soar, as the same mountains block cool breezes from the ocean and trap the baking heat.

Eventually, the Cordillera Cantábrica must be clambered over, as the mountains curve down towards Portugal, blocking the way to Santiago and marking the end of the meseta. Although the western fringe isn't the highest part of the range, it's certainly the wettest section, as the gulf stream brings soggy warm air that clings to northwestern Spain for weeks on end. The mountains have also protected the indigenous people from successive waves of invaders; consequently, this corner of Spain often seems to have more in common with Celtic nations than with the rest of Spain.

Water dominates Galicia—the coastal province gets an average of 2m of rain each year. Deep river valleys have been carved by all that precipitation, and water-loving oak forests cover the land. From Santiago, the lowest point of the camino so far, it's downhill to the ocean at Finisterre, a thin finger of a peninsula that sticks out into the Atlantic towards the setting sun.

Environment

As in much of the rest of Europe, modern development has had environmental consequences. Flush with European Union

cash, Spain embarked on a frenzy of road building, and there are times along the camino where you'll be surrounded by underused, multi-lane roads.

In Galicia, indigenous forests have been torn down to make way for fast-growing eucalyptus. Very few birds and other animals can live in these monocultural stands because the acidic leaves sterilise the soil.

Although it's hard to believe when you're getting soaked by a Galician rainstorm, water is one of Spain's major environmental problems. Not only does the country get less rainfall than it did a few years ago, Spain's per capita water consumption is one of the highest in the world. River flow is decreasing at an alarming rate as water is siphoned off to irrigate agricultural lands and to satisfy thirsty industries and cities. Tourism, destructive in its own right in Spain's coastal region, is also causing water problems as foreign visitors demand emerald-green golf courses even in water-starved areas.

Hunting is a big part of Spanish culture, and Spain gives over much of its land to reservas de caza (hunting reserves). In summer, you'll often hear staccato bursts of gunfire-like noise, although the sound is just as likely to be from fiesta firecrackers as from hunters' rifles. Hunting has eliminated some of Spain's rarer creatures, and the brown bear, found in the Cordillera Cantábrica and the lammergeier, a bird of prey that nests in the Pyrenees, are just clinging to existence. Although the wolf is a protected species, local farmers put their rifles away with gritted teeth, as compensation from the government for lost livestock arrives at glacial speed.

A Glimpse of the Camino

The green movement in Spain is much younger than in most northern European countries, but it has become much more organised and high-profile in the last few years. For links to environmental organisations, see our web site at www.pilipala-press.com.

When to Go

Pilgrims traditionally timed their journey to arrive in Compostela for the Día de Santiago. Now a Galician holiday, July 25 is still the liveliest time to be in the city, when the Plaza de Obradoiro in front of the cathedral is the scene of a magnificent fireworks display.

Summer weather is the most reliable, although it can rain at any time of the year in Galicia, and the meseta can be uncomfortably hot from June to August. Albergues are crowded throughout the peak season, and hotels may be fully booked in destinations popular with tourists. Many regions along the camino come alive from June onwards with traditional festivals; the Navarrese celebrate with particular gusto in July and August. The end of summer marks the start of the harvest, and food-based fiestas pop up everywhere.

Early autumn is the perfect time for wine buffs, as the grape harvest in La Rioja and Navarra gets into swing. It's also wild mushroom season, and an excellent time to see birds heading south for the winter. The weather is often mild, sometimes wet and windy, and there may be the occasional snow flurry at higher elevations.

A Glimpse of the Camino (page 2)

Background information about the camino, walking, geography, food & drink, history and the arts.

A Glimpse of the Camino

English name	Latin name	Spanish name
Iberian wall lizard	*Podarcis hispanica*	*Lagartija ibérica*

Length 15cm
Description Flat head, long tail, upper parts grey to brown
Habitat Dry, stony places, especially walls and ruins
Diet Small insects and worms
Viewing tips Look and listen for them scuttling away as you approach
Did you know? Lays eggs in holes; lives up to 15 years

Green lizard	*Lacerta viridis*	*Lagarto verde*

Length 40cm
Description Males vivid green with tiny black dots; sky blue throat during mating. Females duller and brownish
Habitat Dry, sunny locations with shrubs, especially near walls and along roads
Diet Insects and fruit
Did you know? When threatened opens mouth and bites

White stork	*Ciconia ciconia*	*Cigüeña común*

Description 100cm, long bill and legs, white with black flight feathers, red bill and legs
Habitat Marshes, grassy plains
Voice Hisses and claps bill
Diet Fish, insects
Viewing tips Flies at high altitude, neck straight ahead
Did you know? Nests on buildings and churches along the camino, especially in Navarra, La Rioja and the meseta

Crested lark	*Galerida cristata*	*Cogujada común*

Description 17cm, noticeable crest, stubby tail, sandy colour with white belly
Habitat Flat open land
Voice Klee-tirooo weeooo
Diet Seeds, insects
Viewing tips Common alongside open tracks and on agricultural land
Did you know? Nests on ground; never seen in a flock

English name	Latin name	Spanish name
Bee-eater	*Merops apiaster*	*Abejaruco común*

Description 30cm, bright blue belly, yellow throat and shoulders, black eyebrow
Habitat Open scrubland with some trees
Voice Prruip prruip prruup
Diet Insects
Viewing tips Sociable, likes to perch & watch the world go by. Good flier, with sudden acceleration and graceful glides
Did you know? Breeds in big groups in holes in the ground

Hoopoe	*Upupa epops*	*Abubilla*

Description 30cm, crest on head, pinkish body, barred white and black wings, long bill
Habitat Farmland, open woodland
Voice Pooo pooo pooo
Diet Insects
Viewing tips Undulating flight as it opens & closes wings
Did you know? One of our favourite birds. Nests in ruins and hollows of old trees

Black woodpecker	*Dryocopus martius*	*Pito negro*

Description 45cm, almost all black, red crown, yellow eyes
Habitat Old coniferous and beech forests
Voice Music laugh: kwick-wick-wick-wick
Diet Ants and wood-boring beetle larvae, tree sap
Viewing tips Found in mature forests, listen for call and loud drumming
Did you know? Three separate, isolated populations in Spain

White-backed woodpecker	*Dendrocopos leucotus*	*Pico dorsiblanco*

Description 25cm, white lower back, white bands across wings, pink under tail
Habitat Deciduous forest with lots of rotting logs
Voice tchick
Diet Insects, nuts and seeds
Viewing tips Rare, mainly south-facing Pyrenean slopes
Did you know? Largest spotted woodpecker in Europe

Flora (page 15) & Fauna (page 16)

English, Spanish and Latin names of birds, mammals, reptiles, amphibians and trees. Includes detailed identification tips, quirky facts and illustrations.

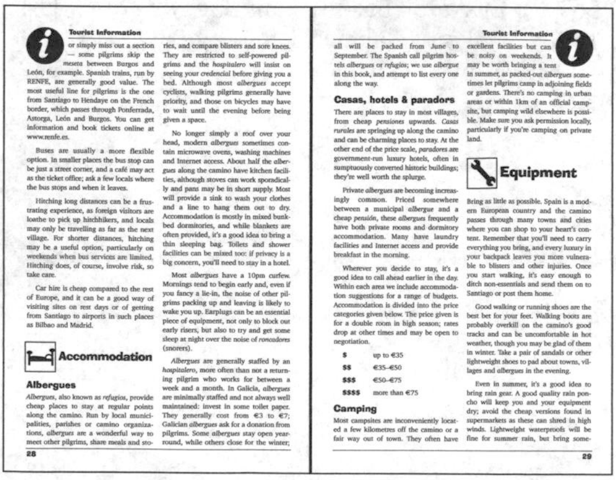

Tourist Information

... or simply miss out a section — some pilgrims skip the meseta between Burgos and León, for example. Spanish trains, run by RENFE, are generally good value. The most useful line for pilgrims is the one from Santiago to Hendaye on the French border, which passes through Ponferrada, Astorga, León and Burgos. You can get information and book tickets online at www.renfe.es.

Buses are usually a more flexible option. In smaller places the bus stop can be just a street corner, and a café may act as the ticket office; ask a local who knows the bus stops and when it leaves.

Hitching long distances can be a frustrating experience, as foreign visitors are loathe to pick up hitchhikers, and locals may only be travelling as far as the next village. For shorter distances, hitching may be a useful option, particularly on weekends when bus services are limited. Hitching does, of course, involve risk, so take care.

Car hire is cheap compared to the rest of Europe, and it can be a good way of visiting sites on rest days or of getting from Santiago to airports in such places as Bilbao and Madrid.

Accommodation

Albergues

Albergues, also known as refugios, provide cheap places to stay at regular points along the camino. Run by local municipalities, parishes or camino organisations, albergues are a wonderful way to meet other pilgrims, share meals and routes, and compare blisters and sore knees. They are restricted to self-powered pilgrims and the hospitalero will insist on seeing your credencial before giving you a bed. Although most albergues accept cyclists, walking pilgrims generally have priority, and those on bicycles may have to wait until the evening before being given a space.

No longer simply a roof over your head, modern albergues sometimes contain microwave ovens, washing machines and Internet access. About half the albergues along the camino have kitchen facilities, although stoves can work sporadically and pans may be in short supply. Most will provide a sink to wash your clothes and a line to hang them out to dry. Accommodation is mostly in mixed bunk-bed dormitories, and while blankets are often provided, it's a good idea to bring a thin sleeping bag. Toilets and shower facilities can be mixed too: if privacy is a big concern, you'll need to stay in a hotel.

Most albergues have a 10pm curfew. Mornings tend to begin early and, even if you fancy a lie-in, the noise of other pilgrims packing up and leaving is likely to wake you up. Earplugs can be an essential piece of equipment, not only to block out early risers, but also to try and get some sleep at night over the noise of roncadores (snorers).

Albergues are generally staffed by an hospitalero, more often than not a returning pilgrim who works for between a week and a month. In Galicia, albergues are minimally staffed and not always well maintained: invest in some toilet paper. They generally cost from €3 to €7; Galician albergues ask for a donation from pilgrims. Some albergues stay open year-round, while others close for the winter.

all will be packed from June to September. The Spanish call pilgrim hostels albergues or refugios; we use albergue in this book, and attempt to list every one along the way.

Casas, hoteles & paradors

There are places to stay in most villages, from cheap pensions upwards. Casas rurales are springing up along the camino and can be charming places to stay. At the other end of the price scale, paradors are government-run luxury hotels, often in sumptuously converted historic buildings; they're well worth the splurge.

Private albergues are becoming increasingly common. Priced somewhere between a municipal albergue and a cheap pensión, these albergues frequently have both private rooms and dormitory accommodation. Many have laundry facilities and Internet access and provide breakfast in the morning.

Wherever you decide to stay, it's a good idea to call ahead earlier in the day. Within each area we include accommodation suggestions for a range of budgets. Accommodation is divided into the price categories given below. The prices given are for a double room in high season; rooms drop at other times and may be open to negotiation.

$	up to €35
$$	€35-€50
$$$	€50-€75
$$$$	more than €75

Camping

Most campsites are inconveniently located a few kilometres off the camino or a fair way out of town. They often have

excellent facilities but can be noisy on weekends. It may be worth bringing a tent in summer, as packed-out albergues sometimes turn pilgrims away. Some turn campers away from the gardens. There's no camping in urban areas or within 1km of an official campsite, but camping wild elsewhere is possible. Make sure you ask permission locally, particularly if you're camping on private land.

Equipment

Bring as little as possible. Spain is a modern European country and the camino passes through many towns and cities where you can shop to your heart's content. Remember that you'll need to carry everything you bring, and every luxury in your backpack leaves you more vulnerable to blisters and other injuries. Once you start walking, it's easy enough to ditch non-essentials and send them on to Santiago or post them home.

Good walking or running shoes are the best bet for your feet. Walking boots are probably overkill on the camino's good tracks and can be uncomfortable in hot weather, though you may be glad of them in winter. Take a pair of sandals or other lightweight shoes to pad about town, village and albergue in the evening.

Even in summer, it's a good idea to bring rain gear. A good quality rain poncho will keep you and your equipment dry; avoid the cheap nonbranded dry; avoid the cheap nonbranded type sold in supermarkets as these can shred in high winds. Lightweight waterproofs will be fine for summer rain, but bring some

Tourist Information (page 26)

Practical information to ease your pilgrimage. What to do before you leave, what to bring, how to get there, where to stay, how much money you'll spend and what to do if things go wrong.

Regional Chapters

regional map →

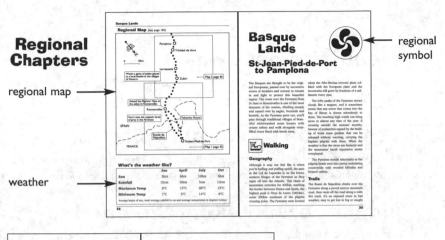

→ regional symbol

weather

Regional Information

regional flora & fauna, people & culture, food & drink and tourist information

Walk Description

camino sketch map includes distances & at-a-glance symbols

camino profile chart

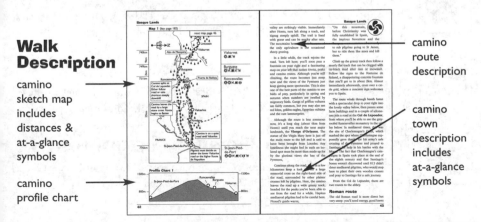

← camino route description

← camino town description includes at-a-glance symbols

Best of the Camino

most magical drink

Jesús Jato's *queimada* ritual at the Ave Fénix *albergue* in Villafranca del Bierzo (page 129), where potent *orujo* is set on fire amidst chants and spells.

best place to eat octopus

At Pulpería Ezequiel in Melide (page 150) you'll be served paprika-spiced *pulpo* (octopus) on a wooden platter, washed down with cloudy Ribeiro wine.

oldest person along the camino

Archaeologists at Atapuerca (page 84) discovered an 800,000-year-old skeleton, said to be *homo antecessor*, an early ancestor of *homo sapiens*.

best place for a splurge

Save your euros for León (page 109), where you can stay at the Parador San Marcos, one of the world's finest hotels, and graze on *tapas* until the small hours.

best place to see birds of prey

The Pyrenees (page 36) are home to golden eagles, short-toed eagles, griffon vultures and black vultures. If you're lucky, you may catch a glimpse of a lammergeier.

most underrated city

Burgos (page 91) is seen by the rest of Spain as dull and grey, but it's a lively city that's also a UNESCO World Heritage Site with don't-miss monuments.

most spectacular mass

At the pilgrims' mass in Santiago's cathedral (page 157), the *botafumeiro*, a huge incense burner, is swung across the transept in a huge, head-skimming arc.

best place to listen to bagpipes

Sitting next to a roaring fire in foggy O Cebreiro (page 133), where many of the bars erupt in impromptu sessions of traditional *gallego* music.

best place to get your feet wet

End the camino in feet-soothing style at the sea in Finisterre (page 166), where you can pick up a scallop shell and visit the end of the world.

oddest-looking bird

On the *meseta*, listen for the pooo-pooo-pooo call of the hoopoe (page 21), and look for its distinctive coral and black crest.

most eerie landscape

The ruined houses of Foncebadón (page 124), a village springing back to life thanks to the camino, are at their spookiest in the area's persistent mists.

best place to be like Hemingway

Ernest Hemingway's favourite weekend retreat was at Burguete (page 45), where he'd stay at the Hostal Burguete and fish for trout in the Río Urrobi.

most spectacular use of glass

León cathedral's acres of stained-glass windows (page 109), a riot of blues and reds and greens.

most topsy-turvy dinner

A long, languid *cocido Maragato* (page 119), where the meat-laden first course is followed by vegetables and then soup. It's enough to feed the hungriest pilgrim.

best mediaeval flashback

Set in mountainous isolation, the atmospheric *albergue* at Manjarín (page 124) lacks beds and electricity, and you'll sleep in the same building as the local cows.

most essential equipment

Don't go anywhere without your *credencial* (page 27), the pilgrims' passport that lets you stay in *albergues* along the camino.

best source of up-to-date information on the camino

See our web site at www.pilipalapress.com for photos, updates and links.

Map of the Camino

(key page 182)

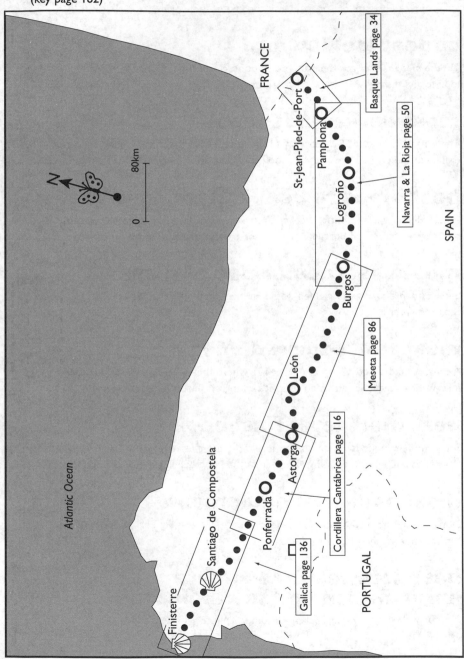

N

0 80km

FRANCE

SPAIN

PORTUGAL

Atlantic Ocean

Finisterre

Santiago de Compostela

Ponferrada

Astorga

León

Burgos

Logroño

Pamplona

St-Jean-Pied-de-Port

Basque Lands page 34

Navarra & La Rioja page 50

Meseta page 86

Cordillera Cantábrica page 116

Galicia page 136

x

An Introduction to the Camino

The Camino de Santiago (the Way of St James) is a glorious amble across the north of Spain, following an ancient pilgrimage route west to the magnificent cathedral at Santiago de Compostela. Tenth-century pilgrims braved bandits and wolves in their quest to revere the bones of St James, entombed in a silver casket in the cathedral. Ancient star-gazing Celts went this way too, heading west towards the setting sun and the solar temple of Ara Solis at Finis Terrae, the end of the earth.

Today, pilgrims walk to Santiago and Finisterre for many different reasons. For some, making a pilgrimage to the Holy City is a lifelong dream borne out of religious faith. Others seek a break from daily routines or want to get back to a simpler way of living, and some want to immerse themselves in Spanish history and culture. You needn't be a hard-core hiker to get to Santiago, as the trails are well maintained and ubiquitous yellow arrows make them easy to follow, and the journey is made easier and more sociable by a centuries-old infrastructure of *albergues* (pilgrim hostels).

This guide leads you step-by-step along the *camino francés*, from St-Jean-Pied-de-Port in the foothills of the French Pyrenees to Santiago de Compostela and on to Finisterre. On the way, you'll pass through a multitude of Spains. You'll see gorgeous Romanesque churches decorated with grotesque gargoyles and elaborate frescoes, ethereal Gothic cathedrals with airy spires and vast interiors, and tiny *ermitas* (hermitages) tucked into cliff faces. We'll steer you towards colourful, riotous festivals, where you can dance to Galician bagpipes or watch crazy, traditional Basque sports like hoe-hurling. We'll help you choose a great bottle of Rioja, order a cheap and hearty three-course dinner, and try regional specialities from white asparagus to spicy octopus. There's spectacular wildlife, too, from wolves and bears that roam northern Spain's mountain ranges, to peculiar, plain-dwelling birds such as great bustards and hoopoes. And we'll smooth your journey with practical information, from accommodation options to useful phrases in *Castellano* (Spanish) and a smattering of *Galega* (Galician) and *Euskara* (Basque).

A Glimpse of the Camino

 **El Camino**

The story of Santiago

Just how Santiago ended up in a remote northwestern corner of Iberia is a strange and marvellous tale.

Santiago, or St James as he's known in English, was one of Jesus' apostles, and after the Crucifixion, he left Judea for Spain to spread the Gospel. Though he preached as far north as Galicia, he didn't have much luck with the native peoples, and attracted a mere seven converts before turning towards home.

While there's no biblical basis for Santiago's visit to Spain, it is clear that Herod Agrippa had him beheaded in AD44 in Jerusalem, making him the first apostle to be martyred. Santiago's friends managed to sneak his body out from under Herod's nose, and put him on a stone boat headed for northwest Spain without oars, sails or crew. After a week-long journey, the body arrived in Padrón on the Galician coast, where his disciples were waiting. They buried Santiago 20km inland in Compostela, after the local queen witnessed a series of miracles and converted to Christianity.

Santiago lay forgotten for a good few centuries, while all around him Spain became Christian through rather gradual, more conventional means. The move to Christianity ended abruptly at the start of the eighth century, when Muslim armies crossed over from North Africa, soon conquering most of the Iberian Peninsula and pushing up into central France. Still, pockets of Christianity remained, notably in northwestern Spain.

In 813, a curious Christian hermit followed sweet music and twinkling stars to a remote hillside in Galicia. The bones he found at Campus Stellae (Compostela) were quickly identified as those of Santiago, and the bishop of nearby Iria Flavia sanctified the discovery. Within a few years, Alfonso II, King of Asturias, visited the site, built a chapel and declared Santiago the patron saint of Spain.

Visions of Santiago multiplied, and the saint became instrumental in the fight against the Muslims. His most famous appearance was at the battle of Clavijo, near Logroño, where he rode a white charger and personally scythed his way through tens of thousands of Moors. This kind of behaviour made him known as Santiago Matamoros (Moor-slayer), to go with his more peace-loving image as Santiago Peregrino (pilgrim).

The history of the camino

Well before Santiago's time, the ancient Celts had their own version of the camino, said to follow the *via lactea* (Milky Way) to the sea at Finis Terrae (Finisterre), the end of the known world and as far west as they could travel without getting their feet wet.

By the ninth century, Christian authorities had seized on the pilgrimage to Santiago as a way to drive out Muslim invaders and to prevent the peoples of northern Spain from falling back on their pagan ways. Local churchmen were also keen on the cash flow that a stream of pilgrims would bring, and their promotion of Santiago de Compostela as a pilgrimage destination was a masterful piece of mediaeval marketing.

The number of pilgrims rose over the next couple of hundred years, particularly after the Turkish capture of the Holy Sepulchre made Jerusalem unsafe for pilgrims. The French were particularly keen, so much so that the main route over the Pyrenees from St-Jean-Pied-de-Port and across Spain is called the *camino francés*.

In 1189, Pope Alexander III declared Santiago de Compostela a Holy City, along with Rome and Jerusalem. Under his edict, pilgrims who arrive during Holy Years (when the Día de Santiago, July 25, falls on a Sunday) can bypass purgatory entirely, while those arriving in other years get half their time off.

It wasn't all voluntary penitence; sometimes people were sentenced to walk to Santiago as punishment for a crime, although wealthy convicts could get around this by paying someone else to walk the pilgrimage. Other pilgrims went on behalf of their villages in an effort to get rid of plagues, floods or locusts, or as a chance to see the world in the days before package holidays.

Churches and pilgrim hospices sprang up along the camino, often built on the site of miracles. Their walls provided havens from a dangerous and arduous outside world, where wolves and bandits thwarted the faithful.

The stream of pilgrims peaked in the eleventh and twelfth centuries, when about half a million people made the pilgrimage and when many of the towns and cities along the camino were built. French pilgrims of this time may well have been guided by the *Codex Calixtinus*, a twelfth-century travel guide usually attributed to Aymeric Picaud, a cantankerous French monk with bile-filled views about almost all the people he met and most of the land he walked through.

The number of pilgrims dropped off once the Christian reconquest was complete, and had fallen considerably by the time that Domenico Laffi, a seventeenth-century Italian pilgrim, wrote his guide to the *camino francés*. The steady decline continued through the eighteenth and nineteenth centuries, and by the mid-twentieth century only a few hardy souls walked the camino.

The camino today

Although the camino had dropped off the world-tourism radar, it wasn't entirely forgotten. Santiago remained the patron saint of Spain, and local people were still able to trace the route of the camino through their villages. In one of these villages in the 1960s, Don Elias Valiña Sampedro, the parish priest at O Cebreiro, began a meticulous labour of love that eventually became *El Camino de Santiago*, the camino's first modern-day guidebook. By the 1980s, the camino's popularity had soared: in 1982, John Paul II became the first pope to visit Santiago de Compostela, then in 1987 the European Union declared the camino Europe's first Cultural Itinerary. UNESCO followed suit in 1993, adding the camino to its World Heritage list.

Today's pilgrims rarely make the complete journey from their homes to Santiago and back, and most prefer to follow one of the standard routes through Spain or France. Some pilgrims walk the *vía de la plata* from Sevilla or the *camino inglés* from A Coruña, but the vast majority join the *camino francés* at some point between France and Santiago.

Any pilgrim who walks the last 100km to Santiago can apply for a *compostela* (a certificate recognizing the completion of the pilgrimage) from the authorities in Santiago de Compostela. The number of pilgrims travelling the camino peaks during Holy Years: 180,000 people reached Santiago in 2004, and future Holy Years are likely to see even more pilgrims. Even in other years, about 70,000 people follow the camino; more than half are from Spain, and most of the rest are from elsewhere in Europe.

Some pilgrim traditions have survived into the modern era. Many pilgrims walk with the aid of a tall staff and wear a scallop shell attached to their pack or their person, mimicking images of Santiago Peregrino. The beaches of Galicia are awash with scallop shells, and mediaeval pilgrims would often collect one as a souvenir of their journey; scallop symbols are also ubiquitous along the route, adorning concrete camino markers, churches and houses along the way. Even some of the pilgrim songs survive, as does ¡*Ultreia*!,

an exhortation to pilgrims to keep going, which you'll see graffitied on walls and underpasses along the way.

 # Walking

Hiking is gaining popularity in Spain, particularly amongst some southern city dwellers, who escape to cooler mountain regions like the Picos de Europa on sticky summer weekends. Around cities such as Pamplona and Logroño, you'll share the trail with recreational walkers, but most northern urbanites prefer the civilized tradition of the evening stroll, browsing in shop windows, sipping Rioja and nibbling at *tapas*. In places like rural Galicia, walking is an integral part of life, whether heading to work in the fields or making for a post-farming glass of wine, and exercise for exercise's sake can be seen as rather ridiculous.

There's a certain snooty hierarchy amongst pilgrims. Many walkers look down on cyclists, often called *peregrinos descafeinados* (decaffeinated pilgrims), and *albergues* (pilgrim hostels) may refuse to admit cycling pilgrims or ask them to wait until early evening before deciding if there's room. Self-propelled pilgrims, even non-religious ones, often dismiss car-pilgrims as "tourists." Pilgrims on horses or donkeys are now a rarity: fewer than 1% of pilgrims travel this way.

 # Trails

The camino heads across Spain on a variety of different surfaces, from narrow paths to wide tracks to tarmac (paved roads). It's mostly easy walking with very few rough or uneven surfaces, although some stone and mud tracks can become slippery after rain. Road walking can be unpleasant, and occasional stretches are dangerous due to narrow shoulders, busy roads and blind corners. Walk in a group on the left-hand side of the road (facing oncoming traffic) if possible.

Trail marking is generally excellent, and it's difficult to lose your way. Almost every turn is marked with a scallop shell or a yellow arrow painted on everything from sidewalks to trees to the sides of houses. Local people will be able to direct you to the camino if you should stray from the route — see our language section on page 169 for helpful walking phrases.

Navigating through cities is occasionally difficult, as new building work or industrial development can obliterate arrows and paths. On the *meseta* there can be long stretches with very little or no shade. The wind on the plains can be strong and quickly sap your energy; you'll need to eat well and drink lots of water, even if it isn't very hot.

 Maps

Most pilgrims don't bother with detailed maps, as the camino is well marked and easy to follow. The sketch maps in this book show the villages, terrain and sights you'll encounter, along with distances and facilities along the way.

If you're determined to weigh down your backpack with maps, Michelin maps 571, 573 and 575 give an overview of the camino, and although they're next to useless for walking, they do mark most of the towns and villages you'll pass through.

There's more detail on the 1:25,000 maps put out by the Instituto Geográfico Nacional (www.mfom.es/ign/) and the 1:50,000 maps published by the Servicio Geográfico del Ejército.

Walking maps are scarce along the camino but can be ordered from the UK before you go. Try Stanfords (☎ 020 7836 1321; www.stanfords.co.uk), the Map Centre in Hereford (☎ 01432 266 322; www.themapcentre.com) or the Map Shop in Upton-upon-Severn (☎ 0800 085 4080; www.themapshop.co.uk).

 Guided Walks

Many tour companies offer guided walks along the camino. Most trips last about two weeks, taking in a selection of regions from Roncesvalles to Santiago. Based in A Coruña, **On Foot in Spain**'s (www.onfootinspain.com) small group tours are highly regarded. Also operating out of Spain, **Iberian Adventures** (www.iberianadventures.com) runs nine-day trips between León and Santiago; the company can also arrange custom tours.

Other companies include **Alternative Travel Group** (www.atg-oxford.co.uk; ☎ 01865 315678), **Experience Plus** (www.experienceplus.com; ☎ 1-800 685 4565), **Saranjan Tours** (☎ 1-800 858 9594; www.saranjantours.com) and **Spanish Steps** (☎ 1-877 787 WALK; www.spanishsteps.com), one of the few companies to offer a continuous camino tour, starting at O Cebreiro.

 Geography

One of the most stunning aspects of walking the camino is the gradual unveiling of the landscape in front of you. As the camino snakes its way across the third-largest country in Europe, you'll traverse everything from high mountain passes to wide river valleys. Although Spain is the second most mountainous country in Europe (after Switzerland), the camino follows the line of least resistance across gently undulating terrain.

The foothills of the Pyrenees are the first obstacle faced by pilgrims. Created by the collision of the Afro-Iberian and European tectonic plates, these mountains continue to rise fractionally every year. On the other side of the mountains, you'll enter the provinces of Navarra and La Rioja, where grapes grow on rolling hills of sun-baked clay and limestone. The land is dominated by the Río Ebro, which drains the water from a vast area of northeastern Spain, and the camino follows a natural corridor into the heart of Spain between the Sierra de la Demanda to the south and the Sierra de Cantábria to the north. The Montes de Oca are the last major hills before the city of Burgos and the *meseta* beyond.

Many pilgrims expect the *meseta* to be a long flat boring expanse of nothing, but the reality is far more interesting. The 800m-high central plateau dominates central Spain, covering almost two-fifths of the country. Treeless for the most part, the horizon seems to stretch endlessly across yellow wheat fields, broken only by views of the spectacular Cordillera Cantábrica, which dictate the *meseta*'s climate. In winter, a strong, cold wind howls down from their snowy peaks, freezing the land for eight months of the year. In summer, temperatures soar, as the same mountains block cool breezes from the ocean and trap the baking heat.

Eventually, the Cordillera Cantábrica must be clambered over, as the mountains curve down towards Portugal, blocking the way to Santiago and marking the end of the *meseta*. Although the western fringe isn't the highest part of the range, it's certainly the wettest section, as the gulf stream brings soggy warm air that clings to northwestern Spain for weeks on end. The mountains have also protected the indigenous people from successive waves of invaders; consequently, this corner of Spain often seems to have more in common with Celtic nations than with the rest of Spain.

Water dominates Galicia—the coastal province gets an average of 2m of rain each year. Deep river valleys have been carved by all that precipitation, and water-loving oak forests cover the land. From Santiago, the lowest point of the camino so far, it's downhill to the ocean at Finisterre, a slim finger of a peninsula that sticks out into the Atlantic towards the setting sun.

 Environment

As in much of the rest of Europe, modern development has had environmental consequences. Flush with European Union

cash, Spain embarked on a frenzy of road building, and there are times along the camino where you'll be surrounded by underused, multi-lane roads.

In Galicia, indigenous forests have been torn down to make way for fast-growing eucalyptus. Very few birds and other animals can live in these monocultural stands because the acidic leaves sterilize the soil.

Although it's hard to believe when you're getting soaked by a Galician rainstorm, water is one of Spain's major environmental problems. Not only does the country get less rainfall than it did a few years ago, Spain's per capita water consumption is one of the highest in the world. River flow is decreasing at an alarming rate as water is siphoned off to irrigate agricultural lands and to satisfy thirsty industries and cities. Tourism, destructive in its own right in Spain's coastal region, is also causing water problems as foreign visitors demand emerald-green golf courses even in water-starved areas.

Hunting is a big part of Spanish culture, and Spain gives over much of its land to *reservas de caza* (hunting reserves). In summer, you'll often hear staccato bursts of gunfire-like noise, although the sound is just as likely to be from fiesta firecrackers as from hunters' rifles. Hunting has eliminated some of Spain's rarer creatures, and the brown bear, found in the Cordillera Cantábrica, and the lammergeier, a bird of prey that nests in the Pyrenees, are just clinging to existence. Although the wolf is a protected species, local farmers put their rifles away with gritted teeth, as compensation from the government for lost livestock arrives at glacial speed.

The green movement in Spain is much younger than in most northern European countries, but it has become much more organized and high-profile in the last few years. For links to Spanish environmental organizations, see our web site at www.pilipalapress.com.

When to Go

Pilgrims traditionally timed their journey to arrive in Santiago de Compostela for the Día de Santiago. Now a Galician holiday, July 25 is still the liveliest time to be in the city, when the Plaza de Obradoiro in front of the cathedral is illuminated by a magnificent fireworks display.

Summer weather is the most reliable, although it can rain at any time of the year in Galicia, and the *meseta* can be uncomfortably hot from June to August. *Albergues* are crowded throughout the peak season, and hotels may be fully booked in destinations popular with tourists. Many regions along the camino come alive from June onwards with traditional festivals; the Navarrese celebrate with particular gusto in July and August. The end of summer marks the start of the harvest, and food-based fiestas pop up everywhere.

Early autumn is the perfect time for wine buffs, as the grape harvest in La Rioja and Navarra gets into swing. It's also wild mushroom season, and an excellent time to see birds heading south for the winter. The weather is often mild, sometimes wet and windy, and there may be the occasional snow flurry at higher elevations.

The weather worsens through the winter. You'll need to carry more equipment to cope with rain at any time and to deal with snow on the mountain passes. It can be an inconvenient and chilly time to travel, as churches and tourist sights may be closed, and those *albergues* and hotels that stay open often lack heating. Despite this, travelling the route in winter can be a fabulous, solitary experience, and there's a definite camaraderie amongst the hardy souls who attempt the camino at this time.

Come spring, the weather improves, although there's still a chance of snow at higher elevations and you'll probably be rained on for at least a few days of your trip. Spring is the best time to see wildflowers, which bloom earlier on the warm *meseta* than in chillier, damper Galicia, and it's also the ideal time to spot migrating birds on their way back north.

The camino is always busier during Holy Years such as 2010 and 2021, when the Día de Santiago falls on a Sunday. Pilgrims who walk the camino in Holy Years get more time off purgatory, and special ceremonies are performed in Santiago and in churches and cathedrals along the way.

How long will it take?

If you're fit and healthy and don't want to stay for more than one night in any of the places along the way, you can walk the camino from St-Jean-Pied-de-Port to Santiago de Compostela in about a month. It's a good idea to allow for extra time in case of any unforseen injuries, an occasional lazy day or a whimsical decision to linger in one of the lovely towns along the way.

If you have less time, or if you're not used to walking long distances, consider starting somewhere closer to Santiago; you only need to walk the last 100km to Santiago to get a *compostela*. Cities such as Pamplona, Logroño, Burgos, León, Astorga, Ponferrada and Sarria are all popular places to start.

Many pilgrims walk the camino in stages, and returning every year or so to walk another two-week stretch is especially popular with French and Spanish pilgrims. For suggested itineraries, see www.pilipalapress.com.

People & Culture

History

The Iberian peninsula was home to some of the earliest known Europeans, and excavations at Atapuerca, on the camino just before Burgos, have uncovered an 800,000-year-old skeleton. Farther north, and a good many years later in 15,000BC, cave dwellers at Altamira created stunning, artistically sophisticated buffalo and deer paintings. Neolithic peoples arrived in Spain in about 5000BC, building some splendid *dolmens* and *menhirs* in Galicia and the Basque country. The Celts came south across the Pyrenees in about 800BC, leaving a string of *castros* along the camino, and an indelible mark on Galicia's culture and architecture.

Things were fairly peaceful on the peninsula until the Romans decided to expand their empire in about 200BC. Resistance from the Celtiberian tribes of northern Spain was so strong that it took a couple of centuries for the Romans to control the country and, even then, peoples like the Basques retained their own distinctive cultures. The Romans, as always, chose the shortest, most logical routes for their roads: the camino follows the Via Traiana, the Roman road that linked Bordeaux and Astorga, for much of its length.

As Roman power waned, northern armies poured into Spain. Like the Romans, the Suevi and the Visigoths made little impact on northern Spain, although a couple of lovely Visigothic chapels remain, and others lie buried underneath the foundations of later, grander churches.

In 711, a small force of Moors landed in Gibraltar and quickly moved north, controlling much of the peninsula in a few short years. But just as the Romans and Visigoths never really got a grip on Spain's unruly northerners, so Muslim strongholds were limited to the south of the country. By the ninth century, while southern Spain was prospering under Muslim rule, pockets of Christian influence were developing in the north.

In 824, the powerful Kingdom of Navarra was formed, becoming strongest during the reign of Sancho el Mayor in the eleventh century, who captured La Rioja and a large chunk of Castilla for the Navarrese Christians. The balance of power was destined to shift west along the camino, however, and by the end of the eleventh century the kingdom of Castilla was the dominant force in Christian Spain.

The camino's popularity peaked in the Middle Ages, when some of the grandest and most glorious churches and cathedrals along the route were built. Meanwhile, Spain's disparate Christian kingdoms were drawing closer together; León, Castilla and Navarra joined forces in 1212 to defeat the Moors at Las Navas de Tolosa, and a more concrete union was cemented in 1479, when Fernando V of Aragón married Isabel I of Castilla.

Fernando and Isabel's reign began a flurry of Spanish exploration and conquest; Columbus discovered the New World in their names and Pizarro set about dominating South America. Back home, the insidious Inquisition was driving almost half a million Jews from the country and was also systematically rooting out Muslims, gypsies and witches.

Meanwhile, Spain's centre of government was moving south, and Felipe II had set up Court in Madrid by the sixteenth century. The north suffered from its lack of political influence, and many of its towns went into gradual decline.

In 1808, Napoleon crossed over the Pyrenees by the old Camino de Santiago, soon installing his brother on the throne of Spain. The Spanish called for help from the British, who were spectacularly unsuccessful at first, and Sir John Moore's troops trashed towns such as Ponferrada and Villafranca del Bierzo as they speedily retreated to A Coruña on the northern coast. It took Wellington's army to drive the French out of Spain, although his troops were just as apt to destroy as liberate the Spanish towns they passed through.

The rest of the nineteenth century is a muddle of coups and counter coups as Spain swung from monarchy to liberal constitution and back again. By the early twentieth century, politics had splintered into factions, and regionalism, anarchism, communism and fascism all gained ground. Almost inevitably, civil war broke out in 1936. The province of Castilla was firmly on Franco's side, and the Nationalists made Burgos their wartime capital. Galicians were also predominantly Nationalist, partly because Franco was a local boy from Ferrol, and partly because of the region's inherent conservatism. The Basques sided with the Republicans, becoming increasingly isolated in the Nationalist north, and in 1937 were finally defeated as Nazi planes carpet-bombed Guernica.

When Franco came to power at the end of the civil war in January 1939, he set about rewarding friendly cities like Burgos, which got a ton of money from the dictator for industrial development. The Basques, meanwhile, were punished severely. *Euskara*, the Basque language, was repressed, and the Basque flag and other Basque symbols were banned. Economically, the country suffered from the costly civil war and the isolation of Franco's fascist regime, but an injection of US investment in the 1950s nudged Spain into the industrial age.

Franco finally died in 1975, wielding influence beyond the grave by nominating King Juan Carlos as his successor. Although Spain flirted with dictatorship and military coups in the late 1970s, by 1982 the country was flinging itself into democracy and capitalism with abandon. Spain's recent economic development has been largely due to its enthusiastic membership in the European Union, which it joined in 1986. European money has flooded into the country, leading to industrial development, agricultural modernization and an unstoppable orgy of road building.

In keeping with European Union philosophy, Spain's modern era has seen a devolution of power to the regions, and the Basques and Galicians in particular have been granted a large measure of autonomy.

Spain today

Spain is not so much a single country as a paella of diverse and disparate cultures. Many Galicians and Basques don't even consider themselves Spanish, and even less autonomous regions are intensely proud of their homelands. Having said this, foreign visitors will notice certain things that are distinctly, and often uniquely, Spanish.

Spain may be in the same time zone as many European countries, but the Spanish day is unrecognizable to those from more northern climates. For a start, things happen later in Spain. A lot later in the case of meals, as restaurant lunches aren't usually served until 2pm, and Spaniards rarely eat dinner before 10pm. Nights out in Spain aren't for the faint-hearted, nor are they for pilgrims curfew-bound by *albergues*, as bars don't get going until midnight, and clubs rarely open before 4am. It's no wonder the Spanish need a long *siesta*, and you'll find that even in the cities, life will grind to a halt from 2pm to 5pm.

Spanish life seems to revolve around eating and drinking. Sunday lunches, in particular, are vast, communal affairs stretching well into the afternoon and involving all members of the family from the oldest to the youngest. Children are universally adored, and more puritanical northern Europeans may be shocked at the extent to which Spanish kids are heard as well as seen in public. Children are positively welcomed in restaurants, and you'll often see youngsters brought along for a late-night stroll or *tapas* crawl.

You won't hear much English spoken along the camino, and even a smattering of *Castellano* (Spanish) will help with communication. Both *Euskara* (Basque) and *Galega* (Galician) are undergoing literary and linguistic revivals. Surprisingly, the noisily nationalistic Basques are less likely to speak their indigenous language than the quieter Galicians, 90% of whom speak some *Galega*.

Spain is an inherently Catholic country, 500 years after the Inquisition drove out Jews and Muslims. Since the 1978 constitution, Spaniards have enjoyed official religious freedom, but there are still fewer than a million non-Catholic souls in the country. In practice, however, secularism is taking hold as church attendance plummets; regular churchgoers are likely to be older, poorer northerners.

You won't pass through any major football towns on the camino, although you may be able to catch an Osasuna game in Pamplona, and Galicians have adopted Deportivo La Coruña as their provincial side. This scarcely seems to dim support for the beautiful game, as almost all Spanish football fans support either Barcelona or Real Madrid as well as their local club, and matches between the two giants of Spanish football will pack bars everywhere in Spain.

Arts

The camino is responsible for and replete with gorgeous examples of Romanesque and Gothic architecture. From the stunning Romanesque frescoes of the Basilica de San Isidoro in León to the gossamer Gothic spires of Burgos and León cathedrals, you'll be dazzled by the wealth and creativity of mediaeval Spain.

Spain's airy Gothic traditions were both continued and splendidly distorted by Gaudí's fantastical swirling confections, seen at their best in Barcelona but with examples in León and Astorga.

Spanish art has very few important schools and movements but a few amazing peaks of individual creativity. In the sixteenth and seventeenth centuries, El Greco, a native Greek who lived most of his life in his adopted Spain, painted passionate and deliberate canvasses of elongated figures and intense contrasts of light and colour. A few decades later, Velázquez, perhaps Spain's greatest artist, painted intricate, life-like portraits of Spanish nobility with meticulous care and flawless technique.

Goya was contrastingly prolific. He was a late starter who began with fairly conventional paintings before spiralling towards embittered and imaginative works as his health declined and the war with Napoleon sent him into depression.

Picasso is probably Spain's best-known artist, although he spent much of his long life in neighbouring France. After flirting with Toulouse-Lautrec's style in his blue period, Picasso moved on to a rose period, when he was influenced by El Greco and Celtiberian sculpture. With Georges Braque, he developed Cubism, a style also adopted by his countryman, Juan Gris. Politicized by the civil war, Picasso portrayed a Basque town's decimation by Nazi bombers in his most famous painting, *Guernica*. The painting has become a symbol of Basque nationalism, and its presence in the Museo de Arte Reina Sofia in Madrid really sticks in the collective Basque throat.

Dalí put the fish in surrealism and was as talented at self-promotion as he was in his bizarre, dream-like art. Alongside him, Spain's other noted surrealist, Joan Miró, seems positively normal.

Spanish film is well respected internationally, but only a handful of directors are household names. Luis Buñuel and Salvador Dalí made many of their films in France, and Buñuel was forced into exile after the civil war. Carlos Maura's bleak, allegorical films subtly undermined the Franco dictatorship during the 1960s and 1970s. In common with many of Spain's younger generation, Pedro Almodóvar sees the Franco years as irrelevant to his work, instead making quirky, controversial and successful films about desire and sexuality.

Spain's folk music is firmly regionalized. Even *flamenco*, the closest Spain has to a national music, is rooted in Andalucía and is rarely heard outside the south, Madrid and Barcelona. Galician and Basque tunes have much in common with Celtic music from northern Europe, and each culture has its own version of the bagpipes.

Modern musicians have moved away from the rigid traditionalism of folk music under Franco and are influenced by styles as diverse as *flamenco* and electronica. Basque and Galician musicians also borrow a lot from each other, swapping instruments and styles with creative abandon.

For more about regional culture, see the People & Culture sections in the regional chapters.

Food

The food of Spain is as varied as the country, but as a rule of thumb it's tasty, substantial and lacking in vegetables. It's also very cheap by northern European standards.

Hungry pilgrims may find it hard to get used to Spanish mealtimes. Restaurants open for lunch at 2pm, and dinner seldom begins before 9pm or 10pm. The best value comes from the *menú del día*, a three-course set meal that includes bread and wine. Many restaurants along the camino will offer a *menú del peregrino* (pilgrim's menu), an early evening *menú* starting at 7pm or 8pm, which is an excellent deal at between €6 and €9 for three courses and wine.

On most menus there's a choice of dishes for each course. The *primer plato* (first course) can be anything from salad to spaghetti and is often more filling than the main course. Soups are fabulous and often meals in themselves. You shouldn't leave Spain without trying *sopa de ajo*, commonly known as the "soup of the poor," a broth of garlic, bread and water topped with a poached egg. You'll have to wait until Galicia to eat authentic *caldo gallego*, a thick soup made of shredded *gallego* (a dark green cabbage), beans and potatoes. Vegetarians be warned: soups are usually made using meat stock, and *caldo gallego* often includes a few slices of *chorizo* (spicy sausage). *Fabada* is a hearty dish made from beans and *chorizo*. The beans are cooked slowly in a stew, soaking up the smoky flavour of the sausage.

The *segundo plato* (second course) is a hefty serving of either fried or roasted lumps of meat with a few chips or boiled potatoes on the side. Chicken, beef, veal and pork are the most common, although fish, usually trout, may also be on offer.

If you still have room, *postre* (dessert) is mercifully small. Usually you'll be offered a piece of fruit, ice cream or yoghurt served in its plastic container, but *flan* (egg custard) is also a good choice.

Most cafés and bars will serve *bocadillos*, substantial sandwiches made from half a baguette stuffed with a range of fillings. *Bocadillos* are often filled with whatever happens to be in the kitchen, usually cheese, *chorizo* or *jamon serrano* (a *prosciutto*-like ham); one of the most fiendishly tasty versions is *tortilla con chorizo* (*chorizo* omelette).

Breakfast can be tricky. In summer, early starts mean that pilgrims often begin walking hours before any of the cafés open. Those bars that are open may serve *pan tostada* (toast) or an assortment of packaged pastries. If you're lucky, there'll be *tortilla* on offer, a deliciously thick omelette made with potatoes, then left to cool and served by the slice with a hunk of bread.

Vegetarians will have a hard time eating out. The *menú del día* is usually devoid of vegetarian options, and even an *ensalada mixta* (mixed salad) will likely contain tuna. Your culinary options are mostly limited to off-menu standards such as *bocadillo con queso* (cheese sandwich), *tortilla francés* (omelette) or potato-based *tapas* treats such as *patatas bravas* and *patatas al alioli*.

The best way to eat well and meet fellow pilgrims is to join in the evening meal at the *albergues*. Some will have a kitchen, where people of different nationalities gather together to cook, generating a fantastic hum as pots boil and bottles of wine are uncorked.

When shopping, look out for typical foods: try *jamon serrano* and *chorizo* or sample wonderful olives such as huge green *manzanillas*. Spain's varied climate means there's a wide selection of fruit and vegetables available year-round. In most shops, you'll need to ask for what you need rather than picking up and squeezing the fruit yourself. Try not to get caught short of food on Sundays, when many shops close.

At least once during the camino, head out for an evening of *tapas* grazing. At its most basic, a *tapa* is just a little bite of food to go with a glass of wine, often offered free by the bartender. In other places, you'll need to order what you like; *pinchos* are small tasters and *raciones* are bigger portions. The best way to sample *tapas* is to embark on a *tapeo* (*tapas* crawl) with a group of friends, hopping from one bar to another and discussing the shortcomings of Real Madrid's latest striker with local bankers and road sweepers.

For more about regional food, see the regional Food & Drink sections.

Drink

Spanish people spend a lot of time in cafés, and days in Spain rarely begin without a caffeine hit. The coffee's excellent, and even the smallest village café will boast a big, shiny espresso machine. Coffee comes in many variations, but essentially you have two options: the strong and espresso-like *café solo* or the long and milky *café con leche*.

Tea is just about drinkable, but hot chocolate can be hard to find and you're more likely to be offered Cola Cao, a sickly, powdery substitute. There's a wide array of soft drinks available, from the usual imports to Spanish sparkling fruity drinks. Fruit juice tends to be sweet and thick, but it's delightfully refreshing when diluted with sparkling water.

Even teetotalling Spaniards drink wine with food: it's considered such a part of the meal that it's not even thought of as alcohol. The Spanish, who have lots of alcoholic proverbs, say, *"comer sin vino es miseria y desatino"* which loosely translates as "a meal without wine is a mean and foolish one."

Foremost among wine regions is La Rioja, the country's most important red wine–producing area. Its smooth, oak-aged wines are well known outside Spain, and fans of Rioja will be delighted by the low prices. There are also some great reds from the Navarra and Ribera del Duero regions.

Galicia's cooler climate is ideal for producing white wine. The region's Albariño whites are unoaked and crisp with flavours of peach and apricot, while cloudy Ribeiro wine rarely makes it outside the province; both perfectly complement the region's seafood. For more about regional wines, see the Food & Drink section in the regional chapters.

Spanish beer is rather bland and tasteless, although brands such as San Miguel, Cruz Campo and Estrella de Galicia can be refreshing on a hot evening. Ask for a *caña* if you want a small draught beer.

Bars are an integral part of Spanish culture, and a 1990s survey found that Spain had 138,200 bars, slightly fewer than the rest of the European Union put together. Bars and cafés in Spain are mostly interchangeable. You can get a great *café solo* at a late-night bar, though it's a bit more of a shock the first time you see locals waking up with a shot of something stronger alongside their morning *café con leche*.

Alcohol in bars is very cheap, with wine and beer usually costing less than €1 a glass, though the glasses may be smaller than you're used to. As always in Europe, bars on main squares will be more expensive than those tucked down a side street. It often costs more to drink at a table, particularly one outside, than standing at the bar.

Long, afternoon-consuming lunches aren't complete without a stiff drink. Northern Spain's favourite tipple is *orujo*, a ridiculously strong spirit made, like Italian *grappa*, from grape skins. Despite the pretty bottles, the manufactured version isn't as good as the rough-and-ready homemade version, known as *orujo casero* and found in unmarked bottles under the counter in bars, restaurants and even bakeries.

In Navarra, end your meal with *pacharán*, a sweet, pinky-orange drink usually served over ice. Avoid spirits such as gin and whisky, particularly the dodgy brands of Scotch made for mainland European tastes.

Flora

Spain is one of Europe's richest botanical regions. The mix of Mediterranean, Atlantic and Continental climates makes for a diverse collection of flowers, shrubs and trees. Geographically isolated from the rest of Europe by the Pyrenees, the Iberian peninsula's plant life developed at its own pace, helped by windblown seeds from North Africa. The results are spectacular, with more than 8000 species of flora in the Iberian Peninsula, a quarter of which are indigenous to the region and occur nowhere else in the world.

Northern Spain was once covered by deciduous forest, dominated by Pyrenean oak and beech. Frequent forest fires and the introduction of faster-growing imported species, such as pine and eucalyptus, are rapidly destroying what little forest survived into the twentieth century.

In the unforested areas that cover much of the central part of the country, the landscape is dominated by dense patches of brambles and wild herbs such as lavender, sage and thyme. At higher altitudes gorse, broom and heather cover the ground and hardy plants such as St Patrick's cabbage, mat grass and sphagnum moss cope with strong winds, deep snow cover and extreme temperature change.

For more about regional flora, see the regional Flora & Fauna sections.

English name	Latin name	Spanish name

Juniper   Juniperus communis   Enebro

Leaves Needle-like, 1.2cm long, in groups of three; sharp, glossy, green-white band on upper surface
Bark Red-brown, peels in thin vertical strips
Fruit Berry-like, 6mm-long cone; becomes black when ripe
Habitat Open spaces from coast to mountains
Height Up to 6m
Did you know? Juniper berries give gin its distinctive taste and are used as a culinary flavouring

Beech   Fagus sylvatica   Haya

Leaves 4–9cm long, oval, with 7–8 parallel veins, silky hairs underneath
Bark Smooth grey
Fruit Triangular brown nuts
Habitat Farmland
Height Up to 40m
Did you know? Planted for timber because it grows tall and straight without knots

English name	Latin name	Spanish name
Pyrenean oak	**Quercus pyrenaica**	**Roble melojo**

Leaves 20cm long, 10cm across, deep lobes, dark glossy green
Bark Pale grey and craggy
Fruit Acorn 4cm long, two years to mature
Habitat Mountains, particularly in the north
Height 20m
Did you know? Produces very strong lumber, used extensively in construction

Olive	**Olea europaea**	**Olivo**

Leaves 2–8 cm long, narrow, grey-green above with delicate silver hairs underneath
Bark Pale grey
Fruit 1–4cm long
Habitat Farmland
Height Up to 15m
Did you know? Fruit is green the first year then turns black when ripe in second year

Sweet chestnut	**Castanea sativa**	**Castaño dulce**

Leaves 10–25cm long, oblong with pointed tip and sharp-toothed edges
Bark Grey ridges that seem to spiral around trunk
Fruit Edible chestnut
Habitat Farmland, plains and mixed woodlands
Height Up to 30m
Did you know? Chestnuts are a staple food in parts of Spain, used as a stuffing for meat or to thicken hearty soups

 # Fauna

Spain is home to an assortment of rare animals. Nooks and crannies hide fire salamanders, genets and wild boar, while large tracts of remote wilderness, especially in Galicia and the Cordillera Cantábrica, offer animals such as the wolf and the brown bear the space to roam unhindered. Agricultural underdevelopment in these areas has preserved unique ecosystems that are now being studied for the first time. Spain is also the main refuelling stop on the north-south bird migration route, and these passages make spring and autumn a great time to visit.

Novice wildlife watchers can greatly increase their chance of seeing animals by going out at dawn and dusk when most animals are active. There's also more chance of spotting animals if you're on the edge of two habitats, like on the fringes of a wood near a river or an open woodland. As you walk along, stop every now and then to sit quietly and wait a few minutes. Allow the animals time to get accustomed to your presence and to resume their normal routines and you'll gradually see undetected animals emerge before your eyes.

For more about regional fauna, see the regional Flora & Fauna sections.

English name	Latin name	Spanish name

Iberian lynx — Lynx pardinus — Lince Ibérico

Length 100cm **Tail** 25cm **Height** 70cm
Description Large and small black spots, black tip on tail, distinctive feathery tufts on head
Habitat Pyrenean and holm oak woods in rocky mountains
Voice Hisses and howls
Diet Birds, young deer, fish, small mammals and reptiles
Viewing tips Very rare and difficult to spot; vast territory
Did you know? Most endangered carnivore in Europe

Wild cat — Felis silvestris — Gato montés

Length 50cm **Tail** 30cm **Height** 35cm
Description Yellow-grey fur with black-ringed tail
Habitat Woodland and scrubland
Voice Purrs and meows
Diet Mice, birds, fish and insects
Viewing tips Active in late afternoon, often sunning itself
Did you know? Persecution of cats in mediaeval times led to spread of black death as rat population exploded

Genet — Genetta genetta — Gineta

Length 50cm **Tail** 40cm **Height** 20cm
Description Pale fur with defined dark spots and tail rings
Habitat Dark woods close to streams
Voice Purrs loudly
Diet Small birds, mammals, insects
Viewing tips Nocturnal, look for footprints near water
Did you know? Lives up to 21 years. Strong swimmer and climber; found at altitudes up to 2500m

English name	Latin name	Spanish name

Badger   Meles meles   Tejón

Length 60cm **Tail** 15cm **Height** 30cm
Description Silver-grey back; black & white striped face
Habitat Scrubland, farmland, woods
Voice Growls
Diet Small rodents, reptiles and plants
Viewing tips Nocturnal; listen for the sound of it digging
Did you know? Foxes and birds of prey often follow
badgers to catch animals they disturb while digging for food

Wild boar   Sus scrofa   Jabalí

Length 150cm **Tail** 15cm **Height** 90cm
Description Pale grey to black; tusks up to 30cm
Habitat Mixed, deciduous woodland; scrubland
Voice Snorts. Female barks and chatters teeth when angry
Diet Roots, vegetables, small mammals, insects
Viewing tips Mainly nocturnal but also active in mornings
Did you know? Litters of 4 to 12 piglets common,
independent after 6 months and can live up to 25 years

Otter   Lutra lutra   Nutria

Length 80cm **Tail** 40cm **Height** 30cm
Description Brown fur; long, slender body with short legs
Habitat Rivers, lakes, marshes, estuaries and sea
Voice Clear whistle, sometimes growls
Diet Fish, birds, frogs and aquatic mammals
Viewing tips Look for remains of meals along riverbanks
Did you know? Good climber and jumper, can walk on
land for long distances

Brown bear   Ursus arctos   Oso pardo

Length 230cm **Tail** 1.5cm **Height** 120cm
Description Very large, heavy build, beige to dark brown
Habitat Mixed woods in the Cordillera Cantábrica
Voice Occasional grunts or howls when angry or frightened
Diet Berries, roots, carrion, insects, occasionally mammals
Viewing tips Very difficult to see, mainly nocturnal
Did you know? Brown bears have an excellent sense of
smell and hearing, but poor eyesight

English name	Latin name	Spanish name

Wolf   Canis lupus   Lobo

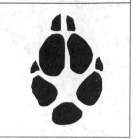

Length 130cm **Tail** 40cm **Height** 80cm
Description Grey, bushy tail, alert ears
Habitat Woods and open country in mountains
Voice Silent when hunting; growls, yelps and long howls
Diet Large and small mammals
Viewing tips Dog-like footprint; visible at dawn and dusk
Did you know? Wolves mate for life. Travel up to 40km per day with a maximum speed of up to 50km per hour

European tree frog   Hyla arborea   Rana de San Antón

Length 4cm
Description Usually green but changes to grey or brown as temperature fluctuates
Habitat Marshland, damp meadows, reed beds
Voice Croaks
Diet Insects and spiders
Viewing tips Easily spotted, active by day and twilight
Did you know? Female lays up to 1000 eggs

Natterjack   Bufo calamita   Sapo corredor

Length 8cm
Description Brown-grey back with huge warts, belly white
Habitat Varied, especially dry sandy soil, up to 1200m
Voice Loud croak
Diet Insects, worms and spiders
Viewing tips Mainly nocturnal, occasionally active in day
Did you know? When the natterjack becomes alarmed, it inflates its body, lowers its head and sticks its bum in the air

Fire salamander   Salamander salamander   Salamandra común

Length 20cm
Description Shiny black; yellow, orange or red markings
Habitat Damp woodlands, streams, meadows up to 1000m
Diet Insects and worms
Viewing tips Emerges at night or in bad weather
Did you know? Don't touch, as the oily slime that covers the body is poisonous. Can live for up to 42 years

English name	Latin name	Spanish name

Iberian wall lizard · Podarcis hispanica · Lagartija ibérica

Length 18cm
Description Flat head, long tail, upper parts grey to brown
Habitat Dry, stony places, especially walls and ruins
Diet Small insects and worms
Viewing tips Look and listen for them scuttling away as you approach
Did you know? Lays eggs in holes; lives up to 15 years

Green lizard · Lacerta viridis · Lagarto verde

Length 40cm
Description Males vivid green with tiny black dots; sky blue throat during mating. Females duller and brownish
Habitat Dry, sunny locations with shrubs, especially near walls and along roads
Diet Insects and fruit
Viewing tips Again, look and listen for scuttling!
Did you know? When threatened opens mouth and bites

White stork · Ciconia ciconia · Cigüeña común

Description 100cm, long bill and legs, white with black flight feathers, red bill and legs
Habitat Marshes, grassy plains
Voice Hisses and claps bill
Diet Fish, insects
Viewing tips Flies at high altitude, neck straight ahead
Did you know? Nests on buildings and churches along the camino, especially in Navarra, La Rioja and the *meseta*

Crested lark · Galerida cristata · Cogujada común

Description 17cm, noticeable crest, stubby tail, sandy colour with white belly
Habitat Flat open land
Voice Klee-treee-weeooo
Diet Seeds, insects
Viewing tips Common alongside open tracks and on agricultural land
Did you know? Nests on ground, never seen in a flock

English name	Latin name	Spanish name

Bee-eater   Merops apiaster   Abejaruco común

Description 30cm, bright blue belly, yellow throat and shoulders, black eyeband
Habitat Open scrubland with some trees
Voice Prruep prruep prruep
Diet Insects
Viewing tips Sociable, likes to perch & watch the world go by. Good flier, with sudden acceleration and graceful glides
Did you know? Breeds in big groups in holes in the ground

Hoopoe   Upupa epops   Abubilla

Description 30cm, crest on head, pinkish body, barred white and black wings, long bill
Habitat Farmland, open woodland
Voice Pooo pooo pooo
Diet Insects
Viewing tips Undulating flight as it opens & closes wings
Did you know? One of our favourite birds. Nests in ruins and hollows of old trees

Black woodpecker   Dryocopus martius   Pito negro

Description 45cm, almost all black, red crown, yellow eyes
Habitat Old coniferous and beech forests
Voice Manic laugh: kwick-wick-wick-wick
Diet Ants and wood-boring beetle larvae, tree sap
Viewing Tips Found in mature forests, listen for call and loud drumming
Did you know? Three separate, isolated populations in Spain

White-backed woodpecker   Dendrocopos leucotus   Pico dorsiblanco

Description 25cm, white lower back, white bands across wings, pink under tail
Habitat Deciduous forest with lots of rotting logs
Voice tehich
Diet Insects, nuts and seeds
Viewing tips Rare, mainly south-facing Pyrenean slopes
Did you know? Largest spotted woodpecker in Europe

English name	Latin name	Spanish name

Chough
Pyrrhocorax pyrrhocorax
Chova piquirroja

Description 40cm, red legs and long, thin, curved red bill
Habitat Rolling hills and mountains
Voice High-pitched cheeeaaah and chuff
Diet Mainly insects
Viewing tips Good flier, tumbles and twists during flight, also frequently seen hopping on ground
Did you know? Nests in caves and on crags

Great bustard
Otis tarda
Avutarda

Description 100cm, pale grey head and upper neck, rufous upper parts. Breeding males have pale fluffy feathers on lower face and fan white tails out in a spectacular display
Habitat Open treeless plains
Voice Not often heard. Low bark in breeding season
Diet Mainly insects
Viewing tips Usually in small flocks on the ground
Did you know? Heaviest bird in Europe

Golden eagle
Aquila chrysaetos
Águila real

Description 90cm, golden feathers on head, white patches on wings and tail
Habitat Mountains, forests, sea cliffs
Voice Seldom-heard kya
Diet Rabbits, reptiles
Viewing tips Soars with wings in shallow V, solitary
Did you know? The largest eagle in the world

Short-toed eagle
Circaetus gallicus
Culebrera europea

Description 65cm, long wings and tail, white underneath except for brown chest
Habitat Mountain slopes, plains and coastal dunes
Voice Noisy; jee or peak-oh
Diet Snakes, lizards and frogs
Viewing tips Resembles osprey but without dark stripes
Did you know? Frequently hovers with legs dangling

English name	Latin name	Spanish name

Booted eagle   Hieraaetus pennatus   Águila calzada

Description 50cm. Two different varieties; can have either dark or white body with black wing edges
Habitat Forest clearings
Voice Keeee
Diet Small birds and reptiles
Viewing tips Always seen near trees; six obvious feathers at end of wings
Did you know? The smallest eagle in Europe

Bonelli's eagle   Hieraaetus fasciatus   Águila perdicera

Description 70cm, white body underneath with dark tail band; wings mostly dark with white patches near wing tips
Habitat Rocky mountains, plains and wetlands
Voice Fast or slow kai kai kai
Diet Rabbits, birds up to heron size
Viewing tips Look for acrobatic courtship display in spring
Did you know? Pairs stay together even when not breeding

Goshawk   Accipter gentilis   Azor

Description 60cm, barred, grey belly, some white near tail and around eyes
Habitat Woods on edge of open country
Voice Pee-lay or kik kik
Diet Wood pigeons and other forest-dwelling birds
Viewing tips Great flier, zooms 2–3m above the ground between and around trees
Did you know? Persistent; chases prey even if ends in crash

Buzzard   Buteo buteo   Busardo ratonero

Description 50cm, dark with barred underside, broad wings and fat, round tail
Habitat Mountains, plains, farmland
Voice Peee-aah
Diet Birds, small mammals, insects
Viewing tips Common over most habitats
Did you know? Seen as the laziest raptor, it rarely chases prey and refuses to fly in the rain

English name	Latin name	Spanish name

Sparrowhawk | Accipiter nisus | Gavilán común

Description 35cm, long tail, barred underparts, grey above
Habitat Woodland and farmland
Voice Varies. Lots of noise especially in breeding season
Diet Small mammals and birds
Viewing tips The sparrowhawk is a common sight hovering over fields looking for food
Did you know? Young birds and captive adults frequently resort to cannibalism

Red kite | Milvus milvus | Milano real

Description 60cm, white head, red-brown upper body, tri-coloured wings, black wing tips and clear white base
Habitat Wooded hills, open country with scattered trees
Voice Hi-hi-heeea
Diet Small vertebrates, insects and sometimes scavenges
Viewing Tips Long, deep wing beats, noticeable forked tail which constantly twists during flight
Did you know? Iberia has the most red kites in the world

Kestrel | Falco tinnunculus | Cernícalo vulgar

Description 35cm, pointed wings, black band at tail base
Habitat Coast, farmland, woodland, cities
Voice Kee kee kee in breeding season
Diet Mainly rodents, but also lizards and small birds
Viewing tips Often seen hovering patiently over fields checking the ground for prey
Did you know? Breeds in old nests of other birds, on cliffs or even buildings

Peregrine falcon | Falco peregrinus | Halcón común

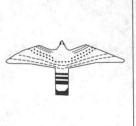

Description 45cm, slate colour, thick black moustache, white speckled belly. Female larger and darker than male
Habitat Open country, mountains, cliffs
Voice Hek hek hek or airk airk airk
Diet Small- and medium-sized birds and mammals
Viewing tips Graceful flier, languid at rest but dramatic dive-bomb as attacks prey
Did you know? Dives at up to 100km/hr

English name	Latin name	Spanish name

Montagu's harrier   Circus pygargus   Aguila perdicera

Description 45cm, dark wing tips, male grey, female brown with black bars underneath
Habitat Marshes, farmland, plains
Voice Chattering kek kek kek
Diet Frogs, small mammals
Viewing tips Acrobatic flier as it patrols territory
Did you know? Winters in Africa and returns to same territory each year to breed

Griffon vulture   Gyps fulvus   Buitre común

Description 100cm, long broad wings, short stumpy tail, light lines under wings
Habitat All types of landscape but usually mountains
Voice Croaks and whistles
Diet Carrion
Viewing tips Flies gracefully by soaring, with only an occasional flap of wings
Did you know? Often breeds in caves

Egyptian vulture   Neophron percnopterus   Alimoche común

Description 60cm, long wings with black edges, white body, wedge-shaped tail
Habitat Mountains and open country
Voice Largely silent
Diet Carrion
Viewing tips Easily confused with high-flying storks
Did you know? Often seen at rubbish dumps

Eagle owl   Bubo bubo   Búho real

Description 65cm, rust colour with streaks and bars, big feathers on top of head look like ears
Habitat Rocky ledges on crags and mountains
Voice Ooo hoo
Diet Small mammals, birds up to game-bird size
Viewing tips Active at dawn and dusk
Did you know? Easily mistaken for buzzard; uses other birds' abandoned nests

Tourist Information

Getting There & Back

Discount airlines may be your most flexible option, as you can fly into one airport and out of another. The most convenient airport for you will depend on where you choose to begin and end the camino. Ryan Air (www.ryanair.com) flies to Biarritz, and Easy Jet (www.easyjet.com) flies to Toulouse, the most convenient airports for St-Jean-Pied-de-Port. From Biarritz, take an airport bus to Bayonne, and from Toulouse head to Bayonne by train. From Bayonne, it's a lovely, hour-long train journey to St-Jean. You may have to stay overnight in Bayonne, as the late evening train to St-Jean doesn't run every day; see www.voyages-sncf.com for up-to-date schedules.

Pilgrims from outside Europe will probably land in Madrid, from where it's easy to get bus or train connections to major centres such as Pamplona, Logroño, Burgos, León, Astorga and Santiago. If you start at Roncesvalles, head first for Pamplona, then catch a frequent bus or taxi.

Many airlines also visit the splendid city of Bilbao; it's easy to get from there to Logroño, Burgos and León. You can also reach Bilbao by ferry from Portsmouth with P&O Ferries (www.poferries.com).

From Plymouth, you can sail to Santander (www.brittanyferries.com), although it's less convenient to get from there to points along the camino.

International buses and trains will get you from northern Europe to most major towns along the camino. They're unlikely to be any cheaper than flying, however, and will take considerably more time. For UK bus fares and schedules, contact Eurolines (www.eurolines.co.uk), and for selected train schedules, visit SNCF's web site at www.raileurope.co.uk.

Getting back

Iberian airlines offer a 50% pilgrim discount on one-way tickets out of Santiago. There are a few trains a day from Santiago to Madrid, and there's also a daily train from Santiago to the French border at Hendaye; change in Vitoria for Bilbao. Flights within Spain have come down in price over the last few years: try SpanAir (www.spanair.com) or Iberia (www.iberia.com). It's also possible to rent a car in Santiago and drop it off in Madrid, Bilbao or any major airport.

Red Tape

EU nationals can stay in Spain indefinitely, and you don't need a visa if you're from

Australia, Canada USA, or New Zealand and you stay for less than 90 days.

EU nationals are covered by reciprocal health care arrangements; UK residents need a European Health Insurance Card (EHIC) available from the Department of Health. Travel insurance will give you extra health protection and also cover your baggage. Be sure to read the fine print, as some policies classify walking as a dangerous activity.

In order to stay at an *albergue* (pilgrim hostel), you must show a *credencial*, a pilgrim passport which gets stamped with a *sello* (stamp) each night by the *hospitalero* (person who runs the *albergue*). You can also get *sellos* in churches, monasteries and even cafés. You can get a *credencial* from your local Camino de Santiago organization before you go (see page 167 for a list of these), or pick one up at the *albergues* in St-Jean-Pied-de-Port and elsewhere along the camino.

To qualify for the *compostela* (certificate of completing the camino), you must show your stamped *credencial* to prove you have walked the last 100km or cycled the last 200km to Santiago.

Money & Costs

Spain is a member of the European Monetary Union, and like the other members its currency is the euro (€). The most convenient way to get cash is to use your debit or credit card in a cashpoint or ATM. Banks often close for the day at 2pm, and *bureau de change* rates are generally unfavourable. Cashpoints frequently dispense €50 notes, which can be hard to

change in small towns and villages on the camino. Visa and Mastercard are widely accepted in restaurants, hotels and larger shops; American Express is less common.

Your cultural and transport costs can go down significantly if you're under 26, over 60 or a student. If you're a student, be sure to get an International Student Identity Card (ISIC) before leaving home, for discounts at certain museums. The Euro<26 card, available for about €10 from youth and student travel agencies throughout Europe, is more widely accepted and gets you a 20% discount on train travel. Spain is a very child-friendly country; as well as being the centre of attention wherever they go, your little ones will get generous discounts on hotels and transport.

If you stay in *albergues*, eat the *menu del día* once a day, and picnic on bread and cheese in the meantime, you can get by on €20 a day. To eat all your meals in cafés or restaurants, and to splurge on a hotel every now and then, allow about €40 a day. Exchange rates vary, but as a rough idea €1=US$1.20.

How much does it cost?

Albergue	€3–€7
Cheap hotel, double room	€25–€35
Menú (3-course meal)	€6–€9
Cheap bottle of wine	€2–€3

Transport

At some point along the way, you may need to recover from injury, catch up time or simply miss out a section — some pilgrims skip the *meseta* between Burgos and León, for example. Spanish trains, run by RENFE, are generally good value. The most useful line for pilgrims is the one from Santiago to Hendaye on the French border, which passes through Ponferrada, Astorga, León and Burgos. You can get information and book tickets online at www.renfe.es.

Buses are usually a more flexible option. In smaller places the bus stop can be just a street corner, and a café may act as the ticket office; ask a few locals where the bus stops and when it leaves.

Hitching long distances can be a frustrating experience, as foreign visitors are loathe to pick up hitchhikers, and locals may only be travelling as far as the next village. For shorter distances, hitching may be a useful option, particularly on weekends when bus services are limited. Hitching does, of course, involve risk, so take care.

Car hire is cheap compared to the rest of Europe, and it can be a good way of visiting sites on rest days or of getting from Santiago to airports in such places as Bilbao and Madrid.

 **Accommodation**

Albergues

Albergues, also known as *refugios*, provide cheap places to stay at regular points along the camino. Run by local municipalities, parishes or camino organizations, *albergues* are a wonderful way to meet other pilgrims, share meals and sto-

ries, and compare blisters and sore knees. They are restricted to self-powered pilgrims and the *hospitalero* will insist on seeing your *credencial* before giving you a bed. Although most *albergues* accept cyclists, walking pilgrims generally have priority, and those on bicycles may have to wait until the evening before being given a space.

No longer simply a roof over your head, modern *albergues* sometimes contain microwave ovens, washing machines and Internet access. About half the *albergues* along the camino have kitchen facilities, although stoves can work sporadically and pans may be in short supply. Most will provide a sink to wash your clothes and a line to hang them out to dry. Accommodation is mostly in mixed bunk-bed dormitories, and while blankets are often provided, it's a good idea to bring a thin sleeping bag. Toilets and shower facilities can be mixed too: if privacy is a big concern, you'll need to stay in a hotel.

Most *albergues* have a 10pm curfew and a morning closing time. Mornings tend to begin early and, even if you fancy a lie-in, the noise of other pilgrims packing up can wake you up. Earplugs can be an essential piece of equipment, not only to block out early risers, but also to try and get some sleep at night over the noise of *roncadores* (snorers).

Albergues are generally staffed by an *hospitalero*, more often than not a returning pilgrim who volunteers for between a week and a month. In Galicia, *albergues* are minimally staffed and not always well maintained: invest in some toilet paper. They generally cost from €3 to €7; Galician *albergues* ask for a donation from pilgrims. Some *albergues* stay open year-round, while others close for the winter;

all will be packed from June to September. The Spanish call pilgrim hostels *albergues* or *refugios*; we use *albergue* in this book, and attempt to list every one along the way.

Casas, hotels & paradors

There are places to stay in most villages, from cheap *pensiones* upwards. *Casas rurales* are springing up along the camino and can be charming places to stay. At the other end of the price scale, *paradores* are government-run luxury hotels, often in sumptuously converted historic buildings; they're well worth the splurge.

Private *albergues* are becoming more common. Priced somewhere between a municipal *albergue* and a cheap *pensión*, these *albergues* frequently have both private rooms and dormitory accommodation. Many have laundry facilities and Internet access and provide breakfast in the morning.

Wherever you decide to stay, it's a good idea to call ahead earlier in the day. Within each area we include accommodation suggestions for a range of budgets. Accommodation is divided into the price categories given below. The price given is for a double room in high season; rates drop at other times and may be open to negotiation.

$	up to €35
$$	€35–€50
$$$	€50–€75
$$$$	more than €75

Camping

Most campsites are inconveniently located a few kilometres off the camino or a fair way out of town. They often have excellent facilities but can be noisy on weekends. It may be worth bringing a tent in summer, as packed-out *albergues* sometimes let pilgrims camp in adjoining fields or gardens. There's no camping in urban areas or within 1km of an official campsite, but camping wild elsewhere is possible. Make sure you ask permission locally, particularly if you're camping on private land.

Equipment

Bring as little as possible. Spain is a modern European country and the camino passes through many towns and cities where you can shop to your heart's content. Remember that you'll need to carry everything you bring, and every luxury in your backpack leaves you more vulnerable to blisters and other injuries. Once you start walking, it's easy enough to ditch non-essentials and send them on to Santiago or post them home.

Good walking or running shoes are the best bet for your feet. Walking boots are probably overkill on the camino's good tracks and can be uncomfortable in hot weather, though you may be glad of them in winter. Take a pair of sandals or other lightweight shoes to pad about towns, villages and *albergues* in the evening.

Even in summer, it's a good idea to bring rain gear. A good quality rain poncho will keep you and your equipment dry; avoid the cheap versions found in supermarkets as these can shred in high winds. Lightweight waterproofs will be fine for summer rain, but bring a more robust rain jacket and rain pants to protect against winter downpours.

Other clothes should be comfortable and fast drying—bring lightweight layers rather than bulky sweaters. You'll be washing clothes most nights, so pack some laundry soap or travel wash and bring a few pegs or safety pins to hang things out to dry.

Bring a sun hat, sunglasses and sunscreen from spring to autumn, and a warm hat and gloves from autumn to spring. It's important to drink fluids throughout the year, and a collapsible bladder holds more water for long, dry stretches and takes up less room than a rigid water bottle.

A lightweight sleeping bag can make your stay in *albergues* more comfortable. Not all *albergues* provide blankets and some, especially those in monasteries, can be chilly at night.

A small torch (flashlight) can be useful at night and for poking around churches, and an alarm clock can get you up in the morning, though unless you're a very heavy sleeper you'll be woken up by the rustling of other pilgrims. To join in the rustling, bring lots of plastic bags, which are also useful for keeping clothes and other equipment dry.

Keep toiletries and first aid to a minimum, but bring something for blisters, and consider packing earplugs to block out the *roncadores* (snorers) and plastic bag rustlers in the *albergues*.

A phrasebook can help you communicate with people you'll meet along the way; choose one with a menu reader to avoid nasty surprises while eating out.

Binoculars can help you identify soaring birds of prey; they're also ideal for looking at lofty cathedral ceilings and windows.

A walking stick is a matter of personal choice; some pilgrims swear by them, while others find them awkward. Unless you bring a telescopic hiking pole, it's best to pick up a stick in Spain, as airlines are wary of passengers carrying weapon-like objects.

Many pilgrims hang a scallop shell, a traditional symbol of pilgrimage, from their packs or around their necks to distinguish themselves from ordinary tourists. If you're starting the camino before Ponferrada, you should also bring a small stone from home to place on the pile at Cruz de Ferro (page 124).

 Health & Safety

Pharmacies are generally open from 9am to 2pm and from 5pm to 8pm. There should be at least one pharmacy open outside these times too; look at the notice posted outside each one. Pharmacists will often speak English, offer more medical advice than in other European countries and be able to prescribe some drugs without a doctor's prescription.

In an emergency, dial 091 or ask for Cruz Roja (Red Cross), who run a national ambulance service. EU nationals are covered by reciprocal health care arrangements; UK residents should pick up a European Health Insurance card (page 27) before they leave, although it's often a good idea to supplement this coverage with private insurance.

Walking Hazards

Although the pilgrimage presents few natural hazards, walking every day will inevitably take a toll on your body — see Training & Fitness (page 32) for more information. Read the description of your day's route before setting out each morning and make sure you are equipped to deal with any problems that may arise.

Ask at the *albergue* or elsewhere about the weather forecast before heading over the mountain passes, and be prepared to delay your start or to detour via an easier route in case of fog or snow. On uninhabited stretches, make sure that you have enough warm and waterproof clothes, and always take more food and water than you think you'll need.

Route-finding is easy along the camino and there will usually be someone around to point you in the right direction but, if you do get lost, take the time to look around you for any obvious natural or man-made landmarks and use these to pinpoint your whereabouts. Better still, return to the last yellow arrow or camino marker that you passed. If you're not sure where you are, if it's getting dark or if visibility is poor, stay put.

Specific health risks

Blisters are the most common health problem you'll encounter. You're more likely to get blisters if your feet are hot, wet or tired, so be sensible about the distance you cover and the speed you walk at.

Vaseline may help prevent blisters, and sheep's wool can help cushion sore feet. If you do get blisters, the best treatment is rest. You'll come across hundreds of folk remedies for blisters, but essentially it's best to drain the liquid from the blister with something sterile, and to dry out the blister with antiseptic lotion.

The other common problem is heat. Wear a wide-brimmed sun hat, take good sunglasses and use plenty of suntan lotion with a high sun protection factor. Treat mild sunburn with cold water, ice or calamine lotion, and consult a doctor in more serious cases.

Drink lots of fluid and acclimatize gradually to hot conditions to stave off heat exhaustion and the more serious heatstroke. Rest often and take things slowly until your body is used to the heat. The Spanish *siesta* for a reason: it can be uncomfortably hot in the afternoon, and many pilgrims choose to finish their day by 2pm. Symptoms of heat exhaustion include cold and clammy skin, nausea and dizziness. Try to get to a cool place, and be sure to sip plenty of water.

With heatstroke, there may be some early sensation of feeling unwell, but the symptoms of flushed skin, dizziness, lack of sweating and restlessness usually occur suddenly. Move the sufferer to a cool place, cover them with wet clothes and fan them constantly. Get medical advice immediately, as the condition can be fatal.

Water from local springs is delicious, and most villages have drinkable water in the fountain (marked *agua potable*); use your common sense about drinking water from streams and purify or boil it if there are villages or farms nearby.

Most Spanish snakes are harmless, but there are a couple of venomous vipers and adders. Avoid poking around in holes or sitting on piles of rocks, and make slow, deliberate movements if you spot a snake. If someone does get bitten, secure and support the affected limb. Seek medical help, armed with a description of the snake, if possible.

Training & Fitness

The most important thing you can do is to wear comfortable, sturdy shoes and walk them in thoroughly before leaving home. A couple of months before you leave, start walking. If you can, try to walk every day, even if it's only for a short while, as this mimics the feeling of the camino and will help you to get used to daily walking. Gradually build up the distance over the next few weeks, then once you start to get fitter, take your pack along with you. A few times before you leave, pack everything you plan to take and go for a long walk; you'll get used to carrying a load, and perhaps leave non-essentials behind.

If you've left things until the last minute, don't make your first day on the camino too tough. Begin at Roncesvalles or Pamplona to avoid the climb over the Pyrenees from St-Jean-Pied-de-Port, or start at León or Triacastela rather than at Villafranca del Bierzo or Rabanal del Camino so you can prepare for or avoid the Cordillera Cantábrica.

Be sensible distance-wise for the first few days, and walk at a gentle pace. Even after you've been walking for a while, there will be days when you'll be lacking in energy. Try to be flexible about how far you travel each day, and be prepared to stop if you're flagging. Consider doing shorter days in wet weather, as you're more likely to get tired if you're soaking, and you'll also give your pack and shoes more time to dry out.

Communication

Post Offices

Correos (post offices) in smaller towns often close at 2pm, while city *correos* reopen after the *siesta* from 5pm to 8pm. It's faster and more convenient to buy stamps at *estancos*, state-run tobacconists. It's easy to send packages overseas, but if you're simply trying to lighten your load, then it's cheaper to send items on to Santiago. Label the package with your name (surname first and in capitals), and address it to *Lista de Correos*, Santiago de Compostela, Galicia. At the post office in Santiago, if nothing's found under your last name, ask the staff to check under any other names too.

Phones

Most public phones will take both coins and *tarjetas de telefónica* (phonecards). If a phone booth posts international dialling codes, then you can make overseas calls: dial 00, then the country code (44 for UK; 1 for Canada and USA; 61 for Australia; 64 for New Zealand). It costs about €2 to make a short call across Europe or to North America.

Mobile phones are ubiquitous on the camino as many companies provide Europe-wide coverage. Many pilgrims check up on each other via text messaging, and *albergue* bathrooms are often sacrilegiously crowded with recharging phones.

Internet

Many *albergues* now offer Internet access. When they don't, you'll find Internet cafés in cities and bigger towns along the camino. These cafés are frequently open late into the evening and are a sociable place to hang out and check e-mail. Most charge very low hourly or half-hourly rates.

For up-to-date information and useful links, check out www.pilipalapress.com.

Opening Hours & Public Holidays

The Spanish take the *siesta* seriously. Most shops, banks and post offices open at 10am, firmly close their doors at 2pm, then open for the evening from 5pm to 8pm. Museums often stay open through the *siesta* and close for the day at 4pm; most also close on Mondays. Mealtimes are later than in northern Europe. Lunch starts at 2pm, while the evening meal is eaten from 10pm. Along the camino, restaurants often cater to pilgrim schedules, serving a set menu at 8pm. For more on Spanish eating habits, see the Food and Drink sections earlier in this book.

Public Holidays

Most shops and banks close on public holidays, and public transport is limited. Restaurants and café-bars usually stay open, and there'll be a packed, holiday atmosphere inside. If you're low on cash, take some out a few days before the holiday, as bank machines can empty fast.

The following public holidays are celebrated in most of Spain. For regional festivals and holidays, see the Events & Festivals section in each regional chapter.

January 1	*Año Nuevo* (New Year's Day)
January 6	*Día de los Reyes* (Epiphany)
March/April	*Jueves Santo, Viernes Santo* (Maundy Thursday, Good Friday)
May 1	*Fiesta del Trabajo* (May Day)
August 15	*Asunción* (Feast of the Assumption)
October 12	*Día de la Hispanidad* (National Day)
November 1	*Todos Santos* (All Saints' Day)
December 6	*Dia de la Constitución* (Constitution Day)
December 8	*Inmaculada Concepción* (Immaculate Conception)
December 25	*Navidad* (Christmas Day)

Regional Map (key page 182)

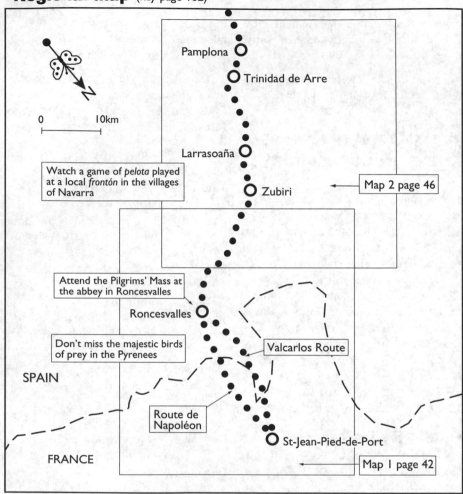

Pamplona

Trinidad de Arre

Larrasoaña

Watch a game of *pelota* played at a local *frontón* in the villages of Navarra

Zubiri

Map 2 page 46

Attend the Pilgrims' Mass at the abbey in Roncesvalles

Roncesvalles

Don't miss the majestic birds of prey in the Pyrenees

Valcarlos Route

SPAIN

Route de Napoléon

St-Jean-Pied-de-Port

FRANCE

Map 1 page 42

0   10km

N

What's the weather like?

	Jan	April	July	Oct
Sun	3hrs	6hrs	10hrs	5hrs
Rainfall	15cm	10cm	5cm	12cm
Maximum Temp	8°C	15°C	28°C	19°C
Minimum Temp	1°C	5°C	14°C	8°C

Average hours of sun, total average rainfall in cm and average temperature in degrees Celsius

Basque Lands

St-Jean-Pied-de-Port to Pamplona

The Basques are thought to be the original Europeans, passed over by successive waves of invaders and content to remain in and fight to protect this beautiful region. The route over the Pyrenees from St-Jean to Roncesvalles is one of the most dramatic of the camino, climbing steeply and soared over by eagles, buzzards and kestrels. As the Pyrenees peter out, you'll pass through traditional villages of whitewashed stone houses with ornate rafters and walk alongside trout-filled rivers lined with beech trees.

 **Walking**

Geography

Although it may not feel like it when you're huffing and puffing uphill, the pass at the Col de Lepoeder is on the lower, western fringes of the Pyrenees as they taper off into the Atlantic. This chain of mountains stretches for 435km, marking the border between France and Spain; the highest peak is Picos de Aneto (3404m), some 200km southeast of the pilgrim crossing point. The Pyrenees were formed when the Afro-Iberian tectonic plate collided with the European plate and the mountains still grow by fractions of a millimetre every year.

The lofty peaks of the Pyrenees attract clouds like a magnet, and it sometimes seems that any storm that comes into the Bay of Biscay is drawn relentlessly to them. The resulting high winds can bring snow at almost any time of the year: if crossing outside the summer months, beware of avalanches caused by the build-up of loose snow pockets that can be released without warning, carrying the hapless pilgrim with them. When the weather is fine the views are fantastic and the mountains' harsh reputation seems overplayed.

The Pyrenees recede reluctantly as the pilgrim heads west into pretty, undulating countryside with wooded hillsides and farmed valleys.

Trails

The Route de Napoléon climbs over the Pyrenees along a paved narrow mountain road, then veers off the road along a wide dirt track. It's an exposed route in bad weather, easy to get lost in fog or caught in snow, and almost every year pilgrims get into trouble along this stretch. Start early from St-Jean, take things slowly and be prepared to take the alternative Valcarlos route in bad weather. After Roncesvalles the camino follows dirt farm tracks with occasional paved stretches.

When to go

The weather in the Pyrenees can be unpredictable at any time of year, and in winter the pass may be snowbound, although it's rarely impassable for long periods of time. Even if there's no snow, fog, high winds and cold can make walking miserable. In the foothills, the weather's changeable in spring and autumn; summers are more settled and the region comes alive with festivals at this time, although the *albergues* will be more crowded.

Flora & Fauna

There's a good chance you'll see **birds of prey** in the Pyrenees. The mountains are home to hundreds of griffon vultures, languidly circling the lower peaks and valleys, often in fairly large groups. There are also black vultures and Egyptian vultures here, as well as golden and short-toed eagles, kestrels and buzzards. The **lammergeier**, called *quebrantahuesos* in Spanish (he who breaks bones) after its habit of dropping animal bones from a great height to smash them and get at the marrow within, is mainly found in the eastern Pyrenees but occasionally ventures this way. Equally difficult to spot are the bouncy chamois, an agile member of

the antelope family, and the marmot, seldom seen amongst rocks and more commonly heard whistling. Rocky terrain is also a favourite of the blue rock thrush, ptarmigan and rock bunting, while the solid, fan-tailed capercaille prefers pine forests. Around 160 plants are indigenous and unique to the Pyrenees; look for gentians, orchids and splendid, carnivorous sundews.

On your way down the mountain into Roncesvalles, you skirt the edge of the **Bosque de Irati**, a beech haven for wildlife that once stretched across the Basque lands to form one of the biggest forests in Spain. The loveliest parts of Irati are further east (see Rest Days & Detours), but along the camino you may see genet, beech marten, wild boar, and red, roe and fallow deer. The forest teems with bird life: listen out for the tap-tap-tapping of woodpeckers, and look for golden orioles, treecreepers, woodcock and ptarmigans.

The valley floors between Roncesvalles and Pamplona have been heavily farmed but willow, poplar, ash and maple stands provide refuge for many songbirds.

People & Culture

Although the camino from St-Jean-Pied-de-Port to Pamplona nominally begins in France and soon enters Spain, many locals insist that it travels through just one country, Euskadi, or the **Basque** lands. The Basque people's fierce independence has helped to preserve unique folk cultures like the *trikitnixa*, a whirling dervish of accordion music, but has also aroused suspicion from Spaniards and other foreigners. Aymeric Picaud, a twelfth-century pilgrim who wrote the *Codex Calixtinus*, was particularly uncomplimentary:

> "This is a barbarous people, different from all other people in customs and in race, malignant, dark in colour, ugly of face, debauched, perverse, faithless, dishonourable, corrupt, lustful, drunken, skilled in all forms of violence, fierce and savage, dishonest and false, impious and coarse, cruel and quarrelsome, incapable of any good impulses, past masters of all vices and iniquities."

Picaud's book was widely circulated in France and did much to sully the reputation of the Basques, culminating in a call for their excommunication by the French church in 1179.

Spanish authorities continued to find the Basque people a little weird. The **Inquisition**, notorious for its decimation of Spain's Jewish population and persecution of other religions, also worked to rid Navarra of the scourge of witchcraft. In a rash of accusations and confessions, stories surfaced of initiation ceremonies run by a toad, along with vampirism, cannibalism and having sex with the devil. By 1611, the Inquisition had uncovered almost 2000 witches in Navarra. Even after the Inquisition died down, many Spaniards continued to believe that the region's women were prone to witchcraft, a natural consequence of their fondness for apples, Eve's forbidden fruit.

Euskara, the Basque language, is the oldest living European language and has no linguistic relative; its origins aren't even Indo-European. About half a million Basques speak the language in Spain, with more *Euskara*-speakers across the Pyrenees in France. Under Franco, spoken Basque was forbidden and *Euskara* publications were forced underground. Furious at the censorship of Basque symbols and frustrated with an older generation who seemed content to wait for Franco to die before taking action, a group of young Basque Nationalists formed an organization in the 1950s that became known as Euskadi ta Astatasuna (**ETA**).

Begun as an intellectual movement primarily promoting *Euskara*, ETA's initial activities were largely peaceful. Activists daubed pro-ETA graffiti on walls and statues and derailed a train carrying people to San Sebastián where a celebration of Franco's 1936 victory was to take place. By the late 1960s, however, ETA attacks and Spanish reprisals (or Spanish attacks and ETA reprisals, depending on your point of view) had escalated into murder.

Although there's widespread condemnation of ETA violence among the Basques, there's also some support for the group's independence aims. And though human rights groups like Amnesty International have protested political arrests and torture of Basque nationalists, the Spanish government and western media continue to portray the complex Basque problem as a one-sided terrorist campaign.

Post-Franco, the Basques have gained some measure of independence, and there's been a revival of interest in traditional Basque culture, with increased attendance at and participation in sports such as goat racing, stone lifting and wood chopping. Still, the most popular Basque sport by far is *jai alai* or **pelota**, a game where two or four players smack a rock-hard ball with their bare hands against high walls. The village *frontón* (*pelota* court) is as ubiquitous as the village church, and you'll see the high-sided concrete courts in almost every inhabited place between the French border and Pamplona. The palm-bruising balls are made from tightly wound rubber tape covered in wool and cotton yarn, all of which is enclosed in goatskin. Once a folksy, machismo pastime, the sport has moved away from its village origins and is now unromantically reliant on TV money.

The camino between the Pyrenees and Pamplona is rife with tales of the exploits of the French king, **Charlemagne**, and his heroic knight, **Roland**, laid out in the epic French tale, the *Chanson du Roland*. According to the story, Charlemagne rode into Spain with his army, determined to win back the Muslim-dominated lands for Christianity. His seven-year-long operation was going pretty well until he reached Zaragoza, where Ganelon, an evil and cowardly knight determined to exact revenge on his nephew Roland, persuaded Charlemagne to accept Muslim peace terms instead of sacking the city. Satisfied with a job well done, Charlemagne headed back to France, but the rearguard of his army was ambushed by a Muslim army, killing Roland and many other brave knights.

It seems more likely that Charlemagne was on his way home after sacking Pamplona in 778, part of a brief campaign to extend French territory, when his army was attacked and defeated by the understandably furious Basques. The battle of Roncesvalles was never actually recorded by Charlemagne, as his only defeat represented a blight on an otherwise victorious military career. The French may even have appropriated the legend of Errolan, a Basque giant of great strength, in creating the figure of Roland. Nevertheless, the *Chanson du Roland* provides some of the more colourful legends of the region.

Food & Drink

Meals in Navarra centre around roast meat, game, trout and *jamón serrano*, a *prosciutto*-like cured ham. The woods provide pheasant, wood pigeon and woodcock, a rare delicacy, and the rivers are home to a seemingly endless supply of trout. Try *trucha a la Navarra*, Pyrenean trout wrapped in *jamón serrano* and then baked, or *chilindrón de cordero*, a delicious and spicy lamb stew made with local peppers.

Navarra **wine** has been produced in vast quantities since the Romans first arrived. Legend has it that when the church in Mendigorría, a few kilometres south of Puente la Reina, was built, the builders used wine instead of water to mix the cement. Navarra wine suffers in comparison with its more famous Riojan neighbour, but the wines are similar, and like Rioja the more robust Navarra depends heavily on the tempranillo grape, usually mixed with garnacha or some other variety.

Wine not your thing? Try the local tipple, **pacharán**, a deep pinky-orange fortified liqueur made from sloes, anise and sugar. *Pacharán* is usually drunk over ice, either neat or with water in a long glass. Often served as an aperitif, and said to aid digestion, it's sweet and tastes dangerously non-alcoholic.

Cheese is made in many places in the Pyrenean foothills. The most famous is the *queso de Roncal*, made from unpasteurized sheep's milk in the western Pyrenees. It's a compact, cylindrical cheese, ivory-coloured or very pale yellow, with a straw-coloured thin rind and a distinctive, creamy flavour.

Tourist Information

Transport

There are buses most days between Pamplona and Roncesvalles; taxis are a reasonable alternative if you can get a group together. A quaint, two-carriage train links St-Jean-Pied-de-Port with Bayonne a few times a day.

Accommodation

The *albergues* are small and evenly spaced, so you'll keep bumping into the same pilgrims and develop a great sense of camararderie. There are few hotels, and those that do exist are usually small, family-run *casas* or *pensiones*.

Events & Festivals

Navarra catches alight for the Noche de San Juan on June 21, a summer solstice festival of bonfires and festivities held in almost all the local villages. In Burguete's version, the whole village dances the *trebolé* and the *torralba del río*, symbolizing the capture of Juan Lobo, a legendary mediaeval bandit. From May to mid-June, there's a *romería* (religious procession) in Roncesvalles every Sunday, involving costumed locals from a nearby village and penitents shouldering huge crosses.

Rest Days & Detours

It's well worth spending the night in **St-Jean-Pied-de-Port**. There are enough things to do to fill the day, and you can stock up on food and then set off rested early the next morning. Although not quite a rest from exertion, the **Bosque de Irati**, just west of Roncesvalles, has some of the best birdwatching in all of Spain, including all seven species of European woodpecker. Hemingway's favourite mini-break when he was tired of running from bulls in Pamplona was a relaxed weekend in **Burguete**, trout fishing on the Río Urrobi.

St-Jean-Pied-de-Port
🅐🅗✗💺€🛈🛒 (776km)

St-Jean-Pied-de-Port is a pretty walled town, attractively located in the French Pyrenean foothills. The town's tourist highlights lie along a single cobbled street, Rue de la Citadelle, which is crowded on both sides with distinctive wooden buildings and uniform souvenir shops.

From the top of Rue de la Citadelle, walk downhill to the gothic **Prison des**

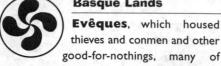

Evêques, which housed thieves and conmen and other good-for-nothings, many of whose victims were hapless pilgrims. It's now a camino and Basque museum. Farther down the street, the elegantly plain fourteenth-century **Eglise de Nôtre Dame** butts against the Porte Nôtre Dame, an imposing town gate with a statue of Santiago Peregrino. There's a scallop shell–decorated fountain in front of the church. The street changes its name to Rue d'Espagne here, then crosses the Rivière Nive over a gently rounded bridge, leading past lots of trinket shops towards the Porte d'Espagne, the gateway to the camino.

Above the town, at the top of Rue de la Citadelle, you can still visit the lower ramparts of the seventeenth-century **citadel**, built on the orders of Cardinal Richelieu and now converted into a college. It's worth coming to St-Jean-Pied-de-Port on a Monday, when the lively Basque open-air market takes over the town.

Turismo Place du Général-de-Gaulle 14 (☎ 0559 370357).

Accommodation
Albergue municipal 55 Rue de la Citadelle, towards the top of town (18 beds, kitchen, open all year). You can pick up a *credencial* here and get advice on walking and weather conditions in the mountains.
Albergue l'esprit de chemin 40 Rue de la Citadelle. €8. Open April to September.
$$ Hôtel Itzalpea, 5 Place du Trinquet (☎ 0559 370366)
$$ Hôtel des Remparts 16 Place Floquet (☎ 0559 371379)
$$$ Hôtel Ramuntcho 1 Rue de France (☎ 0559 370391)
$$$$ Hôtel de Pyrénées 19 Place Général de Gaulle (☎ 0559 370101)

The claustrophobic cobbled streets and tourist bustle of St-Jean-Pied-de-Port are left abruptly behind at the imposing Porte d'Espagne. Almost immediately, you're confronted with a signpost and there's a decision to be made.

There are two routes to Roncesvalles: the Route de Napoléon, which climbs gloriously high and steep over the Pyrenean foothills, and the pretty lower road route via Valcarlos. In mediaeval times, the Route de Napoléon was considered the safer bet, as pilgrims were less likely to be ambushed in the high mountains. On the Valcarlos route, according to Aymeric Picaud,

> "they come out to meet pilgrims with two or three cudgels to exact tribute by improper use of force; and if any traveller refuses to give the money they demand they strike him with their cudgels and take the money, abusing him and rummaging in his very breeches."

Nowadays, there are fewer vagabonds to worry about, and your choice of routes will be dictated mainly by the weather. The Route de Napoléon is exposed and isolated; it can be subject to snow as late as May and cold winds and rain at any time of year. The Route de Napoléon also makes for a very strenuous first day if you go all the way to Roncesvalles. There's almost no water along the way and nowhere to buy food, so bring enough provisions for a long day.

Valcarlos route

The route via Valcarlos is well marked and initially follows the Rivière Petit Nive shadowing the C135 road. You're mostly walking on minor roads through fields, farms and whitewashed buildings. Some

500m before the village of Arnéguy, pass the **Casa Sipilenea** (**$$**, ☎ 948 790129), a lovely *casa rural* right on the camino. After 8km, you'll reach the border at **Arnéguy** (⏣✕⬛€⛟), a pretty whitewashed town with some strangely Bavarian-looking buildings, particularly the church. You can stay at the **Hotel Clementenia** (**$$**, ☎ 0559 373132), but most pilgrims choose to continue for another 3km to Valcarlos. To do so, cross the N135 and take the minor road on its other side. Pass through **Óndarolle**, then head steeply downhill on a narrow lane, cross a river via a bridge and climb up to **Valcarlos** (Ⓐ⏣✕⬛€⛟).

The town's Iglesia de Santiago has a life-size statue of Santiago Matamoros (St James the Moorslayer) inside; outside, there's a sculpture of prematurely exhausted pilgrims. If you need to stay, the basic **albergue** (4 beds, open all year) is hidden underneath the **Casa Marcelino** (**$$**, ☎ 948 790186). You can also stay at the **Hostal Maitena** (**$$**, ☎ 948 790210) or the **Casa Etxezuria** (**$**, ☎ 948 790011), which is 500m out of Valcarlos on the road back to St-Jean.

Leave Valcarlos on the sometimes busy N135, heading uphill. In very bad weather, stay on the road for the 8km to the Col d'Ibañeta. Otherwise, some 2km after a road bridge over the Río Chapitel, veer left down a narrow paved lane signposted **Gañecoleta**. Walk through the tiny, pretty village, then follow a narrow grassy path back to the road. After another 2km of road walking, turn left down a wide grassy track. You'll soon start heading steeply uphill, zigzagging through beech trees. The area's beech forests are the only sites in Europe where you can see all seven species of European woodpecker. Look in particular for the black woodpecker and the white-backed woodpecker, but also keep an eye out for the red-backed shrike and the tiny crested tit.

Return briefly to the road after 2km, then turn left once more to reach the **Puerta de Ibañeta** in another 1km, where you meet up with the Route de Napoléon (page 44).

Route de Napoléon

The more dramatic Route de Napoléon offers fabulous views of the Pyrenees and great wildlife watching: look for eagles, vultures, fox and deer. Although the route is loosely named after Napoleon, his crossing of the Pyrenees into Spain was hardly groundbreaking — the Roman Via Traiana, which you'll follow for much of the next few weeks, went this way, linking Burdegala (Bordeaux) with Asturica Augusta (Astorga).

From the Porte d'Espagne signpost, follow the sign for Chemin St Jacques de Compostelle. The camino soon heads steeply uphill along narrow, quiet minor roads. Look out for lizards in the undergrowth at the side of the road and in walls; listen for rustling sounds to try and spot them.

After about 5km, the road begins to climb much more steeply, and shortly after a sharp hairpin to the left, you'll arrive at **Ferme Ithurburia** (**$**, ☎ 0559 371117), a *gîte* that does bed and breakfast in private and dormitory rooms in the village of **Honto** (⏣). There are dramatic views of the Pyrenees to the east, often snow-capped well into the summer. Behind you, St-Jean-Pied-de-Port and the surrounding valley are strikingly visible

Map 1 (key page 182)

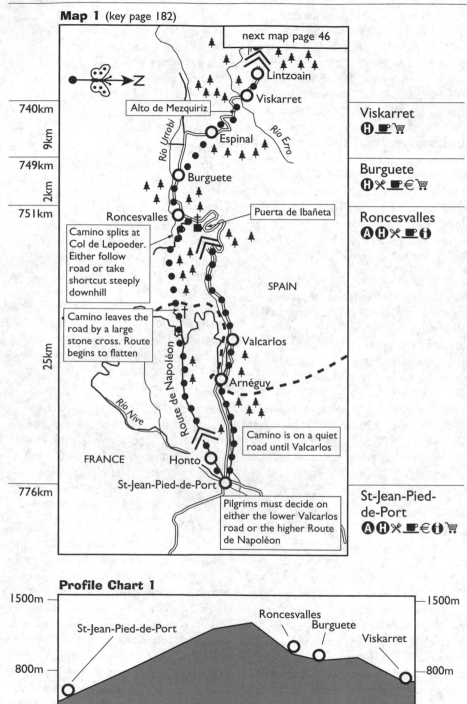

next map page 46

Lintzoain

Viskarret

Alto de Mezquiriz

Espinal

Viskarret
🅗 ☕ 🛒

740km

9km

Burguete

Burguete
🅗 ✕ ☕ € 🛒

749km

2km

Roncesvalles

Puerta de Ibañeta

Roncesvalles
🅐 🅗 ✕ ☕ ❶

751km

Camino splits at Col de Lepoeder. Either follow road or take shortcut steeply downhill

SPAIN

Camino leaves the road by a large stone cross. Route begins to flatten

25km

Valcarlos

Arnéguy

Route de Napoléon

Río Nive

Camino is on a quiet road until Valcarlos

FRANCE

Honto

St-Jean-Pied-de-Port

776km

Pilgrims must decide on either the lower Valcarlos road or the higher Route de Napoléon

St-Jean-Pied-de-Port
🅐 🅗 ✕ ☕ € ❶ 🛒

Profile Chart 1

1500m — — 1500m

St-Jean-Pied-de-Port

Roncesvalles
Burguete
Viskarret

800m — — 800m

when the weather is clear. Immediately after Honto, turn left along a track, and zigzag steeply uphill. The trail is lined with gorse and can be mucky after rain. The mountains here are more barren and the only agriculture is the occasional grazing sheep.

In a little while, the track rejoins the road. Turn left here; you'll soon pass a fountain on your right and a fascinating map on your left that names towns, peaks and camino routes. Although you're still climbing, the route becomes less steep now and the views of the Pyrenees just keep getting more spectacular. This is also one of the best parts of the camino to see birds of prey, particularly in spring and autumn when numbers are swelled by migratory birds. Gangs of griffon vultures are fairly common, but you may also see red kites, golden eagles, Egyptian vultures and the rare lammergeier.

Although the route is less strenuous now, it's a long slog (about 6km from Honto) until you reach the next major landmark, the **Vierge d'Orisson**. The statue of the Virgin Mary here is just off the main route to the left and is said to have been brought from Lourdes. Any loneliness she might feel in such an isolated spot must be more than made up for by the glorious views she has of the Pyrenees.

Continue along the road, then in a few kilometres keep a look out for a large memorial cross on the right-hand side of the road, surrounded by other plainer crosses left by pilgrims. Here, the camino leaves the road up a wide grassy track, headed for the peaks you've been able to see from the road for a while. Hapless mediaeval pilgrims had to be careful here. Picaud's guide warns,

"On this mountain, before Christianity was fully established in Spain, the impious Navarrese and the Basques were accustomed not only to rob pilgrims going to St James, but to ride them like asses and kill them."

Climb up the grassy track then follow a mostly flat track that can be clogged with tar-black mud after rain or snowmelt. Follow the signs to the Fontaine de Roland, a disappointing concrete fountain that you'll get to in about 2km. Almost immediately afterwards, cross over a cattle grid, where a concrete sign welcomes you to Spain.

The route winds through beech forest with a spectacular drop to your right into the lovely valley below, then passes some farm buildings and in a couple of kilometres join a road at the **Col de Lepoeder**, from where you'll be able to see the grey-roofed Roncesvalles monastery in the valley below. In mediaeval times, this was the site of Charlemagne's Cross, which marked the spot where Charlemagne supposedly gave thanks for his army's safe crossing of the Pyrenees and prayed to Santiago for help in his battles with the Moors. The fact that Charlemagne's campaigns in Spain took place at the end of the eighth century and that Santiago's bones weren't discovered until 813 didn't deter mediaeval pilgrims, who would stop here to plant their own wooden crosses and pray to Santiago for a safe journey.

From the Col de Lepoeder, there are two routes to the abbey.

Roman route

The old Roman road is more direct but very steep: you'll need energy, good knees

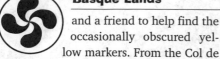

and a friend to help find the occasionally obscured yellow markers. From the Col de Lepoeder, follow the signs to the left for the GR65, cross over the minor road and keep straight ahead downhill through a beech forest. It's a lovely spot, particularly in spring when it's filled with songbirds and bluebells. In a few kilometres, you'll emerge at Charlemagne's Silo, just in front of the Abbey.

Puerta de Ibañeta Route

The second route from the Col de Lepoeder is longer but less steep, and goes via the Puerta de Ibañeta, the spot where Charlemagne heard Roland's horn, asking for help in his battle against the Moors. At the Col de Lepoeder, follow the signs to the right for the GR11, skirting the minor road until you reach the **Puerta de Ibañeta** in about 3km.

The *Chanson du Roland* tells of a great battle between the rearguard of Charlemagne's army, led by Roland, and local troops (probably Basque but often described as Moorish infidels). Roland was told to blow his horn, Olifant, if he got into trouble, but he left it until the last minute, and in any case Charlemagne, who heard Roland's alarm from his camp in Puerta de Ibañeta, was persuaded that the sound was a false alarm. Nowadays it's a pleasant 2km walk from the Puerta de Ibañeta downhill to the abbey at Roncesvalles. In bad weather, though, stick to the road.

Roncesvalles
Ⓐ Ⓗ ✕ 🝙 ⓘ (751km)

Roncesvalles (Orreaga) is a small hamlet, utterly dominated by its imposing abbey.

Pilgrims' Mass is held at 8pm each evening and, as part of the service, the nationality of each pilgrim is read out and pilgrims are invited to the front of the church. The moving ceremony and the communal meals that follow in the hamlet's two restaurants make your stay in Roncesvalles feel like the beginning of an important journey. Having said that, the abbey's strange zinc roof and its location in a sun-starved valley can make Roncesvalles seem rather bleak and grey.

Roncesvalles' attractions are generally related either to Roland and Charlemagne, or to Sancho El Fuerte (the strong), a Navarran king famed for his defeat of the Muslim army at Las Navas de Tolosa in 1212, which marked a turning point in the Christian *reconquista*. Sancho ordered the construction of the Gothic **Real Colegiata**, and his tomb, alongside that of his wife, Doña Clemencia, can be seen in the fourteenth-century chapter house that's annexed to the Colegiata's Cloister. At the foot of his massive tomb (Sancho was said to be well over 2m tall) are the chains of Christian prisoners freed at Las Navas. In the church of the Real Colegiata is a silver-covered wooden statue of the Virgen de Roncesvalles, who was made patroness of Navarra in 1960.

Legend has it that Charlemagne's soldiers, including Roland, were buried in the Capilla de Sancti Spiritus, a simple twelfth-century ossuary in front of the monastery, better known as the Silo de Charlemagne. Whatever the truth of the legend, the ossuary also contains the bones of mediaeval pilgrims who died trying to make it across the Pyrenees. The monastery's museum includes treasures such as Roland's carved ivory horn, Olifant, with which he tried in vain to summon Charlemagne. Charlemagne's chessboard, also in the museum, is actually an intricate fourteenth-century reliquary containing the bones of 32 saints and nothing at all to do with the Frenchman.

There's a small but helpful **turismo** in the old windmill (☎ 948 760301).

Accommodation
Albergue Basic but well-maintained facilities, can be very cold (100 beds, open all year).
$ youth hostel in the monastery (☎ 948 760307)
$$ Hotel La Posada (☎ 948 760225)
$$ Hostal Casa Sabina (☎ 948 760012)

To leave Roncesvalles, turn left and walk down the road. In just 200m, just before the **Cruz de Peregrinos**, a fourteenth-century cross depicting Sancho el Fuerte on the base, turn right down a track marked with yellow arrows and a map of the camino. The flat track runs parallel to the road, through holly and beech trees, then reaches the outskirts of Burguete in a couple of kilometres.

Burguete
Ⓗ✖☐€🛒 (749km)

Burguete (Auritz) is a lovely village of shuttered houses made famous as Hemingway's trout-fishing base in *The Sun Also Rises*. While here, he wrote to F. Scott Fitzgerald that, "heaven would be a big bull ring with me holding two *barrera* seats and a trout stream outside that no one else was allowed to fish in." The writer's presence is less noticeable than camino symbolism such as the house railings decorated with scallop shells and the pilgrim fountain in front of the Iglesia de San Nicolás de Bari. Burguete has an excellent café-*panadería* (bakery).

Accommodation
$ Hostal Juandeaburre (☎ 948 760078)

$ Casa Iturrialdea (☎ 948 760243)
$$$ Hostal Burguete (☎ 948 760005)
$$$$ Hotel Loizu (☎ 948 760008)

In Burguete, turn right 50m after San Nicolás de Bari church, cross a stream over a wooden bridge and join a wide dirt track on the other side. From this broad, flat valley, there are good views of the nearby beech-clad hills.

In a few kilometres, you'll arrive at **Espinal** (Ⓗ✖☐🛒), a small town with distinctive decorative railings, a bar, restaurant, *panadería* and shop. There are a few *casas rurales* in the village: try **Casa Errebesena** ($, ☎ 948 760141) or **Casa Yanborinberri** ($, ☎ 948 790417). In Espinal, turn right at the main road, then turn left in a couple of hundred metres, following the yellow arrows down a broad, semi-paved track.

After a couple of kilometres, cross a road to walk through a beautiful, peaceful beech wood on a path that soon narrows as the road drops steeply away to the left. There's some erosion here and exposed roots in places, and the path can be treacherously muddy in very wet weather, when it's worth sticking to the road. The wood is home to bullfinches, coal tits and robins, and to the more elusive fox.

The camino almost reaches the road at a tight left-hand bend but then veers away to the right, heading uphill on a shady, stony path. After 300m, turn left to walk along a grey, paved track. The government of Navarra is busy "improving" the camino by paving over some of the paths along the route, which can be hard on the feet.

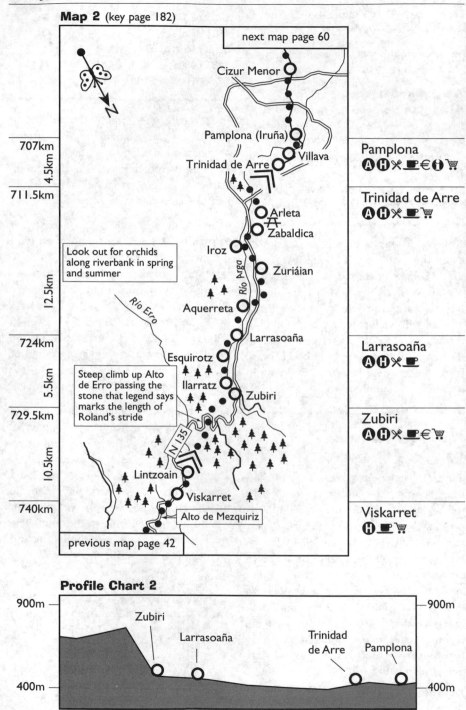

Map 2 (key page 182)

next map page 60

Cizur Menor

Pamplona (Iruña)

Trinidad de Arre

Villava

Pamplona

Trinidad de Arre

707km

4.5km

711.5km

Arleta

Zabaldica

Iroz

Zuriáian

Look out for orchids along riverbank in spring and summer

Río Arga

Aquerreta

Río Erro

Larrasoaña

12.5km

Esquirotz

Larrasoaña

724km

5.5km

Steep climb up Alto de Erro passing the stone that legend says marks the length of Roland's stride

Ilarratz

Zubiri

729.5km

Zubiri

N 135

10.5km

Lintzoain

Viskarret

740km

Alto de Mezquiriz

Viskarret

previous map page 42

Profile Chart 2

900m

900m

Zubiri

Larrasoaña

Trinidad de Arre

Pamplona

400m

400m

You'll emerge in Viskarret's outskirts in a kilometre or so; cross the main road to enter the village proper. **Viskarret** (🅗💷🛒, 740km) is a fascinating village with a distinctive and uniform architecture; look out for wooden balconies, huge wooden roof joists and stone doorways carved with crosses. The stone church has a big bell tower and is a mix of Romanesque and Gothic styles. Just as prominent is the village *frontón*, where the Basque sport of *pelota* is played. You'll see these large concrete courts in almost every village you'll pass between here and Pamplona. You can stay at **Casa La Posada Nueva** ($$, ☎ 948 760173).

At the end of the village, turn left at the shop, ford a stream and pass a cemetery, then take the centre of three narrow paths, pretty with shade and a great place to see and hear songbirds. In 500m, cross the main road and follow a track into the quiet hamlet of **Lintzoain**. Walk past the roofed *frontón*, then turn right to walk under a wooden bridge that links the upper storey of one of the hamlet's gorgeous stone houses with a high-walled garden on the other side of the street.

The camino becomes a dirt track at the top of the village and begins to climb steeply uphill. It's a hot slog in summer, with very little shade initially. Cross a road about 1500m after the village, then a kilometre later, look out for a very low, yellow-painted rock just to the right of the trail; this insignificant-looking monument is said to mark the length of Roland's huge stride.

The trail undulates for a couple of kilometres before reaching the pass at **Alto de Erro**, where the ruins of a pilgrims' inn are now home to local cows, and the nearby fields are a good place for a picnic.

In autumn, there's a feast of mushrooms in the local woods; make sure you ask for local advice before eating anything you don't recognize. The splendid crossbill is a year-round resident, but easiest to see in the winter months when it feeds closer to the ground. From here onwards, it's downhill to Zubiri, some 2km away along a well-marked track. As Zubiri comes into view, the path becomes steeper: watch your footing on the occasional smooth rock sections.

On reaching the first houses in Zubiri, turn right and cross the bridge to reach the village facilities; turn left to continue the camino towards Larrosoaña.

Zubiri
🅐🅗✕💷€🛒 (729.5km)

Zubiri's lovely Gothic bridge, the Puente de la Rabia, crosses the Río Arga to the main part of town. It's said that if cattle are driven around the bridge's central pillar three times, they will be cured of rabies.

Zubiri is a small town with few decent facilities; the *albergue municipal* is a bit run down.

Accommodation
Albergue Municipal (46 beds, open all year)
Albergue Zaldiko (16 beds, March to October, ☎ 609 736420)
$ Hostal Benta Berri (☎ 948 304376)
$ Hostal Usoa (☎ 948 304306)
$$$ Hostería de Zubiri (☎ 948 304329)

Leave Zubiri on a well-marked track through farmland, turn right at a gravel road, then turn left at a minor road 400m later to walk past a massive magnesite factory. After a couple of days of bucolic, timeless walking, the factory is a jarring reminder of the twenty-first century.

As the factory buildings end, turn right to walk down a flight of steps. Head uphill towards the village of **Ilarratz**, which you'll reach in a kilometre and where there's a fountain. Follow minor roads to the hamlet of **Esquirotz**, 1km away, which has a sporadically working fountain. On the other side of Esquirotz, follow a grassy stone track, which soon widens and then crosses a road.

From here, you can see Larrasoaña up ahead. After almost a kilometre, and just as it seems that you have missed the village, you reach a track and a camino map. Turn left to continue the camino, or turn right for Larrasoaña, entering the village via the Gothic, fourteenth-century Puente de los Bandidos, a camino bottleneck where opportunistic bandits would lie in wait for pilgrims.

Larrasoaña

Ⓐ Ⓗ ✕ ☕ (724km)

Although the layout of Larrasoaña's main street dates from the twelfth century, the grand houses that line it were mostly built in the fifteenth and sixteenth centuries. Nothing remains of the village's two hospices, but the Clavería de Roncesvalles, the long low building opposite the thirteenth-century Iglesia de San Nicolás de Bari may have been a monastery warehouse. The village's small bar has a nightly pilgrim *menú* and sells basic provisions.

Accommodation

Larrosoaña's mayor runs the **albergue** (53 beds, kitchen, open all year) with a gentle, caring officiousness. The village's three *pensiones* are all on Calle San Nicolás.

$ Pensión Bidea (☎ 948 304288)

$ El Peregrino (☎ 948 304554)

$$ Pensión El Camino (☎ 948 304250)

At the map of the camino on the far side of the Puente de los Bandidos, head uphill along a gravel track. You'll soon reach **Aquerreta** (Ⓗ), its three-storey houses typical of the region's rural architecture, with the ground floor for animals, the first floor for people and the shallow top storey reserved for pigeons. One of these houses has been converted into the **Hotel Akerreta** (**$$$**, ☎ 948 304572).

Follow a narrow gravel path out of the village, then cross a minor road and continue on a wide gravel track through pine forest. The forest gives way to farmland as you approach the village of **Zuriáian**, where the mediaeval Iglesia de San Millán was restored in the sixteenth and seventeenth centuries. In Zuriáian, cross a modern bridge, then turn left to walk along the main road, taking care as there's not much of a shoulder. In about 500m, turn left down a minor road and re-cross the Río Arga. Take the lane to the right, which soon becomes a gravel track and heads into pine forest, before arriving in a kilometre at the village of **Iroz**, where there's a fountain and the Iglesia de San Pedro.

Follow the road out of Iroz, crossing the humpback Romanesque bridge. Immediately after the bridge, ignore the first lane which goes straight down to the river on the left, and instead take the next single track on the left. This stretch of the Río Arga is a popular fishing spot with both locals and sparrowhawks, and the path is lined with orchids in spring and summer. Walk straight through the village of **Zabaldica**, looking out for the twelfth-century Romanesque Iglesia de San Esteban.

In a few hundred metres, cross the main road at a picnic site, then climb briefly and steeply uphill to follow a dramatic trail high above the river. Soon, the camino arrives at the tiny hamlet of **Arleta**, where there's a graceful manor house and the lovely Iglesia de Santa Marina. After a pretty, kilometre-long stretch, the trail abruptly heads back towards a major road and passes underneath it via a grubby tunnel. From here, follow a paved track downhill, turning around to see your route from Larrasoaña along the Río Arga. At the bottom of the hill, cross over the Romanesque bridge to walk into Trinidad de Arre.

Trinidad de Arre
Ⓐ Ⓗ ✕ 🍺 🛒 (711.5km)

Trinidad de Arre has been a strategic town since Roman times, and the town has a long camino history. The end of the bridge is dramatically marked by the Basilica de la Trinidad de Arre, where there's a monastery, an *albergue* and the remains of an old hospice. Trinidad de Arre's sixteenth-century bylaws, which required each local to provide the pilgrim hospice with half a pound of bread a year, have long since been repealed, but luckily for hungry pilgrims, the main street is now lined with cafés and *panaderías*.

Albergue 34 beds, kitchen, open all year.

$ Pensión Obelix (☎ 948 126056)

$$$ Hotel La Buhardilla (☎ 948 382872)

Turn left at the end of the bridge and head down Calle Mayor. Trinidad de Arre leads seamlessly into **Villava**, famous as the birthplace of Spain's renowned cycling hero, Miguel Induraín. Both villages were swallowed up long ago by suburban Pamplona, and it's a fair way into town through these suburbs. As city approaches go, however, it's surprisingly non-industrial, and there's a pleasant mix of old and new buildings crunched up on either side of the road.

In a couple of kilometres, and just before you reach the river, veer left down a paved walkway. Turn right, initially along a riverside path, then follow a road with no sidewalk. The road ends in about 600m at the Río Arga. Turn right here, then turn left to cross the river over the fourteenth-century Puente de Magdalena, decorated with stone statues and a stone cross donated by Santiago de Compostela in the 1960s. Nothing remains of the leper hospital that once stood at this spot, safely outside the city walls.

Pass a fountain on the far side of the bridge, then cross a busy road and head towards Pamplona's imposing town walls. Walk over a drawbridge and pass through the two magnificent town gates into the old town. You'll reach the *albergue* at the Convento de Adotrices in a few hundred metres.

Regional Map (key page 182)

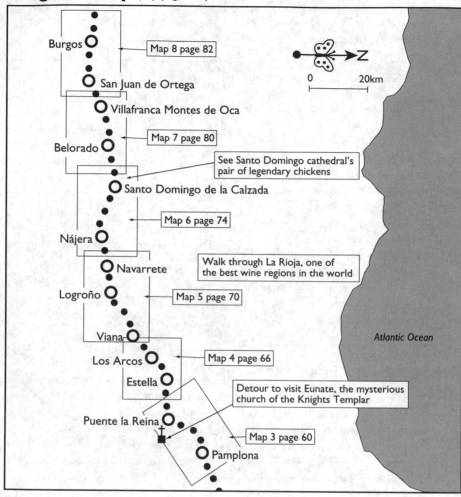

Burgos

Map 8 page 82

San Juan de Ortega

Villafranca Montes de Oca

Map 7 page 80

Belorado

See Santo Domingo cathedral's pair of legendary chickens

Santo Domingo de la Calzada

Map 6 page 74

Nájera

Navarrete

Walk through La Rioja, one of the best wine regions in the world

Logroño

Map 5 page 70

Viana

Los Arcos

Map 4 page 66

Estella

Detour to visit Eunate, the mysterious church of the Knights Templar

Puente la Reina

Map 3 page 60

Pamplona

Atlantic Ocean

0   20km

What's the weather like?

	Jan	April	July	Oct
Sun	3hrs	6hrs	10hrs	6hrs
Rainfall	3cm	4cm	2cm	3cm
Maximum Temp	9°C	17°C	29°C	20°C
Minimum Temp	2°C	7°C	15°C	9°C

Average hours of sun, total average rainfall in cm and average temperature in degrees Celsius

Navarra & La Rioja

Pamplona to Burgos

The camino heads through Navarra and into La Rioja through lovely towns little-changed since mediaeval times and stuffed full of glorious Romanesque churches. You'll also eat and drink like royalty. Rioja wine is smooth, gorgeous and dirt cheap, and the region's Lodosa peppers, white asparagus and veal are known throughout the country.

 **Walking**

Geography

The rolling hills of Navarra soon give way to the fertile Ebro valley. The Río Ebro dominates the landscape, draining an area of more than 85,000 square kilometres. The river is coveted as a source of water for irrigation, with 35 major dams along its length, and the average flow is reduced by a staggering 29% from that of a century ago.

Every inch of Rioja's blood-red soil seems to be covered with vines. The soil needs to be turned frequently, so that any rain that does fall will water the shallow-rooted vines rather than run straight off the dry, hard earth. Concrete drainage channels and aqueducts divert precious water to vines and other crops, and La Rioja's environmental problems are likely to get worse as water-guzzling golf courses become more commonplace.

As pilgrims head towards Burgos they follow a wide natural corridor that separates the high, magnificent Sierra de la Demanda to the south from the smaller Sierra de Cantabria to the north; these peaks are often covered in snow well into April. Just before the flat *meseta* begins at Burgos, the camino climbs up and over the Montes de Oca, a rugged range covered in heather and pine.

Trails

The camino is well marked and is mainly made up of broad gravel or dirt tracks through vineyards and farmland, though there are times when you'll yearn to move away from the N120, which you shadow on and off from Logroño to Burgos. Highlights of the route include the section of well-preserved Roman road between Cirauqui and Lorca and the red tracks that bring you up close and personal to Rioja's unfenced vineyards.

When to go

There's nothing to stop you walking this

section year-round. Spring is particularly lovely and it's not too cold, even though the surrounding mountains are still shrouded in snow. In June or July you can catch one of Navarra's lively festivals, but the best time to visit La Rioja is during the autumn grape harvest.

 # Flora & Fauna

You'll be accompanied by the slow, stately flight of the **white stork** from Puente la Reina to Santo Domingo de la Calzada. In spring, the storks nest on almost every church spire and tower along the route and you'll hear loud clack-clack-clacking as the youngsters demand food. It's less common to see them on the ground, but when you do, they'll be pecking chicken-like at the dirt.

At dawn and dusk, look for the **eagle owl**, a large, buzzard-sized bird with distinctive ear tufts that's strong enough to take on prey the size of a hare. The best way to locate the owl is by its hoot, a continuous oooohu-oooohu-oooohu that can be heard up to 4km away on a still night.

Bonelli's eagles are a lot easier to spot, and the population along this stretch is resident year-round. The birds often hunt in pairs, one bird hovering above while the partner chases a flock of birds, separating and choosing a weak flier, which the hovering bird then swoops down to catch. Both birds share the benefit of their labour. Bonelli's eagles are still hunted here, as their taste for rough-legged partridges irritates local hunters who want the game bird for themselves.

 # People & Culture

Even Picaud, the French camino chronicler who wasn't a big fan of Spain, liked this part of the world: "This is a country full of treasures, of gold and silver, fortunate in producing fodder and sturdy horses and with an abundance of bread, wine, meat, fish, milk and honey." It was a qualified approval, though. "It is, however, lacking in trees, and the people are wicked and vicious."

Western Navarra parties hard, preserving celebrations that date back to before the Roman invasion. **Carnaval**, a pre-Lent celebration with pre-Christian roots, has resurfaced in the last few decades after being banned under Franco, partly because of the distinctly un-Catholic activities involved and partly because Franco's police found it impossible to identify the masked participants. The masquerades usually portray the persecution and killing of something external and dangerous, such as a wolf or a bandit.

The most famous festival is Pamplona's **San Fermín** in July, a week of celebration centred around the lively and controversial *encierro*, when red-scarfed men run through the narrow streets pursued by bulls. The day before the *encierro*, colourful processions of *gigantes* (plaster giants), *cabezudos* (big heads) and *kilikis* (Napoleon-like figures who whack children with foam bats) lollop and dance their way through the city.

Dancing is an essential part of all *fiestas*, and it's said that Navarra has more traditional dances than any other region in Europe. Mixed sex groups jive to the sounds of the Basque *txistu* (flute), *trik-itrixa* (accordion) and *tamboril* (drum). The best-known dance, the *jota*, is a traditional winemakers' dance in honour of Bacchus, the Roman god of wine, whereas other dances evoke grazing, war or honour the Basque flag. El Baile de la Era is a combination of all the traditional dances of the Basque region. Although a relatively recent invention, it's treated as a traditional dance in many festivals in Navarra, particularly in Estella, where composer-choreographer, bagpiper and local boy Julián Romano lives. It's danced as the finale to Estella's San Fermín, which is slightly tamer than Pamplona's version and generously allows women to run with the bulls.

Some traditional and bizarre Basque sports survive in Navarra, including spade races in Puente la Reina and hoe hurling further south. You can watch professional games of *pelota* (page 37) in Pamplona and Estella.

Food & Drink

Wine lovers are in for a treat. Rioja is a smooth, gentle, vanilla-scented wine that's available everywhere at about a third of the price you'd pay outside the country. You'll find a great bottle for around €5, and even €2 will get you a fresh and fruity glugger. Wine's been made here since Roman times but (whisper it softly) Rioja was vastly improved when French winemakers fled south to escape the *phylloxera* that wiped out their own vineyards, helping to make Spanish vines resistant to the disease and improving the native grape varieties.

Traditionally, local farmers simply planted vines in the ground, hacked the plant back to a mere stump in winter and picked the grapes by hand. You'll still see fields planted like this, but modern farmers string the vines along wire fences a tractor's width apart. This makes the vine easier to care for and allows more grapes to survive to maturity. Each vine takes three years to reach productivity and can be harvested for about 50 years.

The longer Rioja spends maturing, the smoother it becomes. Crianza spends a year in oak barrels and a year in bottles, Reserva stays in oak for a year followed by three in the bottle, and Gran Reserva matures for at least two years in barrels and another four years in the bottle.

It might be gorgeous, but a glass of Rioja won't do much to fill that gaping hole in your stomach. South of Estella, Lodosa is famous for **pimientas del piquillo**, horn-shaped red peppers that are dried outdoors or roasted by hand and then preserved in oil. They're delicious on their own, well-salted with slivers of garlic, but can also be stuffed with almost anything; lamb, olive and pine nuts are a particularly good combination.

In spring, you'll see fields of **white asparagus** along the camino, particularly between Pamplona and Puente la Reina. As the asparagus grows under black, light-blocking plastic, soil is gradually piled up around the stems. The government has designated the Valle del Ebro in Navarra, around Logroño, as the *denominación* (official region) for *espárrago de Navarra*. Cooked asparagus is most often seen pickled in jars and is frequently served in restaurants as an anaemic-looking starter, smothered in mayonnaise.

The people of Navarra and Rioja eat a lot of meat. Veal from Navarra is known throughout the country, and Pamplonan *chorizo* is also very good. *Fiestas* are a great excuse to spit-roast pig, kid or lamb, while more economical dishes like *patatas con chorizo* (potato with *chorizo* stew) and *los caparrones* (red bean stew with *chorizo* and scrag ends of meat) help to eke out the meat a little longer.

i Tourist Information

Transport

It's easy to get around by bus and there are frequent services between Pamplona and Estella, Estella and Logroño, and Logroño and Burgos, stopping at sizeable places in between.

Accommodation

Albergues are well maintained and tend to be fully equipped with kitchens, ideal for cooking the local *chorizo* and *pimientas del piquillo* and sampling a glass or two of Rioja. If you fancy a break from the *roncadores* (snorers), splurge at the *parador* in Santo Domingo de la Calzada, a splendidly opulent hotel just across the square from the cathedral.

Events & Festivals

The people of Nájera take to the streets for the Fiestas de San Juan y San Pedro at the end of June, singing and dancing to catchy, militaristic music said to have originated with soldiers in the Carlist wars. Pamplona's famous San Fermín explodes into action on July 6, and Estella's marginally calmer version takes

place on the first Friday in August. At the end of September, Logroño livens up for the week-long Fiesta de San Mateo, worth visiting for the grape-crushing ceremonies in the Paséo del Espolón.

Rest Days & Detours

Just south of Nájera, a trip into the Sierra de la Demanda to visit the two monasteries of **San Millán de Cogolla**, designated as UNESCO World Heritage Sites, will add about 15km or so to your route towards Santo Domingo de la Calzada. Since it's difficult to find somewhere to stay along the way, it may be easier to visit on a day trip from Nájera.

The serene monastery at **Suso**, just above the village, was established in the seventh century and incorporates the hermit caves of San Millán and Santa Oria. Expanded in the tenth century to a pre-Romanesque church, the monastery was rebuilt in the eleventh century in a mix of Mozarabic, Romanesque and Gothic styles.

The cloister-like front porch holds the gruesome, headless remains of the seven Infantes de Lara, princes betrayed by their uncle to the Muslims, who decapitated the Infantes and brought their heads to their father for identification. Inside, the central cave contains San Millán's lovely twelfth-century tomb.

Lower down, the village is dominated by **San Millán de Yuso**, a sixteenth-century Renaissance monastery. The statue on the façade might look like Santiago Matamoros but is in fact San Millán, complete with horse and sword. Plaques in the Salon de los Reyes record the first written use of *Castellano* (Spanish) and Basque in the tenth century.

If it's wine you're after, head to **Haro**, 40km northwest of Logroño, particularly in the last week of June during the festivals of San Juan, San Felices and San Pedro, when the *bodegas* fill the plaza with free samples and bottles at knockdown prices. On June 29, the wine flows even more freely when villagers drench each other with Rioja's finest in the *batalla del vino* (wine battle).

About 20km south of Logroño is **Clavijo**, the eighth-century scene of Santiago Matamoros' first appearance in battle, resplendent on his white charger. Apart from the ruined castle above the hamlet, there's not much to see here. Further southwest, and a few thousand

years earlier, **dinosaurs** roamed the mud around **Arnedillo**, leaving massive prints when the mud hardened to stone. In the Middle Ages, the footprints were said to be those of giant chickens that lived during the times of the Moors, or the hoof marks of Santiago's horse. If you want to learn more, nearby Enciso has a Centro Paleontológico; once you've finished, you can relax at Arnedillo's spa.

About 10km northwest of Los Arcos, the church in the village of **Sorlada** holds the sacred bones of San Gregório, a bishop who rid the surrounding area of a plague of locusts in the eleventh century. On May 9 each year, the anniversary of his death, church officials pour water over his saintly bones, and villagers collect this blessed water to use on their fields.

Pamplona

ⒶⒽ✕�€ⓘ🛒 (707km)

Pamplona (Iruña) is a compact city, its narrow cobbled streets seemingly squashed together to fit within its commanding walls. There's very little modern building in the centre of the city, although there's a fair bit of pro- and anti-ETA graffiti to remind you of current Basque concerns. Pamplona was founded by Pompey, and the city's cathedral is said to be built on the spot of the Roman capitol. Excavations of the cloister have discovered a market, forum and baths. Charlemagne razed Pamplona in 778, which goes a long way towards explaining the rout of his army and the death of Roland at the hands of the annoyed Basques.

Pamplona's Gothic **cathedral** was begun in the late fourteenth century after the earlier Romanesque building collapsed in 1390. The present cathedral's late-eighteenth-century façade stretches up in thick, solid, grey columns more in keeping with a grand mausoleum than a church. The façade is almost universally hated, although it's actually quite impressive in a morose kind of way.

Among the cathedral's highlights are the delicate, fifteenth-century alabaster tombs of Carlos III el Noble and his wife Leonor, and the intricate Gothic cloister, with its glorious, appropriately named Puerta Preciosa (precious door). The kings of Navarra, many of whom were crowned in the cathedral, swore their oaths of allegiance to the laws of the

Pamplona

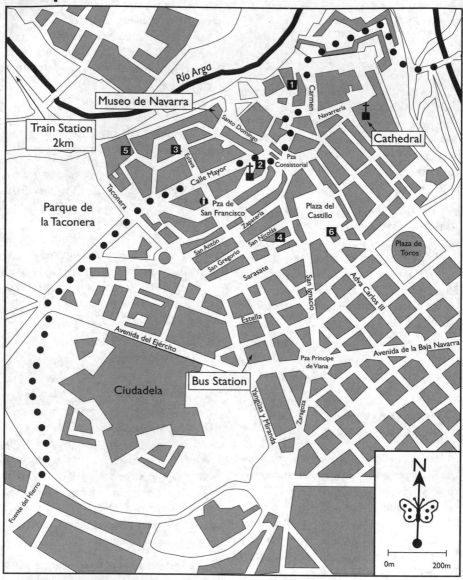

Accommodation

1	Albergue Convento Adoratrices	**4**	Hostal Otano
2	Albergue Iglesia de San Saturnino	**5**	Hostal Eslava
3	Pensión Eslava	**6**	Hotel Europa

land in front of the Romanesque, silvered Virgen del Sagrario, which is now in the main altar. The cathedral's Museo Diocesano is worth a visit, particularly for the exquisite twelfth-century French reliquary. On a more prosaic note, you can also add to your *sello* collection in the cathedral by asking the priest to stamp your *credencial*.

The **Museo de Navarra**, just east of the cathedral on Calle Santo Domingo, is housed in a magnificent former hospice and contains a wealth of information about Pamplona's history, including intricate Roman mosaics and Romanesque capitals from the cathedral.

If sport's more your thing, head to Estadio de El Sadar, Osasuna's **football** ground. The Pamplona club flits in and out of the Primera Liga, but it's the nearest you'll get to a top-class club on the camino.

Pamplona loses its head at the annual **San Fermín** festival from July 6 to 14, and if you've seen pictures of the city before you arrive, it's likely to be of the world-famous *encierro*, the running of the bulls that forms part of this festival. Each year, local men and male tourists race through Pamplona's narrow streets pursued by drugged-to-the-eyeballs bulls; it's a dangerous event in which tourists seem to be disproportionately among the gored. If you're a woman, you'll have to wait until the mixed Estella event on the first weekend in August for your slice of insanity. San Fermín, a 700-year tradition, is a week of processions, music, dancing, fireworks and drinking: apparently, three million litres of alcohol are consumed each year. Procession participants include *gigantes* (giant plaster puppets) and *cabezudos*, big-headed figures who attack onlookers with rubber sticks.

Pamplona's a large city with some excellent restaurants and plenty of bars, shops and banks. The **turismo** is at Calle Eslava 1, Plaza San Francisco (☎ 948 206540).

Accommodation

There are two **albergues** in Pamplona. The most reliable (and most strict) is in the Convento Adoratrices on Calle Dos de Mayo, 4 (94 beds, open April to October). There's also an *albergue* in the Iglesia de San Saturnino on Calle Florencio Ansoleaga (20 beds, kitchen, open April to October), although this is often closed, and a summer-only *albergue* in a school outside town: go to the San Saturnino *albergue* for directions.

Hotels are expensive in Pamplona, and prices during San Fermín usually triple.

$ Pensión Eslava, Calle Eslava 13 (☎ 948 221558)
$$ Hostal Otano, Calle San Nicolás 5 (☎ 948 225095)
$$$ Hostal Eslava, Plaza Virgen de la O, 7 (☎ 948 222270)
$$$$ Hotel Europa, Calle Espoz y Mina 11 (☎ 948 221800)

There aren't many facilities between Pamplona and Obanos, 20km away, so make sure you have enough food and water before leaving Pamplona.

The camino through Pamplona takes you along narrow streets and arrives at the park that surrounds Pamplona's *ciudadela* (citadel), a star-shaped fort surrounded by lovely gardens. From here, pass through the university district, about a kilometre out of town. On the hills up ahead, you can see a line of modern windmills on the Alto de Perdón, which provide some of the region's electricity; you'll pass these later on the camino. Head towards Cizur Menor, a couple of kilometres away, along a broad sidewalk that's popular with promenaders in the evenings and on weekends.

Cizur Menor

Ⓐ✖☕ (702.5km)

The thirteenth-century church of San Miguel, to the right of the main road, is worth a quick look for its Romanesque-Gothic door. It was recently restored, having been used for more than a century as a grain warehouse. More impressive is the church of San Andrés in Cizur Mayor, 2km up this road.

Accommodation

Cizur Menor's small **albergue** (35 beds, kitchen, open all year), just off the main road to the right, is run by the *grande dame* of the village and located in the grounds of her beautiful home. There's also a second *albergue* nearby (27 beds, kitchen, open June to September).

From Cizur Menor, it's a steep climb with stunning views to the windmill-topped Alto de Perdón. Leave the village on the main road, then turn right in 300m at a *frontón*, and walk through a housing estate. Turn right at a tarmac road, then turn left a few hundred metres later. This stretch of the walk marks a transition between the green, rolling hills of the Pyrenean foothills and the wider, more arid wine-growing regions of Navarra and La Rioja.

The camino continues through farmland, bypassing the small hamlet of Galar. Look out for linnets, greenfinches and other songbirds here. In a kilometre or two, you'll pass the dilapidated hamlet of

Guenduláin on your right, which once housed a pilgrim hospice but is now abandoned.

You're still heading up towards the line of windmills on the Alto de Perdón, and there are great views of Pamplona behind you. At the top of a short climb, and about 2km after Guenduláin, you arrive at **Zariquiegui**. This village was decimated in the fourteenth century by an outbreak of bubonic plague, and most of the buildings date from a century or two later. The impressive crests on a few of the houses are worth a look, as are their carved doors. Zariquiegui's Romanesque church of San Andrés is on your right as you enter the village, and there's a fountain here too.

About 500m from the last house in the village, the path curves to the left and becomes narrower and steeper as it heads up to the Alto del Perdón. The low, eerie whoosh that you can hear is from the regimental line of windmills, built to catch the strong winds at the top of the ridge.

Just before the summit, you pass the dry **Fuente Reniega** (fountain of denial). Legend tells of a parched and tired pilgrim who was offered water by the Devil, disguised as a fellow pilgrim, if he renounced his faith. The pilgrim refused, and Santiago appeared to reveal a spring, quenching the pilgrim's thirst from his handy scallop shell. Almost immediately after the fountain, you arrive at the **Alto de Perdón** ridge, home to a pilgrim hospice until the early nineteenth century and now decorated with a cast-iron pilgrim silhouette statue. Cross a minor road at the top of the ridge and follow the stony track on the other side. From here you can see your next destinations: Uterga, Muruzábal and Obanos are clearly visible ahead, and Puente la Reina is just in view to the west of the ridge behind Obanos. At the southeast end of the ridge, there's a circle of pine trees, which hides the octagonal church of Eunate.

The route downhill is stony and steep, and can be slippery in wet weather. In spring, the path is lined with wild hyacinth and orchids. In just under a kilometre, pass through a gate scrawled with ¡Ultreia! (a word of encouragement amongst pilgrims, which roughly translates as "Onward!"). The trail becomes broader from here on and flattens considerably. The landscape is much greener and more fertile here too. In spring, there are long, low tunnels of black plastic in many of the surrounding fields; these are used to grow white asparagus, a regional delicacy that requires careful cultivation to halt photosynthesis.

In a couple of kilometres, and after climbing a slight rise, the lovely stone village of **Uterga** (🅐🅗✕🏠, 690.5km) comes into view. Uterga's **albergue municipal** has just four beds, and is open year round. You can also stay year-round at the **Albergue Camino del Perdón** ($$, ☎ 948 341017) which has 18 dormitory beds as well as some double rooms. Turn right just after the village square, home to a couple of impressive mansions, to visit the church of La Asunción and the village fountain but otherwise, carry straight on.

It's another 2km to **Muruzábal**, following a small ridge lined with wildflowers and olive groves, an ideal place to see hovering kites and kestrels. As you enter Muruzábal, the olive grove on your right is a glorious mass of orchids in spring. Pass a *frontón* and the large, high-walled

church of San Esteban, which has an impressive, colourful sixteenth-century *retablo*. Near the church, a sign points towards Eunate, a unique Romanesque church with a tiny *albergue* next door, well worth the 4km round-trip detour.

Detour to Eunate

Eunate (🅐) is an incongruously located church (usually closed Mondays and for December), surrounded on all its eight sides by dusty fields. It's also one of the most stunning churches you'll see on the camino. Eunate's origins are unknown. Its shape suggests a link with the Knights Templar, one of the earliest Christian military orders, who often built octagonal churches in the style of the Church of the Holy Sepulchre in Jerusalem. It could also be a major funerary chapel on the camino de Santiago, as graves containing scallop shells, presumably those of pilgrims, have been discovered between the church and the outside walls.

Inside, the church is breathtakingly serene. Marble windows let in a gentle light and floor-to-ceiling pillars buttress each octagonal angle, stretching upwards to support an eight-angled roof. Although the simple interior is spartan, you can spend hours outside looking at the gargoyles and faces carved on the church façade and on the arcaded wall that surrounds it. Binoculars will bring ornately carved monsters and musicians, as well as stonemasons' marks into focus, and let you puzzle over capitals carved with men whose beards twist around their ears like ram's horns.

Next to the church is a tiny **albergue**

Map 3 (key page 182)

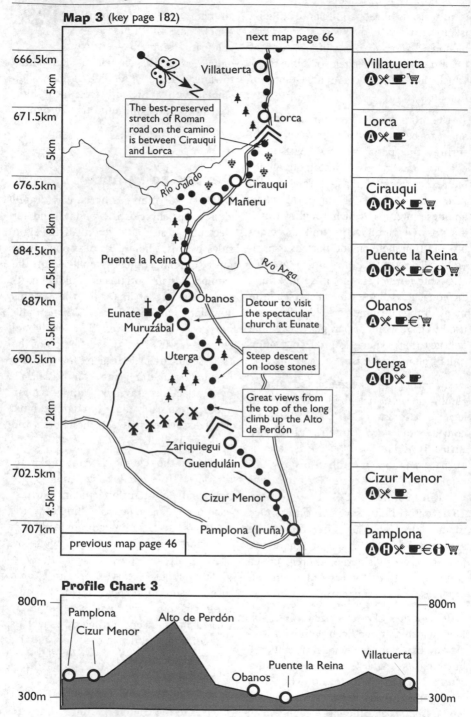

next map page 66

666.5km

5km

Villatuerta

Villatuerta
Ⓐ✕◻🛒

671.5km

5km

The best-preserved stretch of Roman road on the camino is between Cirauqui and Lorca

Lorca

Lorca
Ⓐ✕◻

676.5km

8km

Río Salado

Cirauqui

Mañeru

Cirauqui
ⒶⒽ✕◻🛒

684.5km

2.5km

Puente la Reina

Río Arga

Puente la Reina
ⒶⒽ✕◻€❶🛒

687km

3.5km

†
Eunate ∎

Obanos

Muruzábal

Detour to visit the spectacular church at Eunate

Obanos
Ⓐ✕◻€🛒

690.5km

12km

Uterga

Steep descent on loose stones

Uterga
ⒶⒽ✕◻

Great views from the top of the long climb up the Alto de Perdón

Zariquiegui

Guenduláin

702.5km

4.5km

Cizur Menor

Cizur Menor
Ⓐ✕◻

707km

Pamplona (Iruña)

previous map page 46

Pamplona
ⒶⒽ✕◻€❶🛒

Profile Chart 3

800m

Pamplona
Cizur Menor
Alto de Perdón

Obanos
Puente la Reina
Villatuerta

300m

800m

300m

(4 beds, open all year), as Eunate lies on the branch of the camino that leads from Sangüesa to Puente la Reina. From Eunate, you can return the way you came, or miss out Obanos by following the *camino aragonés* along the Río Robo into Puente la Reina.

If you decide not to visit Eunate, take the right-hand track at a metal cross at the end of Muruzábal. Follow this shady track to the outskirts of Obanos, and soon reach the Iglesia de San Juan Bautista and the *albergue*, which is opposite the children's playground.

Obanos
Ⓐ✗▆€🛒 (687km)

Obanos is a pretty, restful village, and many of its lovely houses are graced by elegant iron balconies. Yet the place is best-known for its legend of sibling love and murder.

Felicia, the sister of Guillermo, Duke of Aquitaine, was so moved by a pilgrimage to Santiago that she decided to live the life of a hermit in northern Navarra rather than return to the French court. Livid, and unsuccessful in persuading Felicia to return to a life of nobility, Guillermo killed her. Overcome with remorse, Guillermo went to Santiago himself and, on his return, decided to spend the rest of his life mourning his sister. Both siblings were beatified, and Guillermo's silver-covered skull now lies in Obanos' neo-Gothic church, where it is used each *Jueves Santo* (Maundy Thursday, the day before Good Friday) to bless wine that is then ceremonially served to villagers.

Each August, the village re-enacts the legend in a play involving 800 locals.

Obanos has a lovely if chilly **albergue** (36 beds, kitchen with limited cooking facilities, open May to September). Near the church, there's a good shop and an excellent butcher.

In Obanos, walk through the arch next to the roundabout, pass the town *frontón*, then leave town along a concrete path. Soon after passing the Ermita de San Salvador on the left, the road becomes a dirt track.

Cross the main road, then turn left about 1km after Obanos at the Hotel Jakue, which is both a hotel and an *albergue* (see Puente la Reina). There's also a modern statue of Santiago Peregrino here, marking the meeting point of the *camino francés* and the *camino aragonés*. Look out for nesting storks on top of the brick chimney to your left, then in about 300m, turn left down Carretera Pamplona just as you reach Puente la Reina. The town's main *albergue* is the first building on the left (on the corner), opposite the Iglesia del Crucifijo.

Puente la Reina
ⒶⒽ✗▆€ⓘ🛒 (684.5km)

Puente la Reina exists, like many other towns you pass through along the camino, solely because of the camino. In the eleventh century, there was no easy way to cross the Arga, and unscrupulous ferry captains charged high prices to carry pilgrims to the other side. It's not known whether the far-sighted queen who commissioned the **bridge** and gave her name to the town was Doña Mayor, wife of Sancho el Fuerte, or her successor, Doña Estefania, wife of Don García de Nájera. Whichever queen was responsible, the result is a gorgeous, six-arched bridge that's a wonderful place to see the sun set.

Puente la Reina lacks the open squares of other towns and villages in Navarra but its pedestrianized main street is a giant meeting place, where children, mothers and grandmothers gather in the early evening. Most of Puente la Reina is found along this Calle Mayor, a canyon-like street of tall buildings whose balconies drip with geraniums: don't walk below them at plant-watering time!

The soothingly simple **Iglesia del Crucifijo**, at the beginning of town, was founded in the twelfth century by the Knights Templar. A second nave was added a couple of hundred years later to display a remarkable, Y-shaped crucifix brought here by a German pilgrim. A restored arch, providing a graceful, intimate entrance into Puente la Reina, joins the church to the monastery that stands opposite on the site of a pilgrim hospice. Further towards the river, on Calle Mayor, the **Iglesia de Santiago** has Moorish influences in its south portal, which is carved with saints, sins and grotesque, hell-guarding monsters. Inside, the flamboyant Baroque *retablo* shows scenes from the life and martyrdom of Santiago, and the left aisle contains a famous Gothic statue of Santiago Peregrino, known in Basque as Santiago Beltza (black Santiago).

Puente la Reina's **turismo** (☎ 948 340845) is beneath the town hall.

Accommodation

There are three **albergues** here: one at the Hotel Jakue, just before town (58 beds, open April to September), one at the far end of town over the bridge (100 beds, open May to October) and the third just as you enter Puente la Reina, on Carretera Pamplona (100 beds, kitchen, open all year). This *albergue* has small rooms, and there's a doctor available for pilgrims in the early evening.

$$$ Bidean (☎ 948 340457)
$$$ Hotel Jakue (☎ 948 341017)
$$$$ El Peregrino (☎ 948 340075)

Leave Puente la Reina via its namesake mediaeval bridge. Turn left at the end of the bridge, then cross the main road 30m later. This section can be steep and muddy, and cyclists should stick to the road.

Pass a convent, then follow a broad, flat track alongside the river, filled with fish, lined with poppies in season and home to vivid kingfishers and dragonflies. After almost 2km, pass to the left of a factory. The camino soon leaves the Río Arga, a river you've followed and crisscrossed since Zubiri. Climb uphill on a track that can be treacherously muddy after rain, then wind through fields until you reach Mañeru. Keep straight on at a sixteenth-century crucifix, following the yellow arrows into the village over a small bridge.

Mañeru (🏠€) is a maze of narrow, angular streets graced with grand houses, stone balconies and imposing stone crests. Turn right to visit the neoclassical Iglesia de San Pedro, otherwise keep straight on to continue the camino, turning left at the Casa Consistorial, then immediately right to leave the village on a narrow tarmac road.

It's a pretty stretch along a flower-lined track through olive groves and vineyards to Cirauqui. Look out for Iberian wall lizards on the stretch flanked by stone walls. Up ahead, you can see the pale grey limestone cliffs of the Sierra de Urbasa in the distance: these have been visible since the Alto de Perdón. The camino enters Cirauqui via a Gothic arch in the town walls; the *albergue* is at the top of a steep climb up the village's cobbled streets.

Cirauqui

Ⓐ Ⓗ ✕ ◧ 🛒 (676.5km)

Built on a distinctive rocky hill, Cirauqui is a beautiful mediaeval village that's a great place to linger over a *café con leche*. The village's name means "nest of vipers," but it's unclear whether the snakes in question were the slithering kind or the ever-present pesky bandits.

Narrow, cobbled streets lead you uphill to the oldest part of the village, where you'll be struck by the **Iglesia de San Román**, a twelfth-century Romanesque church with impressive capitals and a portal resembling the one at the Iglesia de Santiago in Puente la Reina. Next door is a Civil War monument: like all those built during Franco's reign, it lists only Nationalist casualties.

Albergue Maralotx (28 beds, open all year) has a couple of private rooms (**$$**, ☎ 678 635208).

To leave Cirauqui, the camino peculiarly passes through a building, where there's a self-serve *sello* for your *credencial*. The route soon heads across a dilapidated Roman bridge then crosses a main road. You're now walking over rolling, arid hills, and traces of the Roman road disappear and reappear beneath a wide farm track. Look closely, as the section of Roman road from Cirauqui to Lorca is one

of the best preserved of the entire camino.

Walk downhill for about 1km to a mediaeval bridge, now restored. At the top of a short uphill stretch, keep straight on as the farm track curves to the right. Make sure you take the right-hand of two parallel tracks here, as this is the best remaining example of Roman road. You can clearly see the road's central divide and the drainage channels that slice across it every 50m or so.

Some 2km after the last bridge, pass under a sky-high aqueduct, then turn left to cross a mediaeval bridge across the **Río Salado**. The river is noisy with frogs in spring, and the undergrowth alongside the water hides grey Cetti's warblers, although you're more likely to hear a loud, brief burst of song than see the birds. This spot is also the setting for one of Aymeric Picaud's more distressing camino experiences. The twelfth-century guidebook writer warned:

"At a place called Lorca, to the east, there flows a stream known as the Salt River. Beware of drinking from it or of watering your horse in it, for this river brings death. On its banks, while we were going to St James, we found two Navarrese sitting there sharpening their knives; for they are accustomed to flay pilgrims' horses which die after drinking the water. In answer to our question they lied, saying that the water was good and drinkable. Accordingly we watered our horses in the river, and at once two of them died and were forthwith skinned by the two men."

Today, you should be more concerned

about the busy road you'll need to cross in a few hundred metres, before arriving at Lorca about 1km later. In **Lorca** (Ⓐ✕⬛, 671.5km), there's a pleasant square with a fountain, and an **albergue** (14 beds, open April to October) on the main road, slightly off the camino.

Head to Villatuerta, a few kilometres away, along a narrow path that winds through fields next to the busy N111. Pass under a tunnel, walk through Villatuerta's dull outskirts, then cross an arched, Romanesque bridge over the Río Iranzu into the village.

Villatuerta (Ⓐ✕⬛🛒, 666.5km) has a sporadically open **albergue** (30 beds) on Calle Rúa Nueva and the restored, twelfth-century Iglesia de la Asuncíon, reached at the top of the same street. This is a shady spot for a rest; there's a statue of Santiago Peregrino at the front of the church and drinkable water (*agua potable*) in a fountain around the back.

The route out of Villatuerta soon passes near the Ermita de San Miguel, of which little remains. Cross a busy road at a picnic area to a well-marked path on the other side, then curve around a field and cross a stream over a modern wooden footbridge. There are glorious flowers at this spot in spring — the fields near the river are full of irises and poppies.

Up ahead, turn right next to a factory onto a tarmac road, and pass the first houses of Estella. Walk past the Iglesia del Santo Sepulcro, keep straight on under a road bridge, and the *albergue* is on your left, just after the Puente de los Peregrinos.

Estella

Ⓐ🅗✕⬛€🛈🛒 (662.5km)

Estella (Lizarra) is a graceful, compact town, rich in Romanesque monuments, and attractively located on both sides of the Río Ega. While the Basque town of Lizarra had existed for some time on the north side of the river, Estella really got going in the late eleventh century, when Sancho I founded a new town on the opposite bank, at a spot where shooting stars revealed a statue of the Virgin Mary hidden in a cave. Even Picaud, the hard-to-please twelfth-century author of the *Codex Calixtinus*, thought the city, "fertile in good bread and excellent wine and meat and fish and full of all delights."

Estella is a lively place to visit at the end of May, when the Baile de la Era, a festival of traditional dances, comes to town. It all gets a little crazy on the first weekend in August, when Estella is taken over by bull-running, processions and dances for the annual San Fermín festival, only slightly less over-the-top than the famous version in Pamplona.

Estella's clear architectural highlight is the **Palacio de los Reyes de Navarra**, a rare example of civic Romanesque building, with a capital depicting Roland's fight with the giant Ferragut. The Palacio's museum is home to the works of Gustavo de Maeztú, an early twentieth-century Navarrese painter.

Estella's rulers didn't skimp on religious buildings, either; the city boasts no fewer than nine churches, which are generally open only for Mass and the half hour before it. Just above the Palacio de los Reyes de Navarra, the fortified **Iglesia de San Pedro de la Rúa** looms above Estella. Although damaged in 1572 when Felipe II blew up the nearby castle so that it couldn't be used against him, the remains of the cloister contain masterful Romanesque capitals depicting biblical scenes and monsters. The church's Capilla de San Andrés is said to house St Andrew's shoulder bone, brought here by the Greek Bishop of Patras, who fell ill and died in Estella on his way to Santiago.

Most of Estella's bars, shops and banks lie on the opposite bank of the Río Ega. The **Iglesia de San Miguel** looks grandly down on such practicalities from its site above the Puente de los Peregrinos. The portal, which dates from the twelfth century, is an incredible example of Romanesque sculpture, and its depiction of the Last Judgment includes fantastic goat-demons and monkey-musicians.

Cross back over the Río Ega via the delicate, single-arched Puente de los Peregrinos, watching your footing on the slippery cobbles, and turn left to visit the **Iglesia de Santo Sepulcro**. The thick façade, added a couple of hundred years after the twelfth-century church was built, is the first sight that greets pilgrims at the entrance to Estella, and it's a suitably dramatic introduction. Bring your binoculars to get a close look at fantastic carvings of the Crucifixion, the Last Supper and hundreds of quirky beasts, saints, mortals and monsters.

The **turismo** (☎ 948 556301) is in the same building as the Palacio de los Reyes. Estella's Thursday market has been in place since the fifteenth century.

Accommodation

Estella's main **albergue** (114 beds, kitchen) is open all year; the doors open at 3pm.
Albergue de Anfas, Calle Cordeleros 7 (30 beds, open June to September)
Camping Lizarra (☎ 948 551783), next to the Río Ega, also has cheap beds.
$ Izarra, Calle Caldería (☎ 948 550678)
$$ Cristina, Calle Baja Navarra 1 (☎ 948 550450)

$$ San Andrés, Calle Mayor 1 (☎ 948 554158)
$$$ Yerri, Avenida Yerri 35 (☎ 948 546034)

Keep straight on along the lovely, antique shop–lined cobbled road in Estella. Walk across the Plaza San Martín, passing the Palacio de los Reyes on your right. At the end of the cobbled lane, leave the old part of town via a gate with a carved representation of the Crucifixion.

Walk through suburban Estella, climbing uphill to **Ayegui**, then turn left just before a playground to head towards the Monasterio de Irache. In a few hundred metres, reach the **Fuente del Vino**, a tap of free wine provided by the Bodegas de Irache to fortify thirsty pilgrims on the way to Santiago. From here, you can wave to technophile friends back home via a webcam (www.irache.com). Next door, the imposing, twelfth-century **Monasterio de Irache** contains a simple Romanesque church and Plateresque cloister; its pilgrims' hospital was founded in 1050, making it older than the hospitals at Estella and Roncesvalles.

Follow a gravel road lined with vines to **Irache** (**H**), a modern village with a vast campsite and the **Hotel Irache** (**$$$$**, ☎ 948 551150). The new houses you pass come as a bit of a jolt after the uniformly quaint villages of the rest of the camino, where even newer houses were sympathetically designed to fit in with the existing local architecture.

Up ahead, perched high on a hill, you can see the Ermita de San Esteban, which was built from the stones of Monjardín castle. Walk alongside fields and through

Map 4 (key page 182)

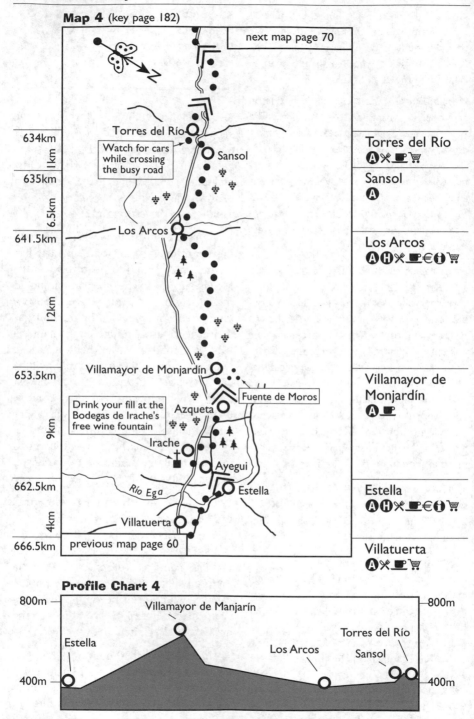

next map page 70

634km

1km

Torres del Río

Watch for cars
while crossing
the busy road

Sansol

635km

6.5km

Los Arcos

641.5km

12km

Villamayor de Monjardín

653.5km

Fuente de Moros

Drink your fill at the
Bodegas de Irache's
free wine fountain

Azqueta

9km

Irache

Ayegui

Río Ega

Estella

662.5km

4km

Villatuerta

666.5km

previous map page 60

Torres del Río

Sansol

Los Arcos

**Villamayor de
Monjardín**

Estella

Villatuerta

Profile Chart 4

800m

Villamayor de Manjarín

Estella

Los Arcos

Torres del Río

Sansol

400m

800m

400m

woodland on dirt tracks and narrow roads. Pass through the village of **Azqueta**, some 3km from Irache, then head uphill towards Villamayor de Monjardín, whose church tower you can see poking above the ridge.

At the top of the climb 1.5km later, and just before the village, you reach the **Fuente de Moros**, an interesting Gothic cistern, recently restored and thought to date back to Islamic Spain. Pass the metallic Castillo de Monjardín winery, and enter Villamayor de Monjardín along the well-signposted street.

Villamayor de Monjardín
Ⓐ ⏻ (653.5km)

Sancho Garcés took the castle above the town from the Moors in the tenth century, although French revisionists claimed that it was captured by **Charlemagne**. In the doctored version, Charlemagne asked God before the battle which of his soldiers would be killed, and the doomed troops were conveniently marked with an illuminated cross on their backs. Determined to save his men, Charlemagne went into battle without the marked soldiers, leaving them to guard his camp instead. When he returned from the victorious battle, he found them all dead. More recently, the castle was used in the Spanish Civil War to control the valley below.

The **Iglesia de San Andrés** is worth a peek for its solidly beautiful Romanesque entrance and seventeenth-century Baroque tower. On the off-chance that it's unlocked, pop inside to see the exquisite silverwork of the Romanesque processional cross.

Villamayor's tiny café open very limited hours. You can stay at the basic **Albergue**

Parroquial (20 mattresses, open all year), or at the Dutch-run **Albergue Hogar de Monjardín** (25 beds, kitchen, open May to October), which has a small café.

The camino to Los Arcos slowly winds its way through a wide valley along red-dirt farm tracks. Watch out for vultures circling high above you looking for food, a disturbing sight when you're on your last legs on a hot day. As you near Los Arcos, there are good views of the Basilica de San Gregorio a few kilometres away to the right, and of the windmills on the distant hills straight ahead. Eventually, follow a gravel road over a rise and see Los Arcos in front of you. There's a fountain at the edge of town for thirsty pilgrims; take the left-hand fork soon afterwards, and follow Calle Mayor into Los Arcos.

Los Arcos
Ⓐ Ⓗ ✕ ⏻ € ➊ 🛒 (641.5km)

Los Arcos is a small town, dominated by the somewhat dour-looking **Iglesia de Santa María de la Asunción**. Inside, the church explodes in a riot of Baroque, and the main, walnut *retablo* is one of the finest and most ornate on the camino; the Gothic cloister is soothing in comparison. Immediately after Mass, pilgrims can climb to the top of the church's Renaissance bell tower. Once a year, in June, the altar is lit by a shaft of sunlight.

Self-catering is a good option, as there's an excellent butcher and fishmonger. The **turismo** is at Plaza Fueros (☎ 948 640077).

Accommodation
Los Arcos boasts four *albergues*. By far the

largest and most popular is the friendly **Albergue Isaac Santiago** (70 beds, open Easter to October), on the far side of town across the bridge. Its kitchen seems to work only sporadically. You can also stay at **Albergue Casa Alberdi** on Calle Hortal (22 beds, open all year), **Albergue Casa Romero** on Calle Mayor (28 beds, open all year) or **Albergue El Fuente** on Travesía del Estanco (48 beds, open all year).

$$ **Ezequiel**, La Serna 14 (☎ 948 640296)
$$ **Mónaco**, Plaza del Coso 1 (☎ 948 640000)
$$ **Suetxe**, Calle Carramendavia (☎ 948 441175)

In Los Arcos, walk past the church, through the archway and across the Río Odrón. Aymeric Picaud, the mediaeval pilgrim who seems to have had something against rivers, said, "through the town known as Los Arcos there flows a deadly river." Assuming you make it across in one piece, the route to Torres del Río is a pleasant one, through farmland and vineyards. If you're lucky, you may see a hovering red kite or kestrel and hear musical bursts of song from a solitary skylark or woodlark.

Sansol (Ⓐ, 635km), about 7km away, has some lovely Baroque architecture, including grand houses decorated with coats of arms, and the simple Iglesia de San Zoilo, from which there are marvellous views to Torres del Río below. The **albergue** has 10 beds and a kitchen. It's less than a kilometre from Sansol to Torres del Río; cross the busy N111 to get there, then head uphill past the church for the *albergues*.

Torres del Río
Ⓐ✕▭⛾

Torres del Río lies tucked into the steep Río Liñares valley, a strategically dubious location for a town that's survived Muslim and Christian battles. The striking, octagonal **Iglesia del Santo Sepulcro** is thought to be Templar in origin, although its function is obscure. As in Eunate, excavations around the church have revealed a number of tombs, so it may have been a funeral chapel, an explanation that seems more likely than the one that suggests Torres del Río's lantern vault acted as a beacon to guide pilgrims, as the town is all but invisible from the surrounding countryside. The church's design echoes that of the mosques of southern Spain, particularly the altar niche and the cupola's crossed arches. If the church is locked, ask for the key in the village, or hang around outside looking pilgrim-like if your Spanish isn't up to asking questions.

There are two *albergues*: **Albergue Casa Mari** (21 beds, kitchen, open all year) at the top of the village, and the **Hospital Peregrino** (32 beds, open January to November), on Calle Mayor.

Heading out of Torres del Río, you pass a graveyard on your left as the road becomes a dirt track. You'll follow this track on-and-off until you reach Viana, criss-crossing the N111 as you do so. There are fabulous views of the route from Los Arcos, and of the surrounding mountains. As you continue, Logroño comes into view up ahead, and the Sierra de la Demanda appear dramatically in the distance. Pass through a mix of farmland and scrubland, where water has eroded deep ravines in the arid landscape.

Just past the road sign for Viana, cross the N111 to enter the town, passing an abstract mural of the camino painted in splendidly garish colours on the side of a building. Follow the camino uphill through town, taking Calle Algorrada through an arch in Viana's town walls, then walk up Rúa de Santa María. Viana's *albergue* is at the end of town, wonderfully located next to the ruined Iglesia de San Pedro.

Viana
ⒶⒽ✕🍴💺€ⓘ🛒 (641.5km)

An attractive town, Viana is circled by high walls and filled with imposing, family crest–decorated mansions. Like many towns in Navarra, Viana was founded in the thirteenth century by Sancho el Fuerte, but its best-known hero is Cesare Borgia.

Although Borgia's political machinations largely took place in his native Italy, he found himself imprisoned in Spain at the beginning of the sixteenth century. Escaping from prison and universally unloved in Italy, Borgia headed for Navarra, where he fought for the King of Navarra at the siege of Viana. He died in a chaotic blaze of glory, rushing out of Viana to single-handedly take on the enemy rearguard, while the rest of the town held back, struggling to understand what was happening.

The **Iglesia de Santa María** no longer holds Borgia's grand mausoleum, whicht was desecrated by vandals in the seventeenth century and replaced with a simple tomb in front of the church. It's difficult to spot the tomb, mostly because your attention is inevitably drawn to the glorious Renaissance façade, combining biblical themes with Greek legends and peculiar animals. The beautiful Gothic interior boasts a Baroque *retablo*.

The church takes up one side of the pretty Plaza de los Fueros, a café-lined square with a fountain in the middle.

Viana has a **turismo** (☎ 948 446302) and is well equipped with restaurants and shops.

Accommodation
Viana's lovely **albergue** has 54 beds (triple bunks), a kitchen and huge dining room, and is open all year.

$$ San Pedro, Calle Medio San Pedro 13 (☎ 948 446221)

$$ Casa Armendariz, Calle Navarro Villoslada 19 (☎ 948 645078)

$$$$ Palacio de Pujadas, Navarro Villoslada, 30 (☎ 948 646468)

Leave Viana under the Portal de San Felices. Turn left down Calle la Rueda, then first right on Calle Fuente Vieja. Keep heading downhill out of town, following the yellow arrows past a school. For the next couple of kilometres the camino passes through fields and beside houses, criss-crossing roads.

A few kilometres after Viana, the camino reaches the Ermita de las Cuevas, a former hermitage that's now a shady spot for a picnic. At the end of the picnic area, follow a track to the artificial **Laguna de las Cañas**. The lake, which you'll reach in 2km, is an important bird-watching area that's home to breeding pairs of purple herons, night herons and bitterns. There's an observatory with telescopes, should you want a closer look.

Turn right at the lake to take a track to the Papelera del Ebro factory, where you pass unceremoniously into the province

Map 5 (key page 182)

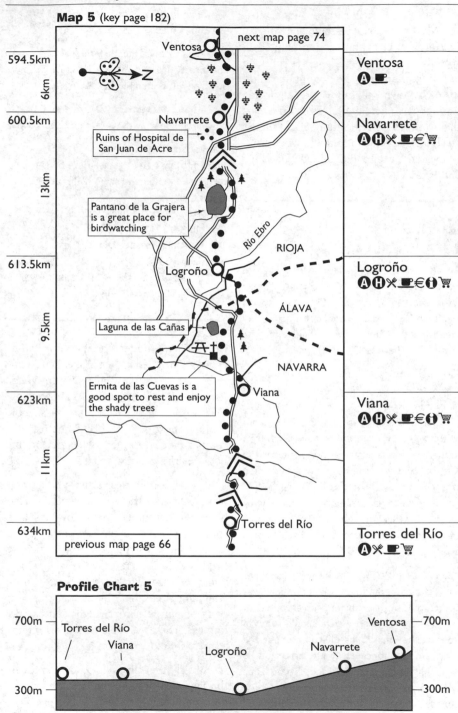

next map page 74

594.5km
6km

Ventosa

Ventosa
Ⓐ ▄▀

600.5km

Navarrete

Navarrete
Ⓐ Ⓗ ✕ ▄▀ € 🛒

13km

Ruins of Hospital de
San Juan de Acre

Pantano de la Grajera
is a great place for
birdwatching

Río Ebro

RIOJA

613.5km

Logroño

Logroño
Ⓐ Ⓗ ✕ ▄▀ € 🛈 🛒

9.5km

ÁLAVA

Laguna de las Cañas

NAVARRA

623km

Ermita de las Cuevas is a
good spot to rest and enjoy
the shady trees

Viana

Viana
Ⓐ Ⓗ ✕ ▄▀ € 🛈 🛒

11km

634km

Torres del Río

Torres del Río
Ⓐ ✕ ▄▀ 🛒

previous map page 66

Profile Chart 5

700m

Torres del Río
Viana
Logroño
Navarrete
Ventosa

700m

300m

300m

pass unceremoniously into the province of La Rioja. Although you'll be hard-pressed to notice any difference, mediaeval pilgrims were suddenly confronted with an entirely different culture, people and currency. Follow a red paved track through a couple of underpasses daubed with pilgrim graffiti and around the flat-topped hill up ahead. The hill contains prehistoric, Roman and mediaeval ruins, and it's just a short detour off the camino to explore the thick walls.

As you head downhill, pass a café that sells snacks and drinks. Turn right 1km later when you join the road, then turn left to cross the Puente de Piedra over the Río Ebro. The bridge dates from the late eleventh century; repairs were made by both Santo Domingo and San Juan de Ortega (see pages 76 and 83 for more about these builder saints). At the end of the bridge, take the second right at a small roundabout to walk down Rúa Vieja. Logroño's *albergue* is about 100m down this road, on the left.

Logroño

Ⓐ Ⓗ ✕ 🛏 € ❶ 🍴 (613.5km)

Although Logroño is the biggest town in La Rioja and the centre of its wine industry, most tourists skip the city in favour of the province's grape-growing centres. A city with a no-nonsense, working feel, Logroño's distinct personalities bump up against each other in its large centre. The airy Plaza del Mercado is home to attractive cafés, and dominated by the stork-nest-topped towers of Logroño's cathedral, the **Iglesia de Santa María la Redonda**. High-class clothes shops line pedestrianized streets in the smarter end of the city around the pleasant Paséo del Espolón, while closer to the

Río Ebro, the cocooned, older part of the city around the Rúa Vieja is grimier and grittier (the *albergue* is directly opposite a police station).

The Gothic **Iglesia de Santiago** lies directly on the camino at the end of the Rúa Vieja. The church takes its name seriously and oozes monuments to the saint: the humble Santiago Peregrino and the impressive, war-mongering Santiago Matamaros that guard the entrance only hint at the plethora of Santiago images you'll see inside. The present building stands on the site of a ninth-century church built to honour the battle of Clavijo, when Santiago Matamoros' timely intervention helped to defeat the Moors.

At the end of September, Logroño livens up for the **Fiesta de San Mateo**, worth visiting for the grape-crushing ceremonies in the Paséo del Espolón.

The **turismo** is in a modern building in the Paséo del Espolón (☎ 941 291260).

Accommodation

Logroño's **albergue** has a bright and spacious first-floor kitchen, free Internet access and a couple of huge, stuffy rooms crammed with 88 bunk beds. It's open all year.

$ Pensión Castellana, Calle San Antón 17 (☎ 941 469017)

$$ Hostal La Numantina, Calle Sagasta 4 (☎ 941 251411)

$$ Hostal Rioja Condestable, Calle Doctores Castroviejo 5 (☎ 941 256861)

$$$$ Hotel Marqués de Vallejo, Marqués de Vallejo 8 (☎ 941 248333)

Walk through Logroño along the Rúa Vieja, passing the Iglesia de Santiago. In front of this grand church is the sixteenth-century Fuente de los Peregrinos, and on the ground is a large painted mosaic, the

Juego de la Oca. This version of a popular, snakes-and-ladders-like board game is full of camino motifs: the board represents the pilgrimage, the squares are the different places and people met along the way, and passing pilgrims are, of course, counters to be moved from square to square.

Pass through an arch in Logroño's town walls. Bear left here, following the road signs to Burgos at the roundabout. After a little over a kilometre, turn left on Calle Portillejo.

For the next few kilometres, you'll walk mostly through parkland along a path popular with promenaders and joggers, which takes you to the **Pantano de la Grajera** (⬛). This reservoir is an ideal spot for birdwatching, particularly in the early morning. Look for herons, rails, ducks and grebes in the water, and woodpeckers, flycatchers, larks and goldfinches in the trees nearby. Follow a wide gravel track that curves around the water, passing shady picnic areas, a café and a birdwatching hide (blind) on your left. As the track moves away from the reservoir, there's a fountain.

The camino heads uphill on a narrow road, then follows a paved path high above and parallel to the main road. This is a dull stretch, enlivened by a large metal outline of a bull and the rustic wooden crosses stuck by pilgrims in the wire fence to the right of the track. At the end of the fence, cross a road, then follow a winding farm track; fields of vines stretch towards the horizon in all directions.

In a kilometre or so, cross the motorway via a pedestrian bridge and arrive almost immediately at the mostly ruined **Hospital de San Juan de Acre**. Founded in the late twelfth century, the church and hospice of Hospital de San Juan de Acre served pilgrims for four centuries. The site has been recently excavated, and although some of the restoration work is clumsy, there's a clear picture of how the hospice was set up. There's also a fountain here. In less than a kilometre, climb some steps to cross a road and enter Navarrete.

Navarrete
Ⓐ Ⓗ ✕ ⬛ € ☕ (600.5km)

Navarrete is a pretty, fortified hillside town where every street corner seems to be daubed with a yellow arrow. The hill itself is pocketed with small caves, used to store Navarrete's plentiful harvests of mushrooms and wine in cool, dark conditions.

The **Iglesia de la Asunción**, near the top of town, is dominated by a Baroque *retablo* of dazzling extravagance, possibly the finest in the country. It may have dazzled the church's other architects and builders too: the church tower was begun in the fifteenth century but not completed until 300 years later. Navarrete's annual highlight is the Fiesta de la Virgen y San Roque in mid-August.

There's a grocery store opposite the *albergue municipal*, and a fabulous *panadería* close by on Travesa Mayor Alta.

Accommodation
Navarrete's **albergue municipal** (40 beds, kitchen, open all year) is at the beginning of town, its entrance hidden in the pretty arcades of the Calle Mayor. There are also two private *albergues*: **Albergue El Cántaro** (16 beds, open all year), which also has private rooms (**$$**, ☎ 941 441180)

and **Albergue Iacobus** (12 beds, open May to October).

$ Hostal La Carioca (☎ 941 440805)

$$ Hostal Villa de Navarrete (☎ 941 440318)

$$$$ Hotel San Camilo (☎ 941 441111)

In Navarrete, turn right up Calle La Cruz to reach the Iglesia de la Asunción. Turn left at the church down Calle Mayor Alta, then keep straight on past a couple of fountains. Make sure you fill up with water, as it's a long, fountain-less stretch between here and Nájera.

Leave town along the road, reaching the town cemetery in about 300m. Although the cemetery was built fairly recently, its stately façade is thirteenth-century Romanesque, brought here from the Hospital de San Juan de Acre on the other side of Navarrete. The marvellous capitals depict great battles, such as Roland's defeat of the giant Ferragut and St George killing the dragon, but also portray gentle, mundane scenes of camino life such as pilgrims eating a meal together and washing each other's hair.

The camino between here and Nájera winds through vineyards and the occasional olive grove, veering right and left to walk around fields lined with cornflowers and poppies in spring, but always staying close to the road. Take a look at the huge pots made in the ceramic factory across the road: Navarrete's potters are renowned for their great use of the region's distinctive red clay soil.

After about 6km, the camino veers away from the road to the hamlet of **Ventosa** (Ⓐ☒, 594.5km), where you can stay at the **Albergue de San Saturníno** (24 beds, kitchen, open all year), which is rather basic. You can also bypass the village by following an alternative route.

Soon after Ventosa, the camino leaves the roadside for a while, heading uphill on a grass farm track. Pass hundreds of precarious piles of shepherd stones left by pilgrims, then keep heading uphill as the path narrows towards the **Alto de San Antón**. From the top of the hill there are views of Nájera, its urban sprawl splayed out to meet nearby villages, and to the right, the ruins of the monastery and pilgrim hospice of San Antón.

Cross the N120 carefully, then follow a level, red-dirt track through vineyards. A few kilometres after crossing the main road, the track leads to the right of a flat hillock topped with radio masts, known as the **Poyo de Roldán**.

According to one legend, the region around Nájera was the home of Ferragut, a giant who was descended from Goliath. Charlemagne sent many brave knights to defeat Ferragut, but all were unsuccessful. It's not clear whether Roland was sent by Charlemagne to fight the giant or if the knight just happened to be passing through but, in any case, Roland reputedly hurled a huge rock at Ferragut, knocking him dead. It's said that the Poyo de Roldán itself is the rock that Roland threw.

The romance surrounding the legend is quickly stifled by the route through semi-industrial Nájera, possibly the most horrible town approach of the whole camino. To relieve the industrial monotony, look left towards the Sierra de la

Map 6 (key page 182)

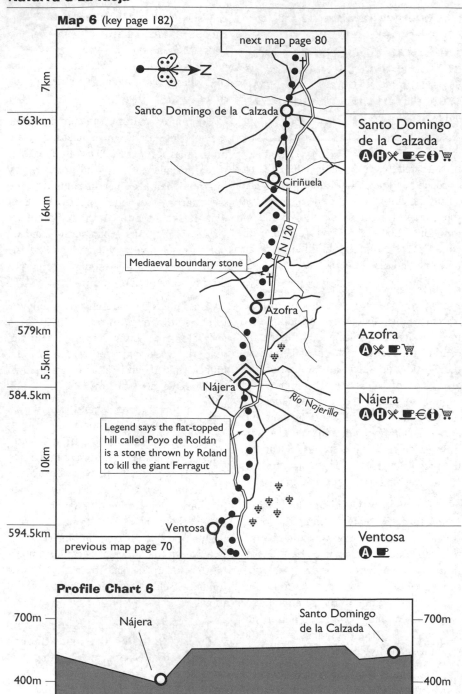

next map page 80

7km

563km

16km

Santo Domingo de la Calzada

Ciriñuela

N 120

Mediaeval boundary stone

579km

5.5km

Azofra

584.5km

Nájera

Río Najerilla

10km

Legend says the flat-topped hill called Poyo de Roldán is a stone thrown by Roland to kill the giant Ferragut

594.5km

Ventosa

previous map page 70

Santo Domingo
de la Calzada
Ⓐ Ⓗ ✕ ⌷ € ⓘ 🛒

Azofra
Ⓐ ✕ ⌷ 🛒

Nájera
Ⓐ Ⓗ ✕ ⌷ € ⓘ 🛒

Ventosa
Ⓐ ⌷

Profile Chart 6

700m

Nájera

Santo Domingo
de la Calzada

700m

400m

400m

Demanda, a dramatic line of mountains rising to more than 2000m. Up ahead, the vegetation on the slopes of the conical, cross-topped Pico de Nájera has been trimmed to form a dove of peace.

When you reach the outskirts of Nájera in a couple of kilometres, follow the signs to Centro Urbano. The tall, nondescript buildings of modern Nájera soon give way to the grimier yet far more attractive old town. The sidewalks here are so narrow that you may have to leap into traffic if you meet an oncoming pedestrian. Turn right to cross a bridge over the Río Najerilla, then turn left at the end of the bridge down the pedestrianized Calle Mayor, following the yellow arrow to the *albergue*.

Nájera
Ⓐ Ⓗ ✕ ♨ € ⓘ 🛒 (584.5km)

Nájera's attractive old town sits squashed between the Río Najerilla and the cliffs behind it, its largely pedestrianized streets home to traditional butchers, bakeries and *pastelarías*. The town's heyday came in the tenth and eleventh centuries, when the Navarrese court moved here en masse after its capital, Pamplona, was destroyed and Sancho III diverted the camino through the new capital.

The old town seems to grow organically from the pink cliffs that rise up behind it, living up to its Arabic name, "the place between the rocks." The **Monasterio de Santa María de Real** is literally built into the cliffs, and its lovely Gothic buildings surround a simple, natural cave where the church's history began.

In 1004, García III was hunting partridge along the banks of the Río Najerilla. He sent his hawk after one bird, and followed the hawk as it chased the partridge into the cave. Inside the cave, he was startled to see a beautiful statue of the Virgin Mary, with a vase of lilies, a burning lamp and a bell at her feet. Close by, the hawk and the partridge were sitting together, at peace.

García saw the miracle as a blessing for the *reconquista*, and spent part of the treasure he captured from the Moors on building a chapel in honour of Santa María. The statue now occupies pride of place in the church's Baroque *retablo*; an early replica and a vase of fresh lilies grace the simple cave. Missing from the *retablo* is the statue's original crown, which was stolen in the fourteenth century and its jewels divvied up: Pedro the Cruel gave Edward the Black Prince a particularly fine stone, and the **Black Prince Ruby** now gleams from the front of the English Coronation Crown.

Flanking the entrance to the cave is the **Panteón Real**, where a sombre line of Renaissance tombs hold the remains of a Who's Who of Navarra royalty from the tenth to twelfth centuries, including the monastery's founder, García III. To the left of the cave, set apart from the rest, is the glorious Romanesque tomb of Sancho III's young wife, Doña Blanca, carved with biblical scenes and images of the dying queen and her grieving family.

Upstairs, the graceful wooden choir-stalls date from the 1490s. The intricate detail of the Gothic carving can be overwhelming, and every surface is covered with monsters, fantastical animals or strange geometric shapes. The sponsor and director of the work were apparently proud of what they had accomplished: both Andrés Amutio and Pablo Martínez de Uruñuela, Nájera's first abbot, are buried beneath lower row seats. Outside

75

the church, reached through a carved walnut Plateresque door, is the peaceful Claustro de los Caballeros, where yet more tombs lie amongst delicate Gothic archways.

The people of Nájera take to the streets for the Fiestas de San Juan y San Pedro at the end of June, singing and dancing to catchy, regimental music said to have originated with soldiers in the Carlist wars.

Turismo Calle Garran 8 (☎ 941 341230)

Accommodation
Nájera's **albergue** (100 beds, open all year) is in a modern building in the old town. It has a small kitchen and a large, cramped dormitory. You can also stay at **Albergue La Judería** on Galle Garrán 18 (19 beds, open all year).
$$ Hostal Hispano, La Cepa 2 (☎ 941 362957)
$$$ Hotel Ciudad de Nájera, Cuerta Calleja San Miguel 14 (☎ 941 360660)
$$$ Hotel San Fernando, Paseo San Julián 1 (☎ 941 363700)

The route from Nájera continues along the dirt farm tracks and through the vineyards and vivid red soil so characteristic of the camino in La Rioja. In a few kilometres, you'll see Azofra. As you approach the village, look out for intricately engineered, gravity-powered water channels, which pass under the road and around fields and vineyards. Since the region is dry and grapevine roots are very shallow, getting water to the plants in this way is an essential part of local farming.

In **Azofra** (Ⓐ✕🍴☕, 579km), look out for the Iglesia de Nuestra Señora de los Angeles, which includes a carving of Santiago Peregrino. The village has two

albergues: the **albergue municipal** (60 beds, kitchen, open all year), and a private *albergue* (14 beds, open all year).

At the far side of the village, there's a modern shrine to the Virgen de Valvanera in a small park, next to the Fuente de los Romeros, a pilgrims' fountain. Turn right at the road here, then left 50m later to walk up a gravel track past small farms. On the right is a stone pillar, a weathered mediaeval cross that marked the boundary between the villages of Azofra and Alesanco. Even though you're next to the main road, the walking is made pleasant by a small stream that attracts lots of warblers and other birds.

Climb up to a plateau, then pass the Rioja Alta Golf Club and a modern housing development. The camino heads through the tiny village of **Ciriñuela** (🍴), then follows minor roads and more farm tracks to Santo Domingo de la Calzada. The outskirts of town are a bit drab and run down, but within a kilometre or two you enter the attractive, compact old town, passing a modern statue of a pilgrim. Walk down Calle Mayor, passing the *albergues* and the cathedral.

Santo Domingo de la Calzada
Ⓐ🅗✕🍴€ⓘ🍷 (563km)

Santo Domingo de la Calzada is a pretty, bustling town, largely established by the tireless work of its founder and namesake, and given its place in camino legend and on the tourist trail by a couple of chickens.

Santo Domingo was a poor shepherd from nearby Viloria who wanted to be a monk but did so badly at his studies that he was rejected by the nearby monasteries. Still, Domingo decided to pursue the religious life, becoming a hermit in the woods around the Río Oja, and for the rest of his life he helped pilgrims by building bridges and improving the camino road, often helped by his disciple, Juan de Ortega. Domingo used a heavy sickle to cut a pilgrim road through the forests between Nájera and Redecilla del Camino, and legend has it that when he stopped to pray, angels miraculously continued to cut a path through the trees.

The town has some grand sixteenth-century buildings and tranquil squares but its undoubted highlight is the **cathedral**. Little remains of Santo Domingo's original church, as it was largely rebuilt in Gothic style a century or so after the saint died.

Most visitors to the cathedral head straight for the **live cock and hen** housed in a Gothic cage on the east side. The legend behind these birds is told in various guises throughout Europe, and even the Santo Domingo miracle has many versions.

In the fourteenth century, a young German pilgrim travelling with his parents spurned the advances of a maid. Furious, the jilted maid planted a silver goblet in the youth's bag, and the youth was caught and hanged for the theft. His distraught parents continued their pilgrimage to Santiago, and on their return were shocked to discover that their son, still dangling from the gallows, was alive. The parents rushed to the *corregidor* (the village's chief magistrate) to tell him of the miracle, but he scornfully replied that their son was as alive as the pair of roast chickens he was about to tuck into for his dinner. The cock and hen miraculously jumped from the plate and began to crow, and the German pilgrim was released.

The live chickens in the cathedral are replaced each month by backups that live behind the *albergue*, and any pilgrim who hears the cock crow will have luck on the journey to Santiago.

Below the chickens, in the crypt, is the tomb of Santo Domingo, a simple Romanesque statue covered by an ornate Gothic temple. The Romanesque pillars that separate the Gothic ambulatory from the main altar are beautifully carved with biblical scenes, including the Wise and Foolish Virgins, the former smugly holding upright lamps and the latter holding their lamps upside down and hanging their heads in shame.

The main altar is dominated by the ornate *retablo*, carved in alabaster and walnut by Damíen Forment in the early sixteenth century, and painted in gaudy, gorgeous, Renaissance style by Andrés de Melgar.

If your knees are up to it, it's well worth climbing the stone steps up to the roof, from where you get a great view of the town and the cathedral's 70m-high **belltower**. The Baroque tower, completely detached from the rest of cathedral, was built after lightning destroyed the first tower and the second was torn down to prevent its imminent collapse.

Next to the cathedral, the town's opulent **parador** is housed in a converted pilgrim hospice originally built by Santo Domingo. Before he built the hospice, Santo Domingo fed passing pilgrims at a long table next to the river, known as the *mesa del santo*.

Santo Domingo is both a working town and a big tourist destination, so you'll find modern, air-conditioned bars serving delicate *tapas* alongside no-nonsense bars with no seats and a day's layer of peanuts and sugar sachets carpeting the floor. Santo Domingo has a couple of supermarkets, some banks and a smattering of restaurants.

The **turismo** is at Calle Mayor 72 (☎ 941 341230).

Accommodation

There are two *albergues* in town. The first is in the **Casa de la Cofradía del Santo**, a beautiful old building often visited by tourists, with single beds rather than bunks (60 beds, kitchen, open all year). The other is the **Albergue del Abadía Cisterciense Nuestra Sra de la Anunciación** (32 beds, kitchen, open May to September).

$ Hostal del Río (☎ 941 340277)
$$ Pensión Miguel (☎ 941 343252)
$$$ Cisterciense (☎ 941 340700)
$$$$ El Parador (☎ 941 340300)

In Santo Domingo, walk down Calle Mayor. You'll soon leave the old town, crossing the Río Oja over Santo Domingo's original bridge, now mostly hidden by concrete additions. Follow farm tracks through mostly flat countryside. Shortly after the track changes to tarmac, you have a choice of routes at a T-junction. If you're in a rush, turn right to walk along the road, but it's much more pleasant to turn left here and continue walking through rolling farmland. The conical hill to your right was an important strategic location, and Celtiberian burials have been discovered there. Whichever option you chose, you'll enter Grañon in a few kilometres.

Grañon
Ⓐ Ⓗ ✕ ⬛ € (557km)

At one time, Grañon boasted two monasteries and a mediaeval pilgrims' hospice, and in the Middle Ages, it was a walled town with an important castle. Nowadays, its only monument is the Iglesia de San Juan Bautista, built over a former monastery and with a gorgeous sixteenth-century Baroque *retablo*.

The old church bell tower houses the town's **albergue** (38 beds, kitchen, open all year), and its communal meals and beautiful surroundings make it a wonderfully relaxing place to stay. You can also stay at the **Casa Jacobeo** ($$, (☎ 941 420684).

Just over a kilometre from Grañon, at the top of a rise, a stone map marks the border of La Rioja and Castilla y León. In another 2km, you'll reach Redecilla del Camino.

Redecilla del Camino (Ⓐ⬛, 553km) is yet another one-street village that grew up with the camino in the eleventh century. Its **Iglesia de Nuestra Señora de la Calle** contains a massive Romanesque baptismal font, the most impressive of the whole camino. A serpent circles the font's base, and the solid bowl is decorated with a city of tall, multi-storeyed buildings, probably a representation of celestial Jerusalem.

Redecilla's **albergue** (50 beds, kitchen, open all year), which stands on the site of the Hospital de San Lázaro, the town's old pilgrim hospice, is a great place to pick up leaflets and gather information about the camino in Castilla y León.

To leave Redecilla, walk down the aptly named Camino de Santiago. You'll arrive at **Castildelgado** (Ⓗ✕⬛) in a couple of kilometres. Although the village contained a monastery and hospice at one time, there's little to detain you nowadays apart from a bar-restaurant, a *panadería* and the **Hostal El Chocolatero** ($$, ☎ 947 588063).

It's just another 2km to **Viloria de Rioja** (Ⓐ, 548km), the inauspicious birthplace of Santo Domingo. Pass a dilapidated church on the left, which still contains the Romanesque font in which Domingo was baptized, although the house where he was born has recently been demolished. Viloria's **albergue** has 18 beds and is sporadically open from April to October. The route to Belorado mostly follows a wide dirt track that's beginning to feel like a pilgrim treadmill as it parallels the main road.

In another 2km, you'll reach **Villamayor del Río** (Ⓐ, 546km). Turn right just before the village for the private **albergue** (52 beds, open all year).

There's little to distract you on the barren 5km stretch to Belorado, although there are still glimpses of the Sierra de la Demanda to your left. Once in town, turn left at the Iglesia de Santa María, then take the first street on the right, and then the first on the left.

Belorado

ⒶⒽ✗▬€🛒 (541km)

Although occupied since Roman times and home to eight churches by the thirteenth century, Belorado is a modern, down-at-heel town, suffering from the gradual demise of its leather industry. The remaining churches of Santa María and San Pedro are less than exciting, but the main square is large and pleasant and Belorado has an incredible number of bars and cafés.

There are good views from the mostly ruined mediaeval castle above the town. The caves below were once home to religious hermits, including San Capraiso, who hid here to escape persecution until a young martyr's courage inspired him to face his executioners.

Accommodation

Belorado's **albergue parroquial** (28 beds, kitchen, open all year) is next to the Iglesia de Santa María. Alternatively, stay at **Albergue Cuatro Cantones** farther along the camino near the main square (60 beds, kitchen, open all year).

$ Hostal Ojarre Calle Santiago 16 (☎ 947 580223)

$ Pensión Toi Redecilla del Campo 7 (☎ 947 580525)

$$ Casa Rural Verdeancho Calle Corro 11 (☎ 947 580261)

$$ Hotel Belorado Avenida Generalisimo 30 (☎ 947 580684)

The walk from Belorado is a pleasant one, heading towards Villafranca Montes de Oca along grass and stone tracks through undulating farmland. Look out for effortlessly circling griffon vultures above you. As you leave town, pass the **Convento de Santa Clara**, said to be built on the site of an *ermita* (hermitage) destroyed by the Moors.

A few kilometres out of Belorado, the camino passes along the top of the hamlet of **Tosantos** (Ⓐ▬, 538km), and you'll need to veer off the route to the right to visit the village café-bar and the **albergue** (40 beds, open April to October). Just before Tosantos peters out, turn left along a dirt farm track, clearly signed. As you climb slightly, look out for the **Ermita de Nuestra Señora de Pena** to your right, built directly into the

Map 7 (key page 182)

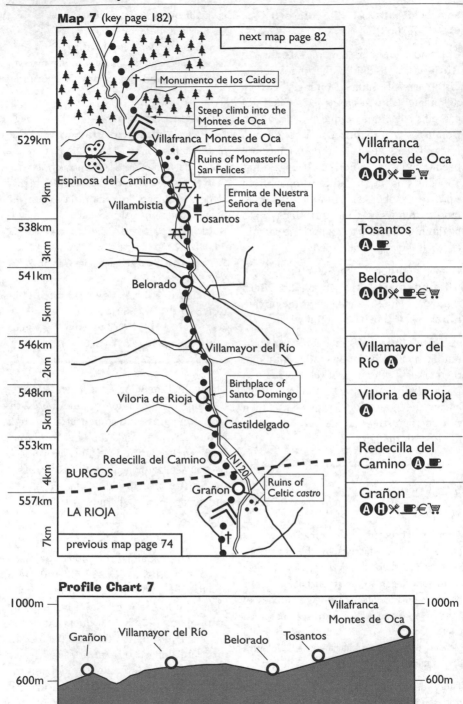

next map page 82

Monumento de los Caidos

Steep climb into the Montes de Oca

529km

Villafranca Montes de Oca

Ruins of Monasterío San Felices

Espinosa del Camino

Ermita de Nuestra Señora de Pena

Villambistia

Tosantos

538km

Belorado

541km

546km

Villamayor del Río

Birthplace of Santo Domingo

548km

Viloria de Rioja

Castildelgado

553km

Redecilla del Camino

BURGOS

Grañon

Ruins of Celtic *castro*

557km

LA RIOJA

previous map page 74

9km
3km
5km
2km
5km
4km
7km

Villafranca Montes de Oca
🅰🅗✕☕🛒

Tosantos
🅰☕

Belorado
🅰🅗✕☕€🛒

Villamayor del Río 🅰

Viloria de Rioja 🅰

Redecilla del Camino 🅰☕

Grañon
🅰🅗✕☕€🛒

Profile Chart 7

1000m

Villafranca Montes de Oca

Grañon   Villamayor del Río   Belorado   Tosantos

600m

1000m

600m

hill and looking as if it's organically part of the landscape.

In just 2km, the camino passes through the hamlet of **Villambistia** (🍺), where there's not a lot to see, and where the modern church, built from large stone blocks, has seen better days. Walk through **Espinosa del Camino** (🍺), less than 2km from Villambistia, past a bar on the left and a fountain on the right.

Walk through rolling, green countryside to the top of a rise, from where you can see Villafranca Montes de Oca ahead. Descend a little, then pass the ruined **Monasterío San Felices** on your right. Although only a single arch remains of this once-important ninth-century Mozarabic monastery, it's an interesting place to poke around in. The ruins hold the bones of Diego Porcelos, who founded Burgos after recapturing it from the Moors.

In another half a kilometre, the track curves left to meet the main road. Turn right to walk along the road, entering Villafranca Montes de Oca.

Villafranca Montes de Oca
Ⓐ Ⓗ ✕ 🍺 🛒 (529km)

Villafranca's beautiful location in a sheltered valley at the foot of the Montes de Oca has attracted settlers for almost 3000 years. Nearby, there's evidence of an Iron Age settlement from 700 BC, while the town's name comes partly from Auca, a large Roman town that once stood here, and partly from the Franks who resettled the area as the camino became popular.

Visit the eighteenth-century **Iglesia de Santiago** to look at the altar's Santiago Peregrino statue and a baptismal font made from a giant Philippine shell. The fourteenth-century **Hospital de San Antonio Abad**, also known as the Hospital de la Reina in honour of its founder, Queen Juana Manuel, sheltered up to 18,000 pilgrims a year in the sixteenth century. It has now been converted back into an **albergue** (23 beds, kitchen, open all year).

There are rooms in **El Pájaro** ($, ☎ 947 582029), a couple of bars and a *panadería* in the village. There's another shop farther down the main road, just off the camino, your last chance to buy anything at all for about 20km and the last place before Burgos with a good selection of food.

In Villafranca, turn right off the main road to walk past a fountain and the church. From here to San Juan de Ortega, it's a steep initial climb followed by a lovely ridge walk through swathes of heather. In spring, there are primroses and songbirds here, but your eye is inevitably drawn to the endless, spectacular stretches of pink and purple heather.

If you're here early in the morning, you may be lucky enough to see fox, wild boar or roe deer. In autumn, when fog often descends, look out for mushrooms, which in seventeenth-century pilgrim Domenico Laffi's words were "of unbelievable size, as big as a straw hat." Luckily for Laffi, who got lost here, they were also plentiful. The route was also a struggle in mediaeval times, when the Montes de Oca's steep, rugged terrain, dense forest, wolves, thieves and murderers made it

Map 8 (key page 182)

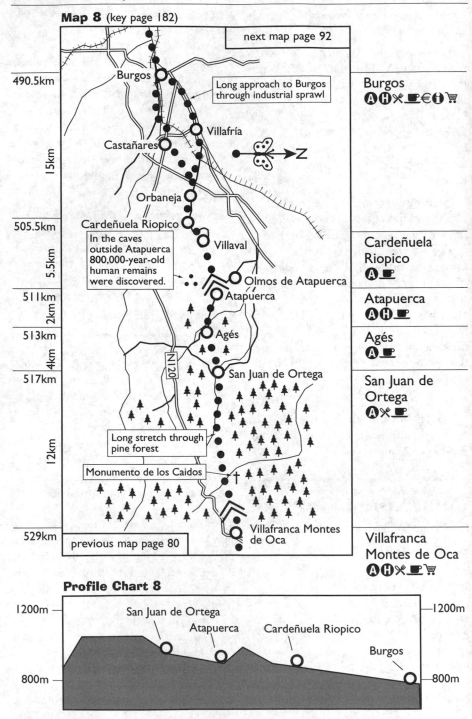

next map page 92

490.5km

Burgos

Long approach to Burgos through industrial sprawl

Villafría

Castañares

→Z

Orbaneja

505.5km

Cardeñuela Riopico

In the caves outside Atapuerca 800,000-year-old human remains were discovered.

Villaval

15km

5.5km

Olmos de Atapuerca

511km

Atapuerca

2km

513km

Agés

4km

517km

N120

San Juan de Ortega

12km

Long stretch through pine forest

Monumento de los Caidos

†

529km

previous map page 80

Villafranca Montes de Oca

Burgos
Ⓐ🅗✕☕€ⓘ🛒

Cardeñuela Riopico
Ⓐ☕

Atapuerca
Ⓐ🅗☕

Agés
Ⓐ☕

San Juan de Ortega
Ⓐ✕☕

Villafranca Montes de Oca
Ⓐ🅗✕☕🛒

Profile Chart 8

1200m —
San Juan de Ortega
Atapuerca
Cardeñuela Riopico
Burgos
— 1200m

800m —
— 800m

one of the most treacherous stretches of the camino.

In a few kilometres, the track heads past the Monumento de los Caidos, a memorial to Spanish civil war victims. From here, it's a long 7km stretch to San Juan de Ortega, following broad, pine-edged tracks through scrub and heather.

Finally, the track starts to descend and soon emerges from the trees at a pastoral countryside setting with the monastery of San Juan de Ortega in the distance. The deciduous trees, fields and flowers are a jolt to the senses after all that pine, and the scene is so pretty and old-fashioned that it seems straight out of an English hymn. Cross a stream and enter the tiny hamlet of San Juan de Ortega.

San Juan de Ortega Ⓐ✕🍵 (517km)

Just like Santo Domingo de la Calzada, the hamlet of San Juan de Ortega is the work of a single man. Juan was a disciple of Santo Domingo, and like his mentor, he improved the pilgrim road and built bridges, hospices and cathedrals. Disaster almost befell Juan as he returned from a pilgrimage to Jerusalem when his boat was shipwrecked in stormy seas, but he prayed to San Nicolás de Barí and was spared to continue his pilgrim work. On his return, Juan dedicated a hospice in the Montes de Oca wilderness to San Nicolás, calling the place Ortega, after the Spanish word for nettle.

San Juan also founded a monasterial order here and built a church. The **Iglesia de San Juan de Ortega**'s twelfth-century apses are said to have been built by the saint himself, and the church is still laid out according to its original Romanesque plan. The church and monastery soon fell into disrepair, but were expanded in the fifteenth century thanks to an injection of cash and the efforts of the bishop of Burgos.

Meanwhile, San Juan garnered a reputation as a patron of fertility after his tomb was opened and a swarm of white bees flew out, surrounded by a beautiful smell. The bees were seen as the souls of unborn children, kept safe by the saint until they could be placed in suitable Christian wombs. Hearing of this, the long-childless Isabel la Católica visited, determined to produce an heir for the Kingdom of Castilla.

When she gave birth to a son, she named him Juan, and when her son died early, Isabel returned to ask for the saint's help once more, this time conceiving a daughter, who she called Juana. Grateful, Isabel ordered the rebuilding of the chapel of San Nicolás de Bari, and commissioned a Gothic baldachin to ornament San Juan's tomb. The alabaster tomb itself is carved with scenes from San Juan's life, including the legend of the bees and the appearance of San Nicolás at sea.

Above you, there's a Romanesque capital showing the battle between Roland and the giant Ferragut, and a magnificent triple capital depicting the Annunciation, the Visitation, the dream of Joseph and the Nativity. Impressive at any time, the capitals literally shine at the time of the Milagro de la Luz, when a shaft of sunlight illuminates the womb of the Virgin of the Annunciation in the late afternoon at the spring and autumn equinox.

Part of the monastery is reserved for the use of pilgrims, and is now an authentic, atmospheric but decidedly chilly **albergue** (58 beds, open all year). The *albergue* is famous for its delicious garlic soup, served to pilgrims at a long, communal table each night after Mass. The tiny hamlet also has a bar, and a fountain that doubles as the *albergue's* clothes-washing facility.

Walk down the road out of San Juan de Ortega. At a bend in the road after 200m, take the well-signposted right-hand track through a pine wood. Reach a flat-topped pasture, criss-crossed by many paths, then head downhill into the village of **Agés** (**A**⬛, 513km). The remains of García de Nájera, who was killed near here by his brother Fernando I of Castilla, were originally entombed at the Iglesia de Santa Eulalia before they were moved to Nájera's Panteón Real. The village has two small *albergues*: **El Pajar de Agés** (42 beds, kitchen, open all year) and **Albergue San Rafael** (36 beds, open all year).

Keep straight on through the village, walking on a narrow paved road that will take you to Atapuerca, a couple of kilometres away. Look out for standing stones on either side of the road — these are modern but were raised using prehistoric means by archaeologists and villagers of nearby Atapuerca. Walk into Atapuerca along the road, passing a water pump to the left of the road.

Atapuerca
A H ⬛ (511km)

Although Atapuerca was one of the first towns wrestled from Muslim control in the *reconquista*, it was a minor stop along the camino with nothing much of interest before archaeologists dug up prehistoric human remains in the nearby hills. Caves were dis-

covered in the Atapuercan massif in the nineteenth century, but it wasn't until the mid-1970s that excavations began in earnest.

These excavations have uncovered some of the best-preserved early human remains ever found. In 1997, archaeologists at the site identified the 800,000-year-old bones as a new species, *homo antecessor*. The site is now a UNESCO World Heritage Site. There's limited information in the village; many of the site's finds are now in the Burgos archaeological museum, and there's also a museum in the nearby village of Ibeas de Jarros, from where guided tours can sometimes be arranged (see www.atapuerca.net).

In Atapuerca itself, you can stay at the **albergue** (20 beds, open all year) next to the church or at the **Turismo Rural Papasol** ($$$, ☎ 947 430320).

There's also an **albergue** (32 beds, kitchen, open all year) and the lovely **Casarrota la Campesina** ($$$, ☎ 947 264966) 2.5km farther along the road in Olmos de Atapuerca. If you choose to stay in Olmos de Atapuerca, there's no need to retrace your steps to continue the camino: just follow the yellow arrows and you'll soon meet up with the route from Atapuerca.

Turn left at the end of Atapuerca to follow narrow tracks over the Sierra de Atapuerca. In spring, look out for wild hyacinths and other flowers as you climb. Head towards a cross on the flat-topped summit, from where you get views of Burgos and of the immense, flat *meseta* that stretches west from the city. Head to the left of the radio towers towards a clump of trees, then walk downhill along a grassy track, passing a quarry on the right.

Just past the edge of the quarry, the camino splits.

Turn left to follow the slightly longer route through pretty villages along narrow, quiet roads, or keep straight on for a shorter, duller route, mostly on tracks through stony pasture dotted with wildflowers. The left-hand route passes through **Villalval** and **Cardeñuela Riopico** (🅐▣, 505.5km), where there's a small **albergue** (20 beds, open all year), before meeting up with the alternative route at **Orbaneja** (▣). At the end of Orbaneja, cross the busy A1 via a bridge. From here, you have two options to get to the *albergue* in Burgos.

By far the nicest way reaches Burgos via a riverside path. To get there, turn left just past the bridge after Orbaneja to follow a red earth track around a military site. Pass a truck dumping area and turn left towards **Castañares** (▣). Carefully cross the busy main road to the Camino Santa María Sendero, then pass a paved park on the left and walk through a brick housing estate. Pass the Campo Futbol el Molinar, cross the river via a blue metal footbridge, and head towards the main road. Turn right and walk on a paved path alongside the road, then pass under the main road. From here, follow a path alongside the Río Arlanzón. This path, popular with joggers and afternoon strollers, leads you right into the centre of Burgos.

A quicker but less pleasant option is to keep straight on, following a minor road towards Burgos' sprawling suburbs. In a couple of kilometres, cross a railway bridge into **Villafría** (🅗✗▣€☕), an ugly town straddling the main road into Burgos. There are a couple of hotels in Villafría, and you're about 8km from the centre of Burgos, but it's better to continue the camino, either on foot or by catching the #8 bus, rather than staying here. Pass a map of the camino after about 4km as the route becomes less industrial, then veer right 1km later, immediately after a military building. Turn left in a few hundred metres at the Centro Comercial Camino de la Plata, then follow Calle Las Calzadas into Burgos.

For the route to the *albergue*, see the city map of Burgos on page 90.

Regional Map (key page 182)

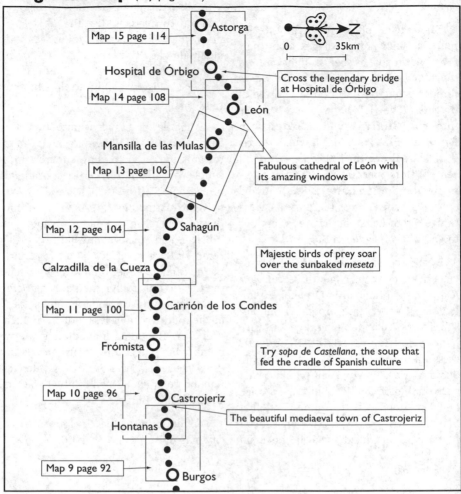

Map 15 page 114 → O Astorga

0 ⊢————⊣ 35km

Hospital de Órbigo O

Cross the legendary bridge
at Hospital de Órbigo

Map 14 page 108 →

O León

Mansilla de las Mulas O

Map 13 page 106 →

Fabulous cathedral of León with
its amazing windows

Map 12 page 104 → O Sahagún

Calzadilla de la Cueza O

Majestic birds of prey soar
over the sunbaked *meseta*

Map 11 page 100 → O Carrión de los Condes

Frómista O

Try *sopa de Castellana*, the soup that
fed the cradle of Spanish culture

Map 10 page 96 → O Castrojeriz

Hontanas O

The beautiful mediaeval town of Castrojeriz

Map 9 page 92 → O Burgos

What's the weather like?

	Jan	April	July	Oct
Sun	4hrs	8hrs	12hrs	6hrs
Rainfall	6cm	5cm	2cm	5cm
Maximum Temp	7°C	15°C	28°C	18°C
Minimum Temp	-1°C	3°C	11°C	6°C

Average hours of sun, total average rainfall in cm and average temperature in degrees Celsius

Meseta

Burgos to Astorga

The *meseta* has a bad reputation. Flat, desolate and the section most likely to be missed out by pilgrims running short of time, the plains can also be hauntingly beautiful. And it's not all desolate wilderness: Burgos and León, the camino's liveliest cities, offer sophisticated restaurants and stunning cultural attractions.

 **Walking**

Geography

The vast expanse and huge skies of the *meseta* are striking and strange, swinging from depressingly monotonous to exhilaratingly infinite in the space of a kilometre. The Cordillera Cantábrica in the north will provide some distraction, but mostly your senses will be overloaded by an endless flatness.

From Burgos, the camino climbs to a flat tableland dented with inhabited valleys and depressions. Towards Frómista, canals drain into poppy-lined wheat fields in a fertile region known as the breadbasket of northern Spain.

Trails

The walking is generally good, although the camino often follows purpose-built gravel tracks alongside the main road, like a dismal, never-ending camino highway. There are a couple of stretches, notably around the lovely village of Calzadilla de los Hermanillos, when you move away from civilization and crunch along thyme-scented tracks with the sparsely inhabited *meseta* all to yourself.

When to go

Summers are hot, and winters are cold, but both can be fabulous times to visit. Start early in summer and you'll miss the worst of the heat and catch a noisy dawn chorus. Wrap up warm in winter to enjoy crisp, cloudless days that make for wonderful walking. The brief spring and autumn seasons are more temperate, although the wind can be bone-chilling.

 **Flora & Fauna**

The wheat fields and scrubland of the *meseta* initially seem lifeless and deserted, but if you stop for a while you'll hear and see a stunning array of birds.

One of the most distinctive is the **great bustard**, a stocky, goose-sized bird that loves the *meseta*'s wide open spaces. In spring, the males coquettishly rustle their tails in a dramatic courtship display; their size and fluffy white feathers making them indistinguishable at a distance from a flock of sheep. Intensive cultivation and tree planting are eroding the bustard's habitat, while a hunting ban may ironically reduce numbers further, as landowners now have no incentive to conserve territory for the former game bird.

Up above, the skies are a bonanza of aerial hunters. You can see kestrels, peregrine falcons, Egyptian vultures, hen harriers and Bonelli's eagles. It takes more patience to look for birds that live low to the ground in fields or scrubland, and at first you're more likely to hear the melodic songs of the *meseta*'s many **larks** — there are short-toed, Dupont's, crested and calandra larks here — than to see the well-camouflaged birds. Much easier to spot is the bold, coral-coloured crest and black and white wings of the **hoopoe**, which flies in such an ungainly, undulating style that it seems to fall from the sky with each wingbeat.

People & Culture

Castilla y León can justly claim to be the cradle of Spanish culture. One of the first regions to be won back by the Christians after the Muslim invasion, Spain is so entwined with **Castilla** that the Spanish even call their language *castellano* (Castilian). As the southern regions came back under Christian control, the power base of the country moved south, leaving the cities of Burgos and León to their glorious Gothic cathedrals. Burgos' second

brief moment in the spotlight came during the civil war, when Franco made the Nationalist city his capital. Just as in the *reconquista*, however, as soon as the southern cities came under Franco's control, the capital moved south to Madrid.

There's not much stone around in the *meseta*, so locals have had to use alternative building materials. Inspired by Muslim architects, intricate **brick** churches were built in many towns, notably in Sahagún, where the recently restored Iglesia de San Tirso is a highlight. More modest folk have been equally creative. In many *meseta* villages, houses are made from adobe, a logical choice in a bone-dry climate, cheap to build and repaired by simply patching the walls with more straw and mud. Hobbit-like underground **bodegas** (cellars) are a common sight on the outskirts of villages and towns, providing cool storage for wine and other produce. The round- or horseshoe-shaped buildings that sit plum in the middle of fields are **palomares** (dovecotes).

Food & Drink

Meat-heavy meals are the norm, often padded out with pulses and rice-blood sausage; most famous of these is Burgos' unappetizingly named *olla podrida* (putrid pot). Castilla y León is also known for its **suckling pig**, traditionally roasted in a baker's oven with pine branches, broom, rosemary and thyme.

Keep vampires away with Castilla's famous **sopa de ajo** or *sopa de castellana*, a soup made by frying bread in paprika and lots of garlic, pouring on stock and cracking an egg on top. A staple food in hard times, *sopa de ajo* is now appearing in the finest restaurants. You'll see plenty of **caracoles** (snails) along the trail, and occasionally spot locals collecting them by the bucketful. *Caracoles* are delicious when boiled with onion, garlic and parsley, a bit of *chorizo* and *jamón* and a splash of white wine.

Ribera del Duero **wines** are a recent introduction to the international scene, and the Duero basin in the south of Castilla y León is now attracting almost as much attention as its more famous Riojan cousin.

Tourist Information

Transport

There are regular buses and trains between Burgos and Astorga, via León.

Accommodation

Albergues vary wildly in quality, space and facilities, from the crammed bunk beds but beautiful setting of Burgos to the spacious, quiet *albergue* in Calzadilla de los Hermanillos. There are plenty of hotels in both Burgos and León if you want to dally in either of those cities, and the Parador de San Marcos in León is one of the best hotels in Spain.

Events & Festivals

Hospital de Órbigo recreates a mediaeval **jousting** competition at the beginning of June each year to honour Don Suero de Quiñones, a knight who defended the bridge at Hospital from all-comers after being rejected by his lady love.

Burgos sheds its dour image during the Fiestas de San Pedro y San Pablo at the end of June. In mid-August, young girls dance through **León**, led by a veiled woman in a turban, celebrating the end of a Moorish law that demanded a sacrifice of 100 maidens from local villages.

Rest Days & Detours

The logical places to take a break are Burgos and León, pleasant cities to wander around, visit spectacular monuments or simply rest sore feet. Farther off the camino, the Gregorian monastery at **Santo Domingo de Silos**, some 70km southwest of Burgos, is well worth a visit. The double-decked Romanesque cloister is breathtaking, with beautifully carved capitals and a gorgeous restored Mudéjar ceiling. The monks have an internationally renowned choir school, and their Gregorian chants broke into the pop charts in the 1990s.

At **Quintanilla de las Viñas**, near Santo Domingo, you can see the lovely seventh-century Visigothic church of Nuestra Señora de las Viñas. North of Frómista, around **Aguilar de Campóo**, you'll find what is said to be the highest concentration of Romanesque churches in Europe. The simple, elegant churches are, for the most part, unrestored, and remain unadorned and untainted by Gothic or Baroque flourishes. Just south of Calzadilla de La Cueza is the **Villa Romana de Tejada**, an excavated Roman villa with mosaic-floor remains.

Burgos

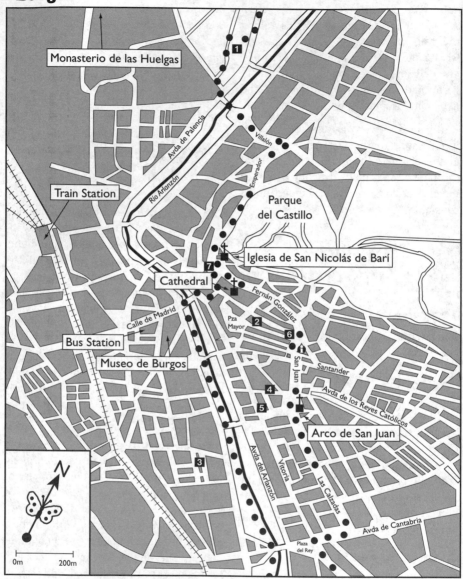

Map labels:
- Monasterio de las Huelgas — **1**
- Villalón
- Avda de Palencia
- Río Arlanzón
- Emperador
- Train Station
- Parque del Castillo
- Iglesia de San Nicolás de Barí
- **7** Cathedral
- Fernán González
- Calle de Madrid
- Pza Mayor — **2**
- Bus Station
- Museo de Burgos
- **6**
- San Juan
- Santander
- **4**
- **5**
- Avda de los Reyes Católicos
- Arco de San Juan
- **3**
- Avda del Arlanzón
- Vitoria
- Las Calzadas
- Avda de Cantabria
- Plaza del Rey
- 0m   200m

Accommodation

1 Main *albergue*

2 Albergue El Parral

3 Albergue de Burgos

4 Pensión Peña

5 Hostal San Juan

6 Hotel Norte y Londres

7 Hotel Del Cid

Burgos

Ⓐ Ⓗ ✗ ▆ € ⓘ 🛒 (490.5km)

Burgos comes as a bit of a culture shock after the mellow, timeless feel of the camino so far. It's a sizeable city with traffic jams, nightlife and noise, and so chock-full of monuments that it's worth staying an extra day or two to see them all. Despite this, the rest of Spain sees Burgos as less than cosmopolitan.

Thanks to famous sons such as El Cid and Fernando III, reconquerer of southern Spain, Burgos had a reputation as a centre of staid military might before the civil war. The city's Nationalist ties during the war and throughout the Franco era simply reinforced the city's image as a bastion of conservative Catholicism. In democratic Spain, the city is trying to cast aside its tarnished reputation: literally so, in the case of Burgos' talismanic cathedral, whose blackened exterior has been polished to gleaming white.

The massive Gothic **cathedral** sits right in the middle of Burgos and is a natural place to begin a tour of the city. Begun by Fernando III at the beginning of the thirteenth century, it was completed in just 22 years, and although there were additions over the next few centuries, the cathedral retains its Gothic style. It's almost impossible to get a complete picture of the cathedral: there's simply no vantage point in Burgos from which you can take in the delicate, air-filled spires, the monumental doorways and arches and the tall, solid towers. The cathedral was made a UNESCO World Heritage site in 1984.

Inside, there's an overwhelming array of stunning sculpture and artwork. The octagonal walls of the late-fifteenth-century **Capilla del Condestable** rise up towards an elegant, star-vaulted dome, whose geometrical carvings show a Muslim influence. The Gothic-Renaissance chapel contains stunning fourteenth-century *retablos* and a beautifully carved marble tomb, replete with realistic details. The Capilla de Santa Tecla contains Burgos' famous **Papamoscas**, a fifteenth-century mechanical clock that springs into action on the quarter hour.

Back in the main body of the cathedral, you can peer into the caged choir to see a gilded Mudéjar lantern vault. You'll also be dazzled by the staggeringly shiny Plateresque Escalera Dorada, which rises from the ground floor of the cathedral to meet the Puerta Alta, some 30m above. El Cid is buried beneath the choir, in a simple tomb brought to Burgos in the 1920s.

Part of the cathedral is reserved for worship rather than tourist gawking. Religious pilgrims can enter the **Capilla del Santo Cristo**, which contains a frankly disturbing statue of its namesake. The statue's hair and fingernails were said to be real and in need of regular trimming, and although the skin was also said to be human, it's now been identified as buffalo hide.

Of Burgos' many smaller churches, the **Iglesia de San Nicolás de Barí**, on Calle Fernán Gonzalez near the cathedral, is worth visiting for its stunning, massive alabaster *retablo*.

Across the Río Arlanzón in the Casa de Miranda, the **Museo de Burgos** has a good prehistory archaeology section, boosted considerably by finds from Atapuerca. Above the town, there's not much left of Burgos' castle, destroyed by successive invaders, including Napoleon who blew it up in 1813, shattering the cathedral's stained glass windows in the process.

The twelfth-century **Monasterio de las Huelgas Reales**, on the western outskirts of Burgos, close to the *albergue*, was

Map 9 (key page 182)

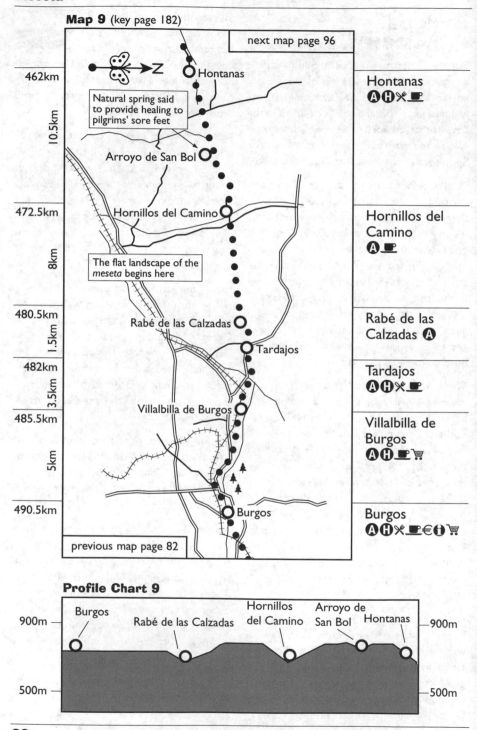

next map page page 96

462km

Hontanas

Natural spring said
to provide healing to
pilgrims' sore feet

10.5km

Arroyo de San Bol

472.5km

Hornillos del Camino

8km

The flat landscape of the
meseta begins here

480.5km

Rabé de las Calzadas

1.5km

Tardajos

482km

3.5km

485.5km

Villalbilla de Burgos

5km

490.5km

Burgos

previous map page 82

Hontanas
A H ✕ ☕

Hornillos del
Camino
A ☕

Rabé de las
Calzadas A

Tardajos
A H ✕ ☕

Villalbilla de
Burgos
A H ☕ 🛒

Burgos
A H ✕ ☕ € ⓘ 🛒

Profile Chart 9

Burgos   Rabé de las Calzadas   Hornillos
                                  del Camino   Arroyo de
                                                San Bol   Hontanas

900m

900m

500m

500m

made famous and powerful by Fernando III, who was knighted into the Order of Santiago here. The statue of Santiago Matamoros used in these ceremonies has a jointed arm so that the saintly sword can be moved up and down. The convent is the final resting place of a good proportion of Castilian royalty, and although the tombs were damaged by plunderers, they contained some beautiful textiles inspired by Islamic designs, which are now displayed in Las Huelgas' Museo de Ricas Telas. Nearby, little remains of the **Hospital del Rey**, which provided food and lodgings for pilgrims from the twelfth century onwards, but it's worth taking in the sixteenth-century gateway.

At the other end of the city, the **Cartuja de Miraflores** stands serenely in beautiful parkland. The fifteenth-century church — the only part of the still-working monastery open to the public — is stamped with the artistic skills of Gil de Siloé and the patronage of Isabel la Católica. The alabaster tombs of Isabel's parents, Juan II and Isabel de Portugal, took four years to complete and are among the most detailed and intricate ever carved; the wall tomb of Alfonso, Isabel's brother, is crafted in similar style. Gil de Siloé's magnificent, overpowering wooden *retablo* is gilded with gold brought back from America by Columbus in the 1490s.

Burgos casts aside its pious image at the end of June during the two-week Fiestas de San Pedro y San Pablo, with bullfighting, feasts, music and street parades with *gigantillos and gigantones*, larger-than-life plaster figures.

Burgos' **turismo** is on Plaza Alonso Martínez 7 (☎ 947 203125).

Accommodation

Burgos' main **albergue** (96 beds, open all year) is attractively located in a park near the university, although the crowded dormitories can be stifling in summer. There are also two smaller *albergues* closer to the centre: **El Parral** on Calle Lain Calvo 10 (18 beds, open all year), and **Albergue de Burgos** on Calle Mateo Cerezo 9 (15 beds, open spring to autumn).

$ Pensión Peña, Calle Puebla 18 (☎ 947 206323)

$$ Hostal San Juan, Calle de Bernabe Perez Ortiz 1 (☎ 947 205134)

$$$ Hotel Norte y Londres, Plaza Alonso Martinez 10 (☎ 947 264125)

$$$$ Hotel Del Cid, Plaza Santa María 8 (☎ 947 208715)

From Burgos' *albergue*, walk through the park, then turn left at the main road. In 300m, just after a roundabout, turn right onto a narrow paved road that soon changes to a dirt track. In no time at all, you've left the city and, as the camino passes through a wood, you can glimpse the jail that held political prisoners during Franco's time on your right. The camino wanders through flat farmland and soon passes near **Villalbilla de Burgos** (ⒶⒽⓁ🛏🍴, 485.5km), where you can stay at the **albergue** (18 beds, open all year) or the **Hostal San Roque** (**$$**, ☎ 947 291229).

After a few kilometres, cross the Río Arlanzón and walk into **Tardajos** (ⒶⒽ✕🍴💊, 482km) along the N120, passing an eighteenth-century stone cross that marks the site of an old pilgrim hospital. There's an **albergue** (22 beds, open all year) in the village and rooms available at **Pensión Mary** (**$**, ☎ 947 451125).

Follow the camino as it winds through a pretty stretch of older terraced houses,

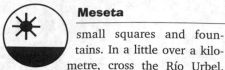

small squares and foun-tains. In a little over a kilo-metre, cross the Río Urbel, where there's good fishing, and veer left on a minor tarmac road, keeping an eye out for larks and magpies near the ground, and kestrels and vultures over-head. There are two *albergues* in **Rabé de las Calzadas** (Ⓐ, 480.5km): the French **albergue** (30 beds, open April to November) and the excellent, friendly **Albergue Danza y Música** (22 beds, open all year). The village bar is open on weekends only.

The camino from Rabé passes through fields and pasture, and alongside streams lined with black poplars and willows. In a couple of kilometres, pass the Fuente de Prao Torre, then climb uphill. At the top of the rise, the scenery is jaw-droppingly, never-endingly flat. Welcome to the *meseta*, treeless, stunningly beautiful, and loud with wind, birdsong and crickets. Calandra larks are difficult to see, except in early spring, when males perform a melodious song flight, wings held stiffly and showing distinctive black wing undersides and a pale belly.

After a few kilometres of flatness, the camino arrives at Hornillos del Camino, hidden from the elements in a hollow and approached by way of a steep downhill track. **Hornillos del Camino** (Ⓐ⚑, 472.5km), is a friendly village of pale, local stone. The **albergue** (32 beds, kitchen, open all year) is on the right, next to a Gothic church built on the site of an Iron Age *castro*, and the Fuente del Gallo, a cockerel-topped fountain.

At the next valley, about 5km after Hornillos, is the **Arroyo San Bol** (Ⓐ), a natural spring just off the camino. Pilgrims who wash their feet in the spring

are said to have no foot problems from here to Santiago. The spring marks the site of San Baudillo, a village mysterious-ly abandoned in 1503, possibly due to disease or possibly after the expulsion of the Jews from Spain. There's a basic **albergue** here (20 beds, kitchen, no bathrooms, open summer-only).

From San Bol onwards, it's a long, flat stretch through fields, a wonderful area for watching birds of prey and listening to noisy choruses of songbirds hidden in wheat fields. Seventeenth-century pil-grims were more concerned about bigger animals: Laffi was warned to only cross the *meseta* in the middle of the day, when shepherds and their dogs provided some protection against marauding packs of wolves. Shepherds still guard against wolves, but these animals are uncommon now and you'd be very lucky to see one.

After a few kilometres of *meseta* walk-ing, the first glimpse of Hontanas, tucked into a valley and named after the large number of local springs, is astonishing. There are gorgeous views of Hontanas' timeless mediaeval rooftops as you walk steeply downhill past dovecotes.

Hontanas
Ⓐ Ⓗ ✕ ☕ (462km)

Hontanas is a one-street village, dominated by the beautiful, looming fourteenth-century Iglesia de la Inmaculada Concepción.

The village has a gorgeous **albergue** (20 beds, kitchen, open all year), located in the beautifully restored Mesón de los Franceses, a former pilgrim hospice. There are two other *albergues*, both open only when the main *albergue* is full: **El Viejo** (14 beds) and **La Escuela** (21 beds). You can also stay at

Mesón-Albergue El Puntido ($$, ☎ 947 378597) which also has bunk beds (30 beds, open Easter to mid-October).
$ Casa Cesar Arnaiz (☎ 947 378521)
$$ Hostal Fuente Strella (☎ 947 377261)

From Hontanas, follow a path that leads along a hillside just above the valley floor, where poplars line the river's edge and the fields are full of sunflowers in summer. Laffi, the seventeenth-century pilgrim chronicler, bemoaned the locusts along this part of the camino: "It moves one to pity to see how people are dying of hunger, and the beasts too, as their pastures are devoured by these insects."

Turn right at a road in 4km, following it for 3km towards the ruins of the Gothic **Convento de San Antón** (Ⓐ, 12 beds, kitchen, open July to September), whose dramatic arch spans the camino. The Orden de los Antonianos rose out of a miraculous cure for San Antón's fire, a burning disease similar to leprosy that was rampant in the Middle Ages.

Hospices like this one were set up all along the camino, treating diseased pilgrims with exercise and red wine as well as the divine hand of San Antón. Locked-out latecomers could sleep in the porch and eat food that the monks left in niches. The niches, visible on the right-hand side of the road, now contain messages scribbled by pilgrims on scraps of paper and held in place by small stones.

Soon after passing San Antón, the ruined fortress perched above Castrojeriz comes into view. In a couple of kilometres, at a sign describing the town's attractions, turn right, walk past the Iglesia de Nuestra Señora del Manzano, then follow the camino signs along the long approach into the centre of Castrojeriz.

Castrojeriz
Ⓐ Ⓗ ✕ ▬ 🛒 (452km)

Castrojeriz is a beautiful town with surprisingly stylish bars and restaurants. The town has been inhabited since Celtiberian times, if not earlier, and it doesn't take much imagination to see this spot as an ideal place for a settlement, near a river and ably defended by a hill with views for miles around. The Romans used its glorious vantage point to guard the route to their valuable gold mines near Astorga and, by the Middle Ages, the town's long main street was packed with hospices and churches. Unusually, the town's tenth-century *fuero* (charter) gave Christians and Jews equal rights, and a murderer of a Jewish resident was to be treated identically to one who killed a Christian.

At the entrance into town, the **Iglesia de Santa María del Manzano** marks a camino miracle. Santiago was so excited to see an image of the Virgin in an apple tree that he leapt heavily on to his horse, leaving behind hoofprints that are embedded in a rock outside the church. The Gothic church, remodelled in the eighteenth century, includes a fine *retablo*, and the thirteenth-century Virgen del Manzano, made famous by miracles ascribed to her in *Cántigas*, the *Galega* poems written by Alfonso X.

The **Iglesia de Santo Domingo** is decorated on the outside with gruesome carved skulls and inside with seventeenth-century tapestries based on Rubens cartoons. The **Iglesia de San Juan de los Caballeros** has lovely Mudéjar ceilings, particularly in the semi-ruined cloister.

Map 10 (key page 182)

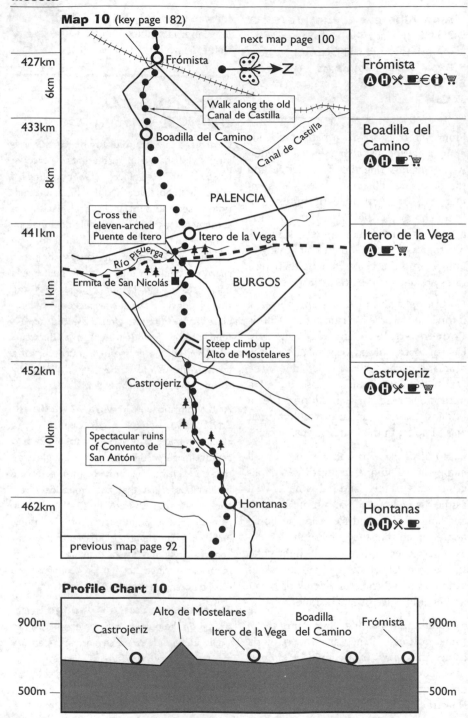

next map page 100

427km

6km

Frómista

Frómista
🅐🅗✕💺€🛈🛒

Walk along the old
Canal de Castilla

433km

8km

Boadilla del Camino

**Boadilla del
Camino**
🅐🅗💺🛒

Canal de Castilla

PALENCIA

Cross the
eleven-arched
Puente de Itero

441km

11km

Itero de la Vega

Itero de la Vega
🅐💺🛒

Río Pisuerga

Ermita de San Nicolás

BURGOS

Steep climb up
Alto de Mostelares

452km

10km

Castrojeriz

Castrojeriz
🅐🅗✕💺🛒

Spectacular ruins
of Convento de
San Antón

462km

Hontanas

Hontanas
🅐🅗✕💺

previous map page 92

Profile Chart 10

Alto de Mostelares

900m

Castrojeriz

Itero de la Vega

Boadilla
del Camino

Frómista

900m

500m

500m

For the best views in Castrojeriz, climb the hill to the ruined **castle**. Although legend claims that it was founded by either Caesar or Pompey, archaeology dates the castle much earlier. The castle changed hands frequently over the centuries from Visigoths to Muslims to Christians, finally ending up as a private residence a few centuries later. The hill beneath is honeycombed with *bodegas*, built to keep locally produced wine cool and linked to each other by tunnels.

Accommodation

There are two *albergues* in Castrojeriz: **San Esteban** is towards the top of town near the Plaza Mayor (25 beds, open May to October) and **Refugio de Castrojeriz** (32 beds, open all year), which is better kept but has stricter rules.

$ Casa Faulin (☎ 947 377051)

$ Méson de Castrojeriz (☎ 947 377400)

$$ La Casa de los Holandeses (☎ 947 377608)

$$$ Hotel la Posada (☎ 947 378610)

Follow the main street to the end of Castrojeriz, then cross a road at a fountain to walk along a gravel track. The route up the Alto de Mostelares is clearly visible straight ahead. About 1km outside town, you come to a wonderfully restored section of raised Roman road, built as a solid route across the boggy Odrilla valley floor. The river is usually fairly dry, although the marshy ground is ideal for bulrushes and reeds, used by craftspeople to make baskets and chairs.

At the start of the climb look to the right to see the remains of old Roman mines; higher up, you'll see the seams of mica more clearly. Below you, the Río Odrilla has slowly carved out the valley from the *meseta*. From this angle it's easy to see how a change in the river's direction thousands of years ago left a pillar of the *meseta* uneroded, providing Castrojeriz with enviable defensive attributes. At the top of the stiff climb, weary pilgrims are rewarded with fantastic views, blasts of wind and an eco-garden, highlighting some of the plants found on the *meseta*.

From the flat top of the **Alto de Mostelares** you can see the camino stretching off into the western horizon towards Puente de Itero, Itero de la Vega and Boadilla del Camino. The massive, open sky is staggering, competing for attention with the spiky church steeples of nearby villages.

In a few kilometres, the camino takes you past the thirteenth-century **Hospital de San Miguel** (Ⓐ), which is now a delightful **albergue** (12 beds, open May to September) run by an Italian confraternity. There's no electricity, and meals are provided under lamp light.

Cross the **Puente de Itero**, a lovely, eleven-arch bridge built on the orders of Alfonso VI. The Río Pisuerga is a tranquil, wide river, a great spot for fishing, bird-watching and paddling. Look out for goldfinches and greenfinches amongst the poplars.

On the far side of the bridge, a stone marker indicates the border between the provinces of Burgos and Palencia. Just after this marker, turn right along a dirt road that initially follows the river before it curves around into the village of **Itero de la Vega** (Ⓐ🛏🍴, 441km). In the village, look for the thirteenth-century Ermita de la Piedad, which contains a statue of Santiago Peregrino. There's a municipal **albergue** here (20 beds, open all year) and the private **Albergue Buen Camino** (18 beds, open all year).

Climb slowly out of the village towards the bumpy ridge ahead. On reaching the top some 4km later, the views are fantastic in all directions. Along this stretch of the camino, ornate dovecotes of all shapes and sizes are a distinctive feature of the landscape. Pigeons are now mainly kept for their droppings, used for fertilizer, though doves and pigeons are also a useful supplement to the local diet.

In another 4km, the camino arrives at **Boadilla del Camino** (Ⓐ Ⓗ ⬛ ☕, 433km), where there's a rest area with benches and a fountain. The **albergue municipal** has 12 beds and is open all year. You can also stay at **Albergue Casa En El Camino** (48 beds, open March to October), next to the sixteenth-century Iglesia de Santa María de la Asuncíon and close to a fifteenth-century village cross decorated with scallop shells, where local criminals were once tried and executed.

The barley fields you'll walk beside as you leave Boadilla are home to finches, skylarks and woodlarks, all inviting prey for the Montagu's harrier. The route soon runs parallel to the **Canal de Castilla**, a feat of eighteenth-century engineering. Although the canal was originally designed to move goods, it was quickly overtaken by the new-fangled railways, and now the canal mainly provides irrigation and electricity for the region's many wheat fields and factories.

In a few kilometres, walk over a canal lock at the entrance to Frómista, then walk up the modern street to a cross-roads. Keep straight on here for the *albergue*, or turn left to continue the camino.

Frómista
Ⓐ Ⓗ ✗ ⬛ € ⓘ ☕ (427km)

Frómista sits proudly in the middle of a rich agricultural region. So dominated by farming, the town was known as the breadbasket of the Roman Empire, and its name may come from *frumentum*, Latin for cereal.

The eleventh-century **Iglesia de San Martín** was once part of the Benedictine monastery built as the town flourished after the defeat of the Muslim armies. Nothing remains of the monastery, and the now-deconsecrated church stands solidly alone in the centre of Frómista. The church was heavily restored around 1900 to much criticism, but although the painted frescoes are gone, the gorgeous Romanesque capitals remain, carved with religious and agricultural motifs.

In the same square, pop in to the **Museo de Queso** to look at antique cheese presses and paddles made of gorgeous worn wood, and stop to sample the cheese over a glass of wine in the adjoining upscale bar.

Frómista's summer-only **turismo** is near the Iglesia de San Martín (☎ 979 810113).

Accommodation
The **albergue** (55 beds, open all year) is also near the Iglesia de San Martín.
$ Pensión Marisa, Plaza Obispo Almaraz 2 (☎ 979 810023)
$$ Hostal San Telmo, Calle Martín Veña 8 (☎ 979 811028)
$$ Hotel San Martín, Plaza San Martín 1 (☎ 979 810000)
$$$$ Hostería de Los Palmeros, Plaza San Telmo (☎ 979 810067)

Leave Frómista on a purpose-built gravel pilgrim track that runs alongside the P980 to Carrión de los Condes. In 3km, the route joins the road and passes the thirteenth-century Ermita de San Miguel on the left, just before the village of **Población de Campos** (**A**, 423km). Turn right down a side road, following the signs to the **albergue** (22 beds, kitchen, open all year), which you'll soon reach. The village street curves around to rejoin the main road. Just before it does, you'll pass the exquisite **Ermita de La Virgen de la Socorro**, a tiny church reached via a set of stone steps. Look for Gothic arches, grooves and tombs in the floor, and a stone sarcophagus.

From here, there's a choice of routes to Villalcázar de Sirga. The gravel pilgrim highway shadows the main road all the way to Carrión de los Condes, a quick if dull, exhaust-filled route to follow. It's far nicer to veer away from the road towards the village of Villovieco, which most pilgrims get to via a farm track. Instead of following this track, we describe a pretty, unmarked route alongside the river.

From La Virgen de la Socorro, follow the raised grassy track to the right-hand side of the river, walking towards a large clump of trees. Follow the track as it heads through the trees, broadens then curves right, still shadowing the river. Shortly after the bend, ignore the bridge to the left, which leads to Revenga de Campos and the road route, and keep walking along the riverbank. In a few hundred metres, turn left at a gravel track to head into **Villovieco**.

Follow the tree-lined river along a tranquil path that feels authentically mediaeval, particularly when you get your first glimpse of the **Ermita de la Virgen del Río** through the trees ahead. The *ermita* contains an alabaster image of Santiago Peregrino as well as a statue of its namesake, which is said to have swum up the Río Ucieza during a flood and stopped at this site. Follow the road into Villalcázar de Sigar, then turn right just before the main road, following the yellow arrows to the *albergue* and the Iglesia de Santa María la Blanca.

The various routes from Frómista converge at **Villalcázar de Sirga** (**AHX▣≜**, 414km). The camino was re-routed via Villasirgar, as it's commonly known, mainly due to Alfonso X's persistent mention of the Virgen Blanca's miracles in his thirteenth-century *Cántigas*. Her achievements include restoring the sight of a blind pilgrim, helping a nobleman recover his favourite hunting falcon, and saving a crew of Italian pilgrims from a storm at sea after their frantic prayers had been ignored by a succession of saints, including Santiago. The chalice they were taking to Santiago is now in Villasirgar's church treasury.

The Romanesque-Gothic **Iglesia de Santa María la Blanca** is thought to have been built by the Knights Templar. The enormous church was once even bigger: the west end was damaged in the 1755 earthquake that flattened Lisbon, and finished off by Napoleon's troops half a century later. The huge, high porch remains, modelled on the Monasterio de Las Huelgas in Burgos. Inside, the Capilla de Santiago's *retablo* shows detailed scenes from the saint's life and holds the statue of the Virgen Blanca in squat Romanesque style with a headless Jesus.

Also in the Capilla are the tombs of Don Felipe, Alfonso X's brother, Doña

Map 11 (key page 182)

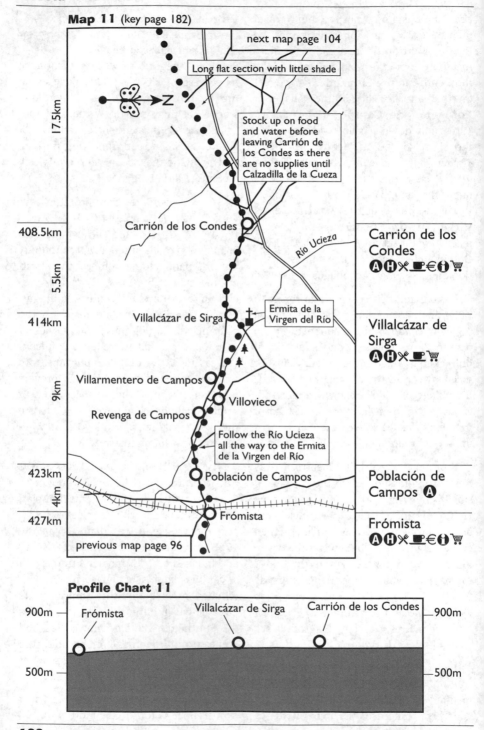

next map page 104

Long flat section with little shade

Stock up on food
and water before
leaving Carrión de
los Condes as there
are no supplies until
Calzadilla de la Cueza

17.5km

Carrión de los Condes

408.5km

Río Ucieza

Carrión de los
Condes
🅐🅗✕⬛€🅘🛒

5.5km

Ermita de la
Virgen del Río

414km

Villalcázar de Sirga

Villalcázar de
Sirga
🅐🅗✕⬛🛒

Villarmentero de Campos

9km

Villovieco

Revenga de Campos

Follow the Río Ucieza
all the way to the Ermita
de la Virgen del Río

423km

Población de Campos

Población de
Campos 🅐

4km

427km

Frómista

previous map page 96

Frómista
🅐🅗✕⬛€🅘🛒

Profile Chart 11

Frómista   Villalcázar de Sirga   Carrión de los Condes

900m —   — 900m

500m —   — 500m

Leonor, Felipe's wife, and a Templar tomb, which is unusual as the knights were generally buried simply, face-down in the earth. Felipe and Alfonso didn't exactly get on: Felipe's first wife was a Norwegian princess promised to and then discarded by Alfonso. Their rivalry eventually spiralled into all-out war, which continued until Felipe died in 1274, possibly murdered by Alfonso's hand.

Villasirgar has an **albergue** (20 beds, kitchen, open all year), and the bar opposite the church makes excellent *tortillas*. You can also stay at **Casa Vidal** ($, ☎ 979 888151), **Hostal Las Cantigas** ($$, ☎ 979 888015) and **Hostal Infanta Doña Leonor** ($$, ☎ 979 888164).

It's a dull walk along a roadside gravel track to Carrión de los Condes. After some 5km, turn left at a church decorated with a large mosaic of Jesus. Follow the main street into town, turning right at the Iglesia de Santa María del Camino for the albergue.

Carrión de los Condes

Ⓐ Ⓗ ✗ ▬ € ⓘ 🛒 (408.5km)

Carrión de los Condes was an important mediaeval town, home to 10,000 people and described by Aymeric Picaud in the tenth century as "an industrious and prosperous town, rich in bread and wine and meat and all fruitfulness." It was also the centre of disputes between Castilla and León, particularly after Alfonso VI of León murdered his brother, Sancho II of Castilla, much to the annoyance of El Cid.

The pro-Castilian epic poem, *El Cantar de mío*

Cid recounts the tale of Castilian nobles from Carrión who married El Cid's daughters, took their fortune and then tied them to oak trees and beat them. El Cid murdered the counts, who gave the town the name *de los Condes* and who are buried in the **Monasterio de San Zoilo**. This lovely monastery, on the far side of town, contains a beautiful Renaissance cloister with a splendidly carved ceiling.

The **Iglesia de Santa María del Camino** celebrates victory over the Moors in a legendary battle on this site. The local Christian Spanish were understandably annoyed at the annual tribute of 100 virgins demanded by their Moorish rulers, and prayed for deliverance. Santa María obliged, sending a herd of bulls to attack the Moors and drive them away, and her Romanesque statue is one of the highlights of the church's interior.

Although the lovely frieze over the **Iglesia de Santiago**'s twelfth-century façade remains, the church's recent restoration is unsympathetic and critics claim that the renovation did as much damage as Napoleon's troops, who blew up the church in the nineteenth century. The **Monasterio de Santa Clara**, at the entrance into Carrión de los Condes, sheltered St Francis of Assisi on his pilgrimage to Santiago. It now has a small museum.

Stock up on food in Carrión, as there are few chances to buy food between here and Sahagún, almost 40km away. The **turismo** is in the Plaza Santa María (☎ 979 880932).

Accommodation
There are two **albergues** in town; one as you come into Carrión in the **Monasterio de Santa Clara** (30 beds, kitchen, open March to November) and the other near the

Meseta

Iglesia de Santa María (54 beds, kitchen, open all year).

$ Hostal El Resbalón, Calle Marqués de Santillana (☎ 979 880433)

$$ Hostal Santiago, Calle Santa María (☎ 979 881052)

$$ Hostal La Corte, Calle Santa María 34 (☎ 979 880138)

$$$ Hotel Real Monasterio San Zoilo (☎ 979 880050)

It's a shadeless treadmill of a route from Carrión to Calzadilla de la Cueza, with the single, glorious distraction of the Cordillera Cantábrica far away to the right.

To leave town, cross the Río Carrión over a sixteenth-century bridge, soon passing the Monasterio de San Zoilo on your left. Keep straight on across a couple of main roads to follow a minor, quiet road through farmland, its unswerving straightness a clue to its Roman origins as the camino once more follows the route of the *Via Traiana*. After about 4km, pass the **Abadía de Abajo**, behind which are the ruins of the Abadía de Santa María de Benevívere.

Along the long route into Calzadilla de la Cueza there are fabulous, endless views, particularly of the Cordillera Cantábrica to the right. There are also some wonderful chances to see birds of prey in these skies: look for hen harriers and buzzards in particular. The occasional marshy sections and man-made ponds on either side of the track are home to herons, mallards and coots. And if you're lucky, you may see the great bustard, once common in continental Europe but now restricted to the Iberian *meseta*.

You spot Calzadilla's church tower long before you reach the village, about 16km from Carrión. **Calzadilla de la Cueza** (❶❶✕☕, 391km) is a tiny, one-street village tucked into a depression in the *meseta*. The **albergue** (60 beds, kitchen, open all year) has a swimming pool, or you can stay at the **Hostal Camino Real** ($$, ☎ 979 883187), also the only place in town to eat.

Leave the village on the unnecessarily named Calle Mayor. Turn right at the main road and take the gravel track to the left of the road. The route shadows the road all the way to Sahagún, with slight detours into the many villages along the way. An alternative, marked route mostly keeps one field south of the main road, and passes through the same villages.

Whichever route you choose, you'll arrive at **Lédigos** (❶☕🛒, 385km) in about 6km, where there's an **albergue** (52 beds, kitchen, open all year). About 3km later, the camino visits the hamlet of **Terradillos de los Templarios** (❶☕, 382km). There's not much here apart from an **albergue** that also serves food (55 beds, open all year) and a distinctive church, built from brick because of the lack of local stone.

Over the next few kilometres, the camino passes through a couple of blink-and-you'll-miss-them hamlets along the side of the main road. **Moratinos**, which you'll reach in 3km, has wonderful underground *bodegas* (cellars) and **San Nicolás del Real Camino** (❶☕, 376km), 2km farther on, is a former Templar village with a reconstructed eighteenth-century brick church and an **albergue** (20 beds, open April to October).

At the top of a rise, after another 4km, you'll get your first view of Sahagún. Soon afterwards, you can detour to the **Ermita de la Virgen del Puente**, which is characteristic of the local Mudéjar style and sits next to a Roman bridge over the Río Valderaduey. To the south you can just make out the fifteenth-century fort at Grajal de Campos.

The approach into Sahagún is a disheartening slog through the town's industrial zone. Once on the outskirts of Sahagún proper, take the first left past the big white grain silo that's dominated the skyline for a while now. Walk past the train station on the left and the bullring on the right, then turn left soon afterwards to cross the railway tracks via a bridge. The *albergue* is on the right as you enter town.

Sahagún

Ⓐ⨀✕⛶€♒ (368.5km)

A busy, no-nonsense town, much more attractive than the grimy approach suggests, Sahagún is at its best during the hustle and bustle of the Saturday morning market.

The town was an important religious and economic centre in the eleventh and twelfth centuries, famous for its plentiful wheat fields, three-week-long markets and the **Vat of Sahagún**, a huge trough of wine. Much of the credit for the town's prosperity must go to Alfonso VI, who showered money and prestige on the town in gratitude for the help he received from the **Monasterio de San Benito** during the war with his brother, Sancho III. It became the most powerful Benedictine monastery in Spain, at its peak controlling almost 100 other monasteries, and home to a prestigious university. But the

glory wasn't to last, and both the town and the monastery were in steep decline by the time a couple of eighteenth-century fires razed much of Sahagún. Today, all that remains of the monastery is a crumbling nineteenth-century tower and the twelfth-century Romanesque Capilla de San Mancio. The arch of San Benito, which formed part of the monastery façade, is now a city gate, straddling a street at the far end of town.

Near the arch is the twelfth-century **Iglesia de San Tirso**, a splendid example of the brick Mudéjar architecture of the *meseta*. Although wheat and vines are plentiful, the region has very little stone, and local craftsmen, many of them settlers from North Africa, devised a brick-based building method as a necessary and creative response to the stone shortage. Look out for the closed, horseshoe-shaped arches and the simple, unornamented design, possibly influenced by Islam's prohibition of human and animal representation.

It's also worth looking at the decorative brickwork and the Muslim influences found in Sahagún's other main churches, the Romanesque-Gothic **Iglesia de San Lorenzo** and the **Santuario de la Peregrina**, a twelfth-century Gothic-Mudéjar church that was once part of a Franciscan monastery.

Accommodation
The **albergue** (85 beds, kitchen, open all year) is on the right after the railway bridge.
$ Pensión la Asturiana, Plaza de Lesmes Franco 2 (☎ 987 780073)
$$ Hostal Alfonso VI, Calle Antonio Nicolás 6 (☎ 987 781258)
$$ Hostal La Cordoniz, Calle Arco (☎ 987 780276)
$$$ Hostal El Ruedo, Plaza Mayor 1 (☎ 987 780075)

Map 12 (key page 182)

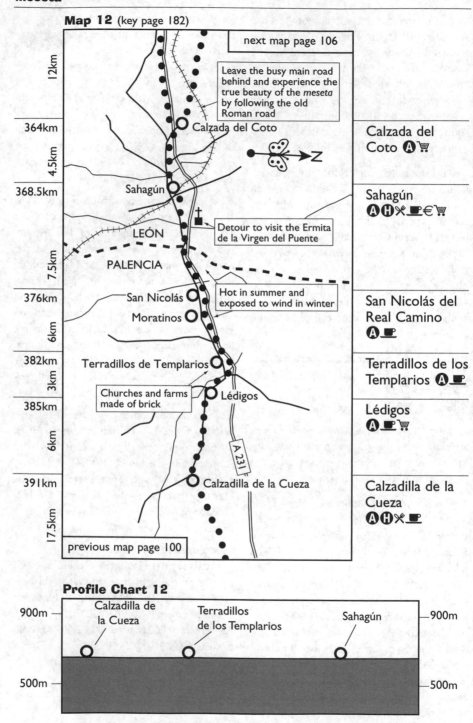

next map page 106

Leave the busy main road behind and experience the true beauty of the *meseta* by following the old Roman road

12km

364km — Calzada del Coto

4.5km

368.5km — Sahagún

Detour to visit the Ermita de la Virgen del Puente

LEÓN

PALENCIA

7.5km

376km — San Nicolás

Hot in summer and exposed to wind in winter

Moratinos

6km

382km — Terradillos de Templarios

3km

Churches and farms made of brick

385km — Lédigos

6km

A 231

391km — Calzadilla de la Cueza

17.5km

previous map page 100

Calzada del Coto Ⓐ🛒

Sahagún Ⓐ🅗✕🍴💻€🛒

San Nicolás del Real Camino Ⓐ💻

Terradillos de los Templarios Ⓐ💻

Lédigos Ⓐ💻🛒

Calzadilla de la Cueza Ⓐ🅗✕💻

Profile Chart 12

900m — Calzadilla de la Cueza — Terradillos de los Templarios — Sahagún — 900m

500m — 500m

Leave Sahagún via the narrow streets of the tiny old town, then cross the stone, arched Puente de Canto, originally built by Alfonso VI in 1085.

The grove of poplars next to the campsite on your right is the site of the eighth-century Legend of the Flowering Lances. Charlemagne's troops, preparing for battle with Aigolando the next day, stuck their lances into the ground. When they awoke the next day, some of the lances had grown bark and were covered in leafy branches, a sign of martyrdom. Although the lances were cut down, the omens proved true as the battle, along with some 40,000 of Charlemagne's men, was lost. The lances again took root, and a large forest grew where they had been planted.

In a couple of kilometres, you'll see the village of Calzada del Coto ahead, and the track ends at a maze of roads, excessive and underused even by Spanish road-building standards. Here, the route splits.

Keep straight on for the original *camino francés*, which mostly follows the road to Mansilla de las Mulas, passing through **Bercianos** (🅰️🅷💻) in 5km, where you can stay at the *albergue* (37 beds, kitchen open all year) or at the **Hostal Rivero** ($$, ☎ 987 744287). In another 8km, you'll reach **El Burgo Ranero** (🅰️🅷✕💻), where you can stay at the *albergue* (26 beds, kitchen, open all year), the private Albergue El Nogal (25 beds, open all year) or the **Hostal El Peregrino** ($, ☎ 987 330069). From here, it's 13km to **Reliegos** (🅰️💻) where the *albergue* has 70 beds and a kitchen and is open all year, and another 6km to Mansilla de las Mulas.

More pleasant, though with fewer facilities, is the Calzada de los Peregrinos, a route that heads along dry, thyme-scented tracks across the *meseta*. Turn right and cross a road bridge to follow this route. In a couple of hundred metres, you'll arrive at **Calzada del Coto** (🅰️🛒, 364km), a small village with a tiny, basic **albergue** (24 beds, open all year) next to the football field. Follow a wide dirt road across a flat landscape of close-cropped grass and scrubland, crossing a railway bridge in a couple of kilometres and reaching Calzadilla 6km later on a mostly obscured Roman road. Sheep have been the region's agricultural staple since the Middle Ages, when flocks of up to 40,000 were commonplace.

Calzadilla de los Hermanillos (🅰️💻🛒, 352km) has a small **albergue** (16 beds, kitchen, open all year) that's a lovely, little-visited place to stay. There's a tiny village shop, and a wonderful bar-café at the entrance to the village. Calzadilla is one of the friendliest villages on the camino, and it's a fascinating place to wander around, checking out the adobe architecture and getting lost amongst the maze-like streets.

The route out of Calzadilla is so straightforward that all you have to do is keep straight ahead for more than 20km. There are no villages along the stony track, and nothing to distract you on the flat, endless expanse apart from whiffs of lavender and wild thyme and a variety of birds: look out for hoopoes, with their dramatic crests, whoop-whoop call and loping flight.

At the end of this quiet stretch, after about 20km, turn left at a narrow tarmac road, then turn left again on reaching the N625 about 1km later. In another 1km, you'll pass through the Puerta de

Map 13 (key page 182)

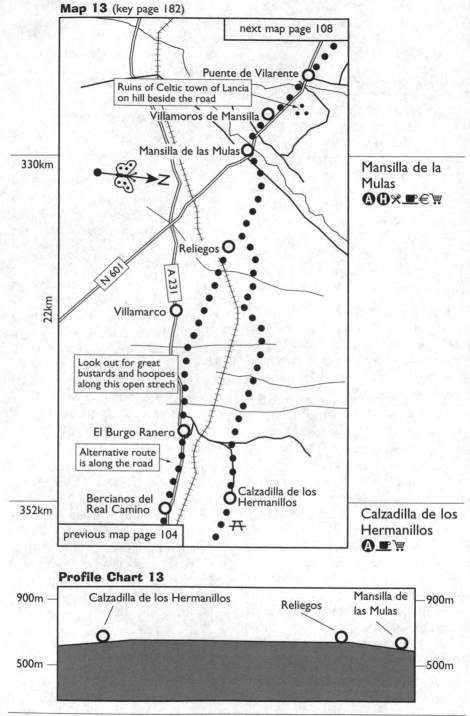

next map page 108

Puente de Vilarente

Ruins of Celtic town of Lancia
on hill beside the road

Villamoros de Mansilla

Mansilla de las Mulas

330km

Reliegos

N 601

A 231

Villamarco

Look out for great
bustards and hoopoes
along this open strech

El Burgo Ranero

Alternative route
is along the road

Bercianos del
Real Camino

352km

Calzadilla de los
Hermanillos

previous map page 104

Mansilla de la
Mulas
Ⓐ Ⓗ ✕ 🛏 € 🛒

Calzadilla de los
Hermanillos
Ⓐ 🛏 🛒

Profile Chart 13

900m —

Calzadilla de los Hermanillos

Reliegos

Mansilla de
las Mulas

— 900m

500m —

— 500m

Santiago into the old walled centre of Mansilla de las Mulas. The *albergue* is on the main street, just past the square.

Mansilla de las Mulas

ⒶⒽ✗🍽€🛒 (330km)

An elegant town of pleasant plazas, Mansilla de las Mulas is circled by mediaeval walls. The fancy *pastelarías* that line the main square might seem ostentatious after the simple adobe houses of Calzadilla de la Cueza, but their sweet, gooey offerings are sublime. *Mansilla* may derive from the Spanish for "hand" and "saddle," and the town's crest depicts a hand resting on a saddle; *Mulas* refers to the town's mule market.

The **walls**, in some places an impressive three metres thick, were successively built, destroyed and rebuilt in the Middle Ages. Much of the wall is still intact and it's worth walking all the way around town to get a closer look. Highlights include the stretch of wall alongside the Río Esla, and the Arco de la Concepción, the only surviving gate.

Accommodation
Albergue (70 beds, kitchen open all year).
$$ Hostal Las Delicias, Calle Los Mesones 22 (☎ 987 310075)
$$ Hostal Albergueria del Camino, Calle Concepción 12 (☎ 987 311193)
$$ Hostal El Gallo, Carretera Cistierna 17 (☎ 987 310359)

The long approach into León from Mansilla de las Mulas is an uninspiring one, mostly following the busy N120. To leave Mansilla, walk past the *albergue* and keep straight on across the stone bridge

over the Río Esla, looking behind you for fabulous views of the city walls. There are hills ahead and mountains in the distance, a welcome break for the eyes after the flat *meseta*. The hill on your right was the site of Lancia, the last holdout of the Celtic Asturians before the city was captured by the Romans in 26BC.

In 4km you pass through **Villamoros de Mansilla**, then 2km later cross the Río Porma over the rickety, much-restored 20-arch bridge that leads into Puente de Vilarente. **Puente de Vilarente** (**Ⓗ✗🍽€🛒**, 325km) has shops, restaurants and upmarket cafés, although the donkey taxi that once took sick pilgrims from the old hospice at the end of the bridge into León no longer exists. If you want to stay, try **Hostal El Delfín Verde** (**$**, ☎ 987 312065), **Pensión Casablanca** (**$**, ☎ 987 312164) or **Hostal La Montaña** (**$$**, ☎ 987 312161).

From Puente de Vilarente, walk uphill to **Arcahueja** (**🍽**), passing a playground, and then ignore the track to the left about 1km later that detours to the village of **Valdelafuente** (**🍽✗**). Climb uphill past factories, then about 1km after the turn off to Valdelafuente, turn left on reaching a minor road.

In about 300m, take great care when crossing the N120 at a particularly busy stretch, then turn right to walk along the road's left-hand side. At the top of the hill there are fabulous views of León spreading out into the *meseta*, with the glorious backdrop of the often snow-tipped Montes de León and the Cordillera Cantábrica. Despite the views, this is one of the nastiest stretches of the camino, following an exhaust-choked major road.

Map 14 (key page 182)

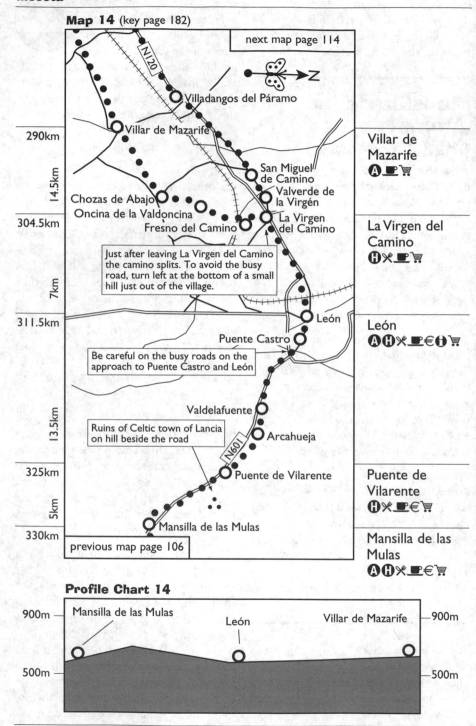

next map page 114

Villadangos del Páramo

Villar de Mazarife

290km

14.5km

San Miguel
de Camino

Valverde de
la Virgén

Chozas de Abajo

Oncina de la Valdoncina

La Virgen
del Camino

Fresno del Camino

304.5km

Just after leaving La Virgen del Camino
the camino splits. To avoid the busy
road, turn left at the bottom of a small
hill just out of the village.

7km

311.5km

León

Puente Castro

Be careful on the busy roads on the
approach to Puente Castro and León

Valdelafuente

13.5km

Ruins of Celtic town of Lancia
on hill beside the road

Arcahueja

N601

325km

Puente de Vilarente

5km

330km

Mansilla de las Mulas

previous map page 106

Villar de
Mazarife
🅰💻🛒

La Virgen del
Camino
🅗✕💻🛒

León
🅐🅗✕💻€🛈🛒

Puente de
Vilarente
🅗✕💻€🛒

Mansilla de las
Mulas
🅐🅗✕💻€🛒

Profile Chart 14

900m — Mansilla de las Mulas   León   Villar de Mazarife   — 900m

500m —   — 500m

In another few hundred metres, just as you get your first view of León's cathedral, veer left down a track to cross a footbridge and head downhill along a wide street. You'll soon find yourself in **Puente Castro** (✕☕♨, 325km), now merged into suburban León, where there are plenty of café-bars and the dilapidated Iglesia de San Pedro. The bridge that gives Puente Castro its name is originally Roman but was rebuilt in the eighteenth century; cross the Río Torío over a pedestrianized bridge 50m farther on.

At a roundabout soon afterwards, turn left for León's municipal *albergue*, but keep straight on for the second *albergue*, the city centre and the camino. See the map on page 110 for the way into León.

León
ⒶⒽ✕☕€ⓘ♨ (311.5km)

León is a delightful city of open squares, wide pedestrianized boulevards and narrow, café-crammed winding streets. By day, office workers stride meaningfully about town, but in the evening the city noticeably relaxes as families, couples and friends slowly promenade in their stylish finery, window-shopping and *tapas* bar–crawling until the early hours.

Founded by the Romans in the first century to guard the gold mines farther west, León was used as a base to subdue the pesky, dogged inhabitants of what are now Galicia and Asturias. León's heyday came about a millennium later, beginning when Ordoño II transferred the Christian capital from Oviedo to León in the tenth century, building monuments and settling on a site for the cathedral. Just 80 years later, the city was destroyed by al-Mansur's Muslim troops, but León's momentum was unstoppable, and the city that grew from the ruins became bigger and more important than ever. As León's kingdom became unwieldy and difficult to govern, the kingdom of Castilla was created, with a capital in Burgos. The two kingdoms officially united under Fernando III in 1252, but León was quickly subsumed into her younger, bigger offspring. This still rankles with *Leóneses*, and although separatism isn't as strong a movement as in the Basque Lands or Galicia, you'll see *León sin Castilla* (León without Castilla) and *León solo* (León alone) graffiti scrawled on road signs.

León's glorious, light-filled **cathedral** is a masterpiece of Gothic architecture, its stunning walls of **glass** stretching upwards in a riot of colour. Serene in cloudy weather and dazzling in the afternoon sun, the cathedral's open, French design allows beams of light to play across the nave, leading the eye upwards to a sumptuous feast of blues and reds and greens. You'll get a crick in your neck from wandering around and around the cathedral to take in the gorgeous, luminous whole, so it's worth bringing binoculars to get a better look at the windows' fine detail. Stained glass was popular with patrons; guild-funded windows depict craftsmen and other workers, and others place noble benefactors next to saints and religious figures.

Back at ground level, almost every surface of the wooden fifteenth-century **choir-stalls** is carved with religious imagery and personification of the vices. Look for gluttony heaving his belly in a wheelbarrow, a lusty priest spanking a naked boy, and an avaricious noble being led into hell for his gambling sins. The cathedral's **chapels** are lovely and contain some beautiful Gothic tombs, including those of Ordoño II and Bishop Martín Rodríguez el Zamorano, one of the driving forces behind the cathedral's construction.

León

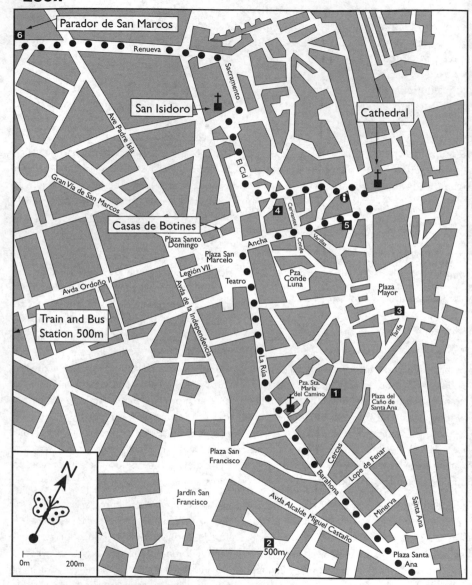

Accommodation

1 Albergue Monasterio de las Benedictinas

2 Albergue Municipal

3 Pensión Puerta del Sol

4 Hostal Guzmán el Bueno

5 Hostal Albany

6 Parador de San Marcos

The most interesting exhibits in the **Museo Diocesano**, reached through the Gothic cloister, are the intricate black-and-white prints of the cathedral's stained-glass windows, a fascinating testament to the artisanship of the glassmakers and beautiful in their own right.

Once you've had your fill of the cathedral's Gothic glory, saunter down Calle Ancha, turn right at Gaudí's **Casa Botines**, a fairytale palace that's tame by the architect's flamboyant standards, and arrive at the **Basílica de San Isidoro**, home to the best-preserved and most splendid Romanesque **frescoes** in Spain. The church, built on the site of a Roman temple to Mercury, was commissioned by Fernando I and constructed in the eleventh century to house the bones of San Isidoro, a Visigothic archbishop, scholar and author of the world's first encyclopaedia.

It's not exactly clear why the remains of San Isidoro, who was from Seville, came to be in León, although the romantic view is that the saint's bones could not rest once he heard of the *reconquista*, and demanded to be moved from Muslim southern Spain to the Christian north. Another version has Fernando accepting saintly relics from the Moors as a price of surrender; the bishops of León and Astorga made the trek down south to collect the bones of Santa Justa, but somehow ended up with San Isidoro instead.

The church itself is worth visiting for its carved capitals and the **Puerta del Perdón**, the first Door of Pardon on the camino, through which sick pilgrims could pass and be granted the same absolution as pilgrims who reached Santiago.

Next door is the **Panteón de los Reyes**, magnificent resting place of a string of monarchs from Fernando onwards until Napoleon's troops desecrated the tombs.

Although the bodies are gone, the Romanesque frescoes remain, thick with intense colour and vivid imagery.

The frescoes date from the beginning of the thirteenth century and are unrestored — it's staggering to think that these paintings have been in place for almost 800 years. Most of the ceiling and arches are taken up with various scenes from the life of Jesus, from the flight into Egypt to Christ in heaven. One of the frescoes shows a month-by-month representation of the farming year: in October, a man harvests acorns, a couple of pigs standing happily at his feet, but by November, one of the pigs is done for, slaughtered for food.

The capitals at the far end, flanking the original entrance to the church, depict Lazarus' resurrection and the curing of a leper; this is probably the earliest example of figurative sculpture in Spain. Above the Panteón, the museum displays valuable treasures from the church, including the silver reliquary of San Isidoro, and the small library holds a collection of massive, illuminated books from as early as the tenth century.

The **Hospital de San Marcos**, along the camino on the way out of town, was a hospice from the twelfth to the fifteenth centuries, and served as a monastery and headquarters of the Knights of Santiago for even longer. The current building, fronted by a magnificent Renaissance façade and topped by a Baroque Santiago Matamoros, is now a luxury *parador* with a sumptuous, antiques-filled interior. The chapterhouse contains an archaeological museum that includes Roman weapons from León and Maragato artefacts from around Astorga, and there are also mediaeval treasures in the church sacristy.

León is a big city with all facilities, some excellent restaurants and wonderful *tapas* bars. The **turismo** is on Plaza de Regla 4, opposite the cathedral (☎ 987 237082).

Accommodation

León has two *albergues*. The **albergue municipal** (64 beds, open all year) at the entrance into the city, and another at the **Monasterio de las Benedictinas** (125 beds, open all year) closer to the centre.

$ Pensíon Puerta del Sol, Calle Puerta del Sol 1 (☎ 987 211966)

$$ Hostal Guzmán el Bueno Calle Lopez Castrillon 6 (☎ 987 236412)

$$$ Hostal Albany, Calle La Paloma 9 (☎ 987 264600)

$$$$ Parador de San Marcos, Plaza San Marcos 7 (☎ 987 237300)

It's a long exit out of León through suburbs and an industrial zone, but you'll eventually find yourself in a familiar landscape of red soil and endless horizons. It's clear that the *meseta* is coming to an end, though, and greener sections and undulating hills lighten the monotony.

A bus tour–style trip past León's famous sights leads you out of town. From the cathedral, follow the scallop shells to San Isidoro and on to Hospital de San Marcos. Cross the old Puente de San Marcos that spans the shallow Río Bernesga. Follow the main road then, in a little under a kilometre, take a modern footbridge up and over the train tracks.

At the other side of the bridge, the camino rejoins the main road at **Trobajo del Camino** (🅗✕💺€🛒), passing the Ermita de Santiago. If you want to stay, try **Hostal El Abuelo ($$, ☎ 987 801044)** or **Hostal La Gárgola ($, ☎ 987 806180)**. Pass some quirky *bodegas*

on the outskirts of Trobajo, turning around for great views of León as you head uphill and into an ugly industrial zone. In about 2km, turn right on meeting the N120 again and put your life into the hands of the speeding drivers who make this short 400m section into La Virgen del Camino nerve-racking.

La Virgen del Camino
🅗✕💺🛒 (304.5km)

In the early sixteenth century, the Virgin Mary appeared to a local shepherd and demanded that he build her a shrine. The bishop of León was unconvinced by the vision until the shepherd used his slingshot to hurl a pebble that turned into a boulder on striking the ground. The cult of the Virgin took off rapidly. In 1522, a merchant was held captive by the Moors in North Africa, chained inside a strongbox. The Virgin, knowing of the merchant's desire to visit her shrine, miraculously transported him, chains, box and all, to La Virgen del Camino.

The façade of the modern 1961 church is dominated by a massive, modernist sculpture of the Virgin and the Apostles, with Santiago pointing towards Compostela. Inside, the merchant's box and chains are held in the sacristy. The Virgen del Camino's feast days are on September 15 and October 10.

Accommodation
$$ Hostal Plaza (☎ 987 302019)
$$ Hostal Soto (☎ 987 802925)
$$ Hostal Central (☎ 987 302041)
$$$ Hostal Villa Paloma (☎ 987 300990)

At the church, cross the N120 and take

the small paved road downhill, parallel to the main road. In 100m, the camino to Hóspital de Órbigo splits.

The authentic *camino francés* shadows the main road, some 28km of cars whistling by at 100kph. Along the way, you'll pass through **Valverde de la Virgén** (✖️💺) in 4km, then follow the road for a nasty stretch to **San Miguel del Camino**, less than 2km away. At the edge of the village, a local man leaves sweets, nuts and other treats for pilgrims. Pass through a long, industrial stretch lined with factories and soulless salesperson's hotels. In **Villadangos del Páramo** (🅰️🅗✖️💺€🛒), you can stay at the **albergue** (85 beds, kitchen, open all year) or at **Hotel-Restuarante Libertad** ($$, ☎ 987 390123), a far better option than the hotels on the way into town.

In another 4km, you reach **San Martín del Camino** (🅰️✖️💺🛒). There are two *albergues* here: the **albergue municipal** (60 beds, kitchen, open all year) and **Albergue Ana** (12 beds, open April to October). Follow a roadside track for a further 6km, then turn right to follow a dirt track and arrive at the foot of the fabulous mediaeval bridge into Hospital de Órbigo.

The more peaceful route heads along minor country roads and farm tracks towards Hospital de Órbigo. To follow this route, turn left at the junction in La Virgén del Camino. Skirt the modern hamlet of **Fresno del Camino**, then follow a minor road into **Oncina de la Valdoncina**. Climb slightly to the flat-as-a-pancake *meseta*, where the scrubland is punctuated by occasional vineyards and fields, and pilgrims are keenly watched by swallows and black kites.

In a few kilometres, you'll pass through **Chozas de Abajo** (💺). Follow a flat minor road all the way to **Villar de Mazarife** (🅰️💺🛒, 290km), about 4km away. On the way into Villar de Mazarife there's a splendid mediaeval-style mosaic on the right, showing pilgrims on their way to Santiago. There's an **albergue** (50 beds, kitchen, open all year), a quirky museum on the right as you enter the village, and a small park as you leave, ideal for picnics.

It's a long, shade-free 10km stretch from Villar de Mazarife to **Villavante** (💺🛒), where the UFO-shaped water tower seems to hover extra-terrestrially above the church. Just past the village, cross some train tracks, stopping to wave at eastbound trains, as they'll likely be carrying pilgrims on their way home from Santiago. The route eventually crosses the N120 and arrives about 300m later at the bridge into Hospital de Órbigo.

Hospital de Órbigo
🅰️🅗✖️💺€🛒 (275.5km)

Hospital de Órbigo is a strategic town, located on a bank of the Río Órbigo. The river crossing was the scene of a vicious battle between the Suevi and the Visigoths in 452, and Alfonso III defeated the Moors here in the late ninth century. Puente de Órbigo, the multi-arched Gothic bridge that's one of the most important of the camino, was built in the thirteenth century, and though it has been destroyed by floods many times since, its appearance remains resolutely mediaeval.

The most famous episode in the bridge's history is the quest of the lovelorn Don Suero de Quiñones. In 1434, rejected by his lady

Map 15 (key page 182)

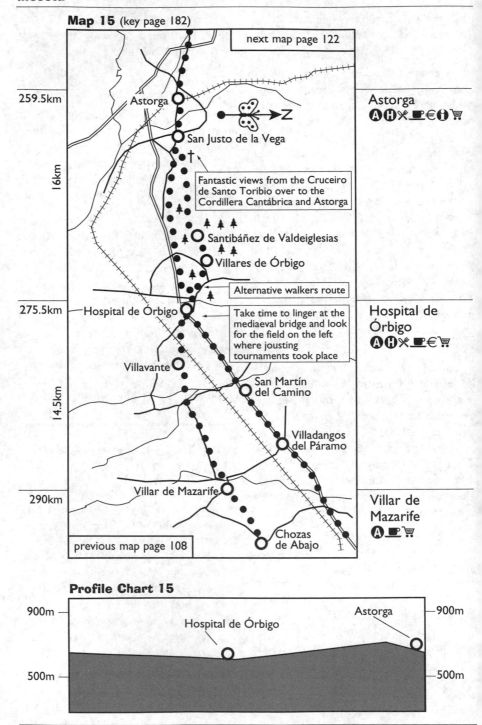

next map page page 122

259.5km — Astorga

San Justo de la Vega

†

Fantastic views from the Cruceiro de Santo Toribio over to the Cordillera Cantábrica and Astorga

Santibáñez de Valdeiglesias

Villares de Órbigo

Alternative walkers route

275.5km — Hospital de Órbigo

Take time to linger at the mediaeval bridge and look for the field on the left where jousting tournaments took place

Villavante

San Martín del Camino

Villadangos del Páramo

290km — Villar de Mazarife

Chozas de Abajo

previous map page 108

16km

14.5km

Astorga

Hospital de Órbigo

Villar de Mazarife

Profile Chart 15

900m — | — 900m

Astorga

Hospital de Órbigo

500m — | — 500m

love, Suero put an iron collar around his neck as a sign that he was still shackled to her. He vowed to keep the collar on until he had broken 300 lances in fights on the bridge with the best knights in Europe.

Many knights rose to the challenge, and Suero and his friends were kept busy fighting them off. The tournament took place during a Holy Year and began a couple of weeks before the Día de Santiago on July 25, the peak time of year for pilgrim traffic. Suero successfully defended the bridge against all-comers and eventually reached his 300-lance target. Taking off his iron collar, Suero journeyed to Santiago and deposited his lady's jewelled bracelet; it now encircles the neck of the statue of Santiago Alfeo in the cathedral. It's said that Suero's story may have inspired Cervantes' *Don Quixote*. The jousting tournament is recreated at the beginning of June each year next to the bridge.

Accommodation
Hospital de Órbigo has three *albergues*: the **municipal albergue** (18 beds, kitchen, open all year) at the river is reached by turning right at the end of the bridge. The wonderful **Albergue San Miguel** (40 beds, open all year) and the **German albergue** (60 beds, kitchen, open all year) are both on the main street.
$$ Hotel Paso Honroso (☎ 987 361010)
$$$ Hostal Don Suero de Quiñones (☎ 987 388238)

To continue the camino, keep straight on down Hospital de Órbigo's main street. At the end of the village, the camino to San Justo de la Vega splits into two; both routes are signposted.

Keep straight on to follow the road route, mostly walking on a gravel track alongside the N120. The mountains up ahead are getting much closer, signalling the imminent end of flat *meseta* walking. In spring, look out for nesting birds in the red cliffs to your right. At the Cruceiro de Santo Toribio, just outside San Justo de la Vega, the two routes meet.

The walkers' route to San Justo is a far more pleasant option. Turn right when the route splits outside Hospital. Head to **Villares de Órbigo**, 2km away, on a broad dirt road. Just outside the village, there's a modern pilgrim monument, and on the hill above is an Iron Age *castro* now renamed *El Santo*. In 2km, you'll reach **Santibáñez de Valdeiglesias** (Ⓐ), where there's an **albergue** (60 beds, open March to November). It's a lovely walk from here to San Justo. Look out for birds of prey overhead, circling the plentiful rabbits in the fields. Meet up with the road route at the Cruceiro de Santo Toribio just outside San Justo.

From the cross, walk downhill into **San Justo de la Vega** (Ⓗ▤☗), where you can stay at **Hostal Juli** ($, ☎ 987 617632). It hardly seems worth it, though, as you'll reach Astorga in just a few kilometres. Follow a stone track that winds through factories, gardens and fields. As town entrances go, this one is very low key and non-industrial. Cross the train tracks and turn left 200m later to walk down a side road. Enter Astorga proper at Puerta Sol, walk past the *ayuntamiento* (town hall), the Bishop's Palace and the Cathedral, and arrive at the *albergue* on Calle San Javier Portería.

Regional Map (key page 182)

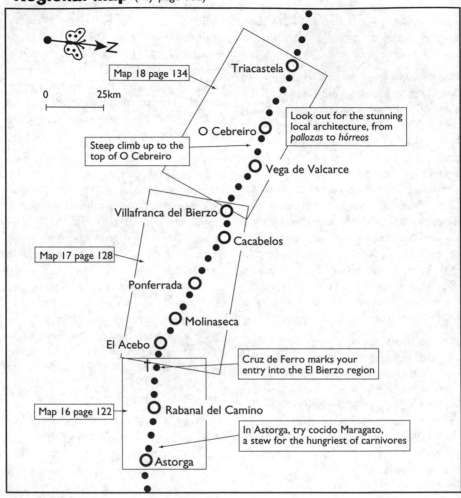

Map 18 page 134

0   25km

Steep climb up to the top of O Cebreiro

Triacastela

Look out for the stunning local architecture, from *pallozas* to *hórreos*

O Cebreiro

Vega de Valcarce

Villafranca del Bierzo

Cacabelos

Map 17 page 128

Ponferrada

Molinaseca

El Acebo

Cruz de Ferro marks your entry into the El Bierzo region

Map 16 page 122

Rabanal del Camino

In Astorga, try cocido Maragato, a stew for the hungriest of carnivores

Astorga

What's the weather like?

	Jan	April	July	Oct
Sun	3hrs	5hrs	7hrs	5hrs
Rainfall	30cm	19cm	6cm	19cm
Maximum Temp	6°C	13°C	24°C	14°C
Minimum Temp	-2°C	3°C	15°C	5°C

Average hours of sun, total average rainfall in cm and average temperature in degrees Celsius
Figures are for the mountains; it's warmer, drier and sunnier in the Bierzo valley

Cordillera Cantábrica

Astorga to Triacastela

From Astorga to Triacastela you'll haul yourself over a couple of misty mountain passes, walking through the land of the Maragatos, Spain's ancient muleteers, and passing into Galicia. Sandwiched between these passes is the fertile El Bierzo valley, home to delicious wine, a Templar castle at Ponferrada and the most enchanting *albergue* of the camino at Villafranca del Bierzo.

 Walking

Geography

The Cordillera Cantábrica curl down from Asturias in the shape of a ram's horn, their slate, schist, quartzite and sandstone foothills jutting into the camino's way. High winds batter the mountains whatever the season and inhibit the growth of all but the hardiest of life, while the proximity of the Atlantic means that heavy rain or even snowstorms can move in without warning at almost any time of the year.

In contrast to the mountains, the El Bierzo valley is an oasis of calm and warmth, a sunny microclimate protected by the mountains from wind and rain. It can be as much as 15 degrees Celsius warmer at the bottom of the valley than at the top of the mountains. The climate is warm enough to grow grapes, and El Bierzo is fast developing into a respected wine-growing region.

Trails

Narrow tarmac roads make up the majority of the route. The climb up and over O Cebreiro is on an old stony path, heavily used by local cattle traffic and the piles of dung they leave behind can make it slippery when wet. From Villafranca del Bierzo onwards, you'll begin to see adverts for taxis to carry you or your belongings, while you walk unencumbered. Pilgrims are firmly divided on whether this is a sensible way to lighten your load or immoral cheating unworthy of pilgrims.

When to go

It can rain at any time of year in the mountains. Summers are sunniest but the camino becomes very crowded as you get closer to Santiago, and *albergues* can be a bit of a squash from June to August. In winter, it's not uncommon for snow to cover some sections of the camino, and the lack of heating in *albergues* can make things a bit chilly.

Flora & Fauna

The mountain moorland consists of hardy, low-growing plants such as heather, broom and wild thyme. Out of the wind and lower down the mountains, silver birch, sweet chestnut and oak grow in protected pockets.

The **wolf** is at the apex of the food chain here and, despite years of persecution by hunters, there are thought to be a couple of thousand animals left in Iberia. Wolves need open space to roam, as they can cover anything from 20 to 40km in a single day, smell prey or a potential mate up to 2km away and, incredibly, hear sounds from up to 10km away. While the wolf feeds mainly on wild boar and roe deer, the smaller **beech marten**, which looks like a large, stocky weasel, patrols mature woodlands looking for voles, shrews and mice.

In good weather, birds of prey can be seen soaring above. The pale-breasted **short-toed eagle** likes to ride thermals and is often spotted hovering with its legs dangling down ready to swoop, and the **golden eagle** is able to crush a rabbit in its powerful feet. The **sparrowhawk**, which also hunts in these mountains, is often seen perched on a stump, holding its prey down with one foot and tearing at the flesh with its beak. At the edge of forests the **honey buzzard** hunts for wasps, its main prey.

Less violent birds are also commonly spotted. The **black woodpecker**'s characteristic dipping flight is seen in woodland areas, whereas lower down, the less elegant **grey partridge** is more likely to waddle away than fly off when surprised. The songs of whinchats, stonechats and wheatears often serenade pilgrims in the mountains, and the splendid **capercaille** makes its home in the woodlands of the western Cordillera Cantábrica.

People & Culture

The Cordillera Cantábrica have provided refuge to people for thousands of years, and although in recent times people have been leaving the mountains, the rebirth of the camino is drawing people back to remote areas. Villages such as O Cebreiro and Rabanal have sprung back to life as camino tourism takes over from agriculture as a major source of income.

One of the most mysterious groups of people found along the camino is the **Maragatos**, who live in the mountains west of Astorga. Their origins are shrouded in debate. Some historians believe they are related to the North African Berbers, while others point to archaeological excavations in the village of Santo Colomba de Samoza, where an ancient necropolis showed cultural links with the Phoenicians. Still others say they were slaves brought by the Romans to dig for gold in the local mountains.

Wherever the Maragatos came from, they survived to become the muleteers of mediaeval Spain, humping produce and other goods from the northern ports to the rest of the country. If you're lucky, you may catch a Maragato wedding outside the town hall in Astorga, where the wedding party, dressed in traditional costume, listens to Maragato musicians and watches the bizarre spectacle of the bride running the length of the town square towards the wedding cake. The best example of traditional Maragato **architecture** is in the recently restored village of Castrillo de los Polvazares, just west of Astorga.

The mountains of O Cebreiro mark the beginning of the land of the Galicians, and your entrance into **Celtic Spain**. It's not uncommon to sit in a bar in O Cebreiro and be serenaded by bagpipes, and you'll also see *hórreos* (granaries) and *pallozas* (straw-roofed stone houses), Galicia's traditional architecture. There's more about Galicia in the next chapter.

Food & Drink

Cocido Maragato is a vast lunchtime meal and a Maragato tradition dating back thousands of years. The topsy-turvy courses are eaten in a very strange order. The lunch starts with a platter of meat: ham, chicken, pork, *chorizo*, venison ear, pork fat (those cubes aren't potato!) and many other things with hair and skin still attached, fill a large platter on the table. This orgy of flesh is followed by a second course of deliciously prepared vegetables, usually chickpeas and Gallego cabbage, then soup. Dessert, more conventionally, ends the meal. Don't plan on doing anything else for at least four hours after eating, as you'll need all your energy for digestion!

A glass or two of red wine is sure to help slice into the richness of *cocido*. As in much of the country, the Romans can be thanked for introducing **wine** to El Bierzo. A *Denominacion de Origen* region since 1989, the best wines are made from Mencía grapes, although Prieto Picudo and Garnacha varieties are also added. Things have certainly changed since Künig von Vach wrote, "when you get there, drink wine sparingly as it burns like a candle and can scorch your very soul."

Queimada is a fiery potion made with *orujo* (Galicia's favourite spirit, which we describe in the Galicia section), caster sugar, lemon peel, a few coffee beans and a good dose of magic. The whole mixture is set on fire, then shared amongst friends. There's nothing quite like sitting in a dark room while a true Galician chants spells and incantations. Jesús Jato, the *hospitalero* at Ave Fénix in Villafranca del Bierzo (page 129) often treats pilgrims to a *queimada* ritual.

For a more healthy option, try the delicious *reineta del bierzo* **apple**. Short-stalked, squat and chunky, this apple has dull skin with rusty speckles.

Tourist Information

Transport

Astorga and Ponferrada are easy to reach by bus or train from major centres in Spain. To get up and over the mountains you'll need to hire a taxi.

Accommodation

Albergues are plentiful, and this stretch has some of the weirdest and best on the camino. Ponferrada's modern *albergue* has comfortable, four-person dormitories, and you'll be pampered and entertained at Ave Fénix in Villafranca del Bierzo. If you're hankering for a mediaeval experience, head for the *albergue* at Manjarín, where you'll meet a healer and sleep with cows and fleas.

Events & Festivals

Along with much of the rest of Spain, Astorga celebrates Carnaval and Semana Santa (Easter week) with parades and feasts. Later in the year, the **Fiestas de Santa María** in the last week of August honour the city's patron saint with a huge market, games and, of course, a massive *cocido Maragato* lunch.

Ponferrada's **Fiesta de la Virgen de la Encina** takes place at the beginning of September, closely followed by El Santísimo Cristo de la Esperanza, a festival held in Villafranca del Bierzo.

Rest Days & Detours

At **Las Médulas**, a UNESCO heritage site 20km southwest of Ponferrada, flame-red mountains hide the remains of Roman gold mines. More than 300km of canals were built to channel water from the Río Cabrera, almost 30km away. Archaeologists guess that about 60,000 slaves worked as miners, hauling the ore out through tunnels and then washing it in huge sluices. Today, you can visit some of the tunnels on a guided tour and find out more in an interesting summer-only museum.

Farther east, the gorgeous, isolated **Valle del Silencio** lies below the Monte Aquiana, a ghostly pale mountain revered by the ancient Celts. At the head of the valley, you can visit Peñalba de Santiago, which has a wonderful, tenth-century Mozarabic church.

Astorga

⒜ ⒣ ✕ 🍴 💶 ❶ 🛒 (259.5km)

At Astorga, the *camino francés* meets up with the *vía de la plata*, an alternative *camino* that snakes up from Sevilla. The town's strategic location near the foothills of the Cordillera Cantábrica has long made it an important centre, and it once had more than 20 pilgrim *hospitals*, more than any place apart from Burgos. From the ancient capital of the Astur tribe, it developed into Asturica Augusta, an important Roman and Christian centre that left murals, walls and other tangible remains. The gradual decline of the region in the eighteenth century has preserved much of Astorga's ancient feel and, unlike many other places of its size along the camino, it remains unblighted by industrial development.

You can easily while away an afternoon visiting Astorga's sights. The well laid-out **Museo Romano** is built over the Ergástula cave, which may have been the entrance to the old Roman forum. The intimidating city walls still stand in places and, throughout Astorga, you can peer into ongoing excavations and try to figure out the layout of this Roman frontier town. The *turismo* has a leaflet of Roman walking tours.

The town is also the capital of the **Maragatos**, a mysterious, isolated race of muleteers who preserved their culture for centuries but are now sadly losing their unique identity. Head to the Plaza de España on the hour to see traditionally dressed mechanical Maragatos banging on the **ayuntamiento** (town hall) bell. The figurines have been at it since 1748 and portray Pero Mato, the Maragato folk hero who fought at the battle of Clavijo alongside Santiago.

The jewel in Astorga's crown is undoubtedly Gaudí's **Palacio Episcopal**. Construction of a palace for the bishop began in 1889, but once it was finished he refused to live in it, afraid of the scandals surrounding the extravagant cost and the fantastical, whimsical architecture. Gaudí resigned in disgust before the building was finished, vowing "I wouldn't cross Astorga even in a hot-air balloon." The palace stood empty for years, briefly serving as the headquarters of Franco's *Falange* during the civil war. It finally found a more permanent tenant in the late 1960s, when the **Museo de los Caminos**, a collection of disparate images of St James and some mediocre art, was established.

The nearby **cathedral** took even longer to settle in: begun in 1471, it wasn't completed for more than three centuries. Although it's somewhat overpowered by its ostentatious neighbour, there are a few gems inside. The main *retablo* is by Gaspar Becerra, a follower of Michelangelo and Raphael, and the sweeping movement of the characters shows that he was sitting in the front row of his art class. Fill up your *credencial* with a *sello* from the

ticket office at the **Museo Diocesano** next door, worth a peek for its varied exhibits.

If all this culture is making your blood sugar plummet, head for a fix at the **Museo del Chocolate**, a museum that celebrates Astorga's chocolate industry, which thrived in the eighteenth and nineteenth centuries on the back of the Maragatos' mule trains.

Astorga's **turismo** is at Calle Eduardo de Castro 5, across from the Palacio Episcopal (☎ 987 618222).

Accommodation
Astorga's best *albergue* is the **Albergue San Javier** (120 beds, kitchen, open all year), near the cathedral. There is also an *albergue* in Plaza Marques (200 beds, open April to October); at certain times of year overflow pilgrims are led to a school about 1km away.

$ **Pensión Garcia**, Calle Bajada del Postigo 3 (☎ 987 616046)
$$ **Hostal La Peseta**, Plaza de San Bartolomé (☎ 987 617275)
$$$ **Hotel Gaudí**, Plaza Eduardo de Castro 6 (☎ 987 615654)
$$$ **Hotel Astur Plaza**, Plaza España 3 (☎ 987 618900)

Follow the yellow arrows out of town, passing the modern Iglesia de San Pedro, which is decorated with a mosaic of the camino. The quiet Calle de los Mártires, named after the Confraternity of the Martyrs who ran a pilgrim hospice here, leads into **Valdeviejas**. In a couple of kilometres, the camino splits and you have two ways to get to Santa Catalina de Somoza.

Most signs direct you left to the village

Map 16 (key page 182)

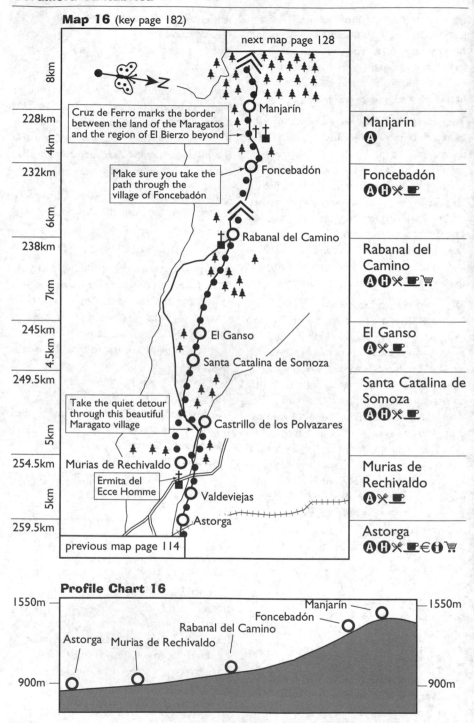

next map page 128

8km

228km — 4km

Cruz de Ferro marks the border between the land of the Maragatos and the region of El Bierzo beyond

Manjarín

232km — 6km

Make sure you take the path through the village of Foncebadón

Foncebadón

238km — 7km

Rabanal del Camino

245km — 4.5km

El Ganso

249.5km

Santa Catalina de Somoza

Take the quiet detour through this beautiful Maragato village

Castrillo de los Polvazares

254.5km — 5km

Murias de Rechivaldo

Ermita del Ecce Homme

Valdeviejas

259.5km — 5km

Astorga

previous map page 114

Manjarín
Ⓐ

Foncebadón
ⒶⒽ✕☕

Rabanal del Camino
ⒶⒽ✕☕🛒

El Ganso
Ⓐ✕☕

Santa Catalina de Somoza
ⒶⒽ✕☕

Murias de Rechivaldo
Ⓐ✕☕

Astorga
ⒶⒽ✕☕€ⓘ🛒

Profile Chart 16

1550m — Manjarín — 1550m
Foncebadón
Rabanal del Camino
Astorga   Murias de Rechivaldo
900m — 900m

of **Murias de Rechivaldo** (🅐✕🍴🛏, 254.5km), where you can stay at the **Albergue Las Águedas** (60 beds, kitchen, open all year) or the **albergue municipal** (22 beds, open all year). Murias' eighteenth-century Iglesia de San Esteban has a carving of the Virgen del Pilar above the door, and the belltower stairs are exposed to the elements, a common local feature. At the end of the village, the camino follows a wide track and takes you to Santa Catalina de Somoza.

Your second option is to turn right when the camino splits, following a second set of yellow arrows towards **Castrillo de Polvazares** (🅗✕🛏), which you'll reach in a couple of kilometres. The village has been carefully and attractively restored, preserving the typical stone-walled, slate-roofed houses. You can stay at the **Hostería Cuca la Vaina** ($$$, ☎ 987 691078) or **Casa Coscolo** ($$$, ☎ 987 691984). Follow the main cobbled street to the end of the village, turn left then climb slowly uphill and meet up with the route from Murias de Rechivaldo, just before Santa Catalina de Somoza.

The friendly village of **Santa Catalina de Somoza** (🅐🅗✕🛏, 249.5km) is less perfectly preserved than Castrillo de Polvazares, but lovely nonetheless. The modern church of Santa María is said to contain a relic of San Blas, who looked after pilgrims' welfare. Modern-day pilgrims have a number of accommodation options. The **albergue municipal** (35 beds, open all year) has received mixed reports, but there are bunk beds and private rooms at the **Hospedería San Blas** ($, ☎ 987 691411), **Casa Rural La Calista** ($, ☎ 987 159053), **El Caminante** ($, ☎ 987

691098) and at **El Arriero Maragato** ($).

Walk through land once cultivated but now overgrown with pine and brambles. In spring and summer this area is a favourite habitat of the red-backed shrike, a rusty-coloured bird with a distinctive black eye strip and the gruesome habit of impaling its captured prey on thorns.

After another 4km on the gravel track, you come to the village of **El Ganso** (🅐✕🛏, 245km). A few houses in the village boast ancient thatched roofs made from the broom that grows all over this region, but such roofs are slowly going out of fashion, giving way to easier-to-build ones made of iron or slate. The modern **Iglesia de Santiago** hints at the camino's early popularity here; by 1142 a church and hospice were up and running to minister to the tide of pilgrims who flowed through the village. The basic **albergue** (16 beds, open all year) has no running water or bathrooms.

It's another 7km to Rabanal del Camino, alongside a narrow paved road. Enter Rabanal on Calle Mayor, veering left for the village's three *albergues*.

Rabanal del Camino
🅐🅗✕🛏🛒 (238km)

Rabanal del Camino is slowly becoming a pilgrim bottleneck. Everyone seems to stay here, resting in one of the village's three *albergues* before tackling the mountains. Traditionally the ninth stop in the *Codex Calixtinus*, this beautiful village is springing back to life as the modern camino revival continues. The houses are enclosed by high

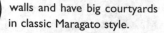

walls and have big courtyards in classic Maragato style.

The Iglesia de Santa María has Romanesque templar origins hidden under centuries of serious renovations. Legend has it that Anseis, one of Charlemagne's knights, married a Saracen bride here, although it's unlikely he even made it this far west.

Accommodation

There are three *albergues* in Rabanal. The wonderful **Refugio Gaucelmo** (42 beds, kitchen, open March to October), just off Calle Mayor, was converted from the ancient Hospital de San Gregorio, where Aymeric Picaud stayed in the twelfth century. **Nuestra Señora del Pilar** (52 beds, kitchen, bar, open all year) is on the main square to the left of Calle Mayor. It opens earlier than Refugio Gaucelmo and has a lovely dining room with an open fire. The **municipal albergue** (100 beds, open May to September) is used as overflow when the other *albergues* are full.

There are also bunk beds and rooms in the private **Posada El Tesin** ($) at the entrance to the village.

$$ Hostal El Refugio (☎ 987 691274)
$$ La Posada de Gaspar (☎ 987 691079)

The camino follows a narrow paved road and tracks uphill to the Fuente del Peregrino, where you can replenish your water supply. Some 5km from Rabanal you'll reach **Foncebadón** (🅐🅗✕🗲, 232km), an eerie and affecting place that features heavily in the camino accounts of Shirley Maclaine and Paulo Coelho. The houses are built from local slate, with thick walls to block the wind and steeply angled roofs to deflect snow. Many of the roofs are thatched with local broom, and wooden beams were often hammered into place with primitive wooden pegs rather than nails. It's often cloudy here, snow is common in winter, and when it's too warm for snow, the mountains are drenched with rain or obscured by fog. Still, Foncebadón is undergoing something of a revival as romantically minded former pilgrims decide to settle here. If you decide to settle too, you can stay at the **albergue** (20 beds, open April to October) or the **Hostal Foncebadón** ($$, ☎ 987 691245). As you leave Foncebadón, the ruins to your left are those of a pilgrims' hospice and church built by Gaucelmo, the twelfth-century hermit who gave his name to the *albergue* in Rabanal.

In a couple of kilometres, the camino reaches the **Cruz de Ferro**. This massive, conical pile of stones marks the pass over Monte Irago and the border between La Maragatería and El Bierzo. Across Europe, Celts traditionally laid stones at peaks and passes like this one to calm the mountain gods and ask for safe passage through the mountains. Romans in the area continued the tradition, calling the stones *murias* after Mercury, their god of travellers.

Adding a stone to the pile at the Cruz de Ferro is an important camino ritual; many pilgrims bring stones from home to place here, and others pick one up along the way. If you climb to the top of the pile, you'll see scribbled messages to friends, family and spiritual beings, and pebbles painted with names and home towns from all over the world. The iron cross on the top is a later addition, placed here to make this pagan tradition more palatable to the Catholic church.

In a couple of kilometres you'll reach **Manjarín** (, 228km), a remote hamlet home to Tomás the *hospitalero*, and his unique **albergue** (20 beds, open all year) is a throwback to what *albergues* must have been like in earlier times. What the *albergue* lacks in basic amenities, such as beds, privacy and cleanliness, it more than makes up for in character and personality: Tomás will feed you, heal your injuries and charm you with camino stories. As you leave in the morning, he rings the large bell at the door to let Santiago know that you're on your way.

From Manjarín, you'll walk on a narrow path, hemmed in on either side by tall, gorgeous heather. Keep an eye out for alpine choughs — black, acrobatic, crow-sized birds with a vivid yellow bill and a piercing call. To your left, there are fabulous views of the Meruelo valley.

Within a couple of kilometres and shortly after passing the military station which innocuously marks the highest point of the camino at 1517m, you'll start to head downhill towards El Acebo. The views open up ahead as the road descends to the wide and fertile El Bierzo valley. The Sierra de Gristredo and the Cordillera Cantábrica, which have shadowed the camino since Navarra, tower above the outline of Ponferrada while, to the west, you can see the summits of O Courel and Los Ancares.

El Acebo's (🅐🅗✕🍴, 220km) importance as the gateway to the mountains was recognized in mediaeval times, when it was excused from paying tax for as long as the villagers maintained the hundreds of foul weather poles that guide pilgrims on this remote alpine section. Today, El Acebo is a pretty collection of slate-roofed stone houses typical of the El Bierzo region, with overhanging wooden balconies reached by external stone staircases.

The Iglesia de San Miguel has a large-headed statue of Santiago Peregrino. El Acebo has many small private *albergues* and *casas rurales*. Try **Albergue de la Junta Vecinal** (12 beds, open all year) or **Albergue Mesón El Acebo** (24 beds, open all year). You can also stay at **Hostal La Trucha** ($, ☎ 987 695548) and **La Casa de Monte Irago** ($$, ☎ 987 970028). In 2005, a new *albergue* was being built next to the church.

There are great views on the lovely descent through hamlets and river valleys to Molinaseca. In little more than 3km, you arrive at **Riego de Ambrós** (🅐🅗✕🍴, 216km) via a landscape of broom and wild lavender. The slate roofs and rural craftsmanship make walking through this village a delight. The sixteenth-century Iglesia de Santa María on the edge of the village has an interesting Baroque *retablo*. Riego's **albergue** (50 beds, kitchen, open all year) is along the camino, and there are also rooms at the **Ruta de Santiago** ($, ☎ 987 695190) and the **Pensíon Riego de Ambrós** ($, ☎ 987 695188).

Head downhill out of Riego on a path of broad slate rocks. This is one of the loveliest stretches of the whole camino, where horse chestnut trees line the route, providing shelter for songbirds like the crested tit. Keep heading downhill, soon seeing the slate roofs of Molinaseca up ahead and the main road far below. Join the road just outside Molinaseca and turn right. Pass the **Capilla de la Virgen de las Angustias** on the right as you enter town, where Galician migrant workers once left their sickles on their way from the harvest in Castilla y León. You can peer through the iron grille to see the beautiful statue of the Virgin inside. Soon afterwards, cross the Puente del Peregrino into Molinaseca.

Molinaseca

Ⓐ Ⓗ ✖ 💻 🛒 (211.5km)

Molinaseca is a mellow town that lies prettily alongside the wide Río Maruelo. The gorgeous location attracted the wealthy and the titled, who left behind houses that still bear elaborate coats of arms. It's said that Doña Urraca, an eleventh-century Queen of Castilla y León and Galicia lived here, as did the aristocratic Balboa family. Historically, the town's importance came from its strategic location on the first flat, open land this side of the mountain pass, and ancient bridges helped make it a control point along the Roman gold road. Molinaseca was a significant town in mediaeval times, too, and once boasted four pilgrim *hospitals*.

Today's attractions include the **Iglesia de San Nicolás**, which contains an image of San Roque Peregrino, and a weekly street market. In summer, it's a lovely overnight stop, as the dammed Río Maruelo becomes a focal point of the village.

Accommodation
Molinaseca's **albergue** is a kilometre out of town (85 beds, kitchen, open all year).
$$ **Hostal El Palacio** (☎ 987 453094)
$$ **La Casa del Reloj** (☎ 987 453124)
$$ **Casa San Nicolás** (☎ 929 793053)
$$ **Posada de Muriel** (☎ 987 453201)

Leave Molinaseca on the main road,

heading gradually uphill. At the top of the rise, turn left to follow a minor road through the hamlet of **Campo**, which in mediaeval times was Ponferrada's Jewish district. Beautifully restored slate and stone houses line the route, and there's an elaborate coat of arms on one such house.

Follow narrow roads through fields and Ponferrada's suburbs. After a few kilometres, cross the Río Boeza over a narrow stone bridge. From here, turn left to continue the camino, passing under a railway and soon reaching Ponferrada's magnificent castle. Alternatively, keep straight on for the *albergue*, crossing the railway over a long bridge and turning right soon afterwards.

Ponferrada

Ⓐ Ⓗ ✖ 💻 € ❶ 🛒 (203.5km)

Once an ancient Celtic village, Ponferrada grew steadily under the Romans to become Interamnium Flavium, a large city in the middle of one of the Roman Empire's richest mining districts. Destroyed twice over the next 500 years, first by Visigoths in the fifth century and then by Muslims in the ninth, Ponferrada got its modern name from the long-gone iron bridge built by the bishop of Astorga in 1082. The arrival of the railway in the nineteenth century spurred Ponferrada's development, and coal mining fuelled a modern boom a few decades later. Today, the city's pretty old quarter contrasts with a mass of ugly tower blocks.

On the south bank of Río Sil is the magnificent **Castillo de los Templarios**, a must-see sight that's worth a visit even if you're not spending the night in Ponferrada. Erected by the Templars in the thirteenth century to help protect pilgrims from bandits, it's a grand, triple-ramparted, fairy-tale castle. As you crawl around the castle, up stairs and over walls, try to spot Templar crosses carved into the stone.

Excavations show that the castle was built over the remains of a Celtic *castro*, a Roman fort and a later Visigothic fort. While the Templars were clearing forest to build their castle, legend says that they discovered a statue of the Virgen de la Encina in a holm oak. The statue can now be seen inside the **Basílica de Santa María de la Encina**, and the Virgin was declared Patroness of El Bierzo in 1958. The massive Templar cross on the outside of the church boldly declares the church's origins.

The **Museo del Bierzo** is fascinating, with lots of exhibits packed into the walls of the former jail. The display of weaving tools and old looms is accompanied by a video showing local women using traditional weaving methods, and the finds from local *castros* make this museum well worth a visit.

Ponferrada's **turismo** is next to the castle, on Calle Gil y Carrasco (☎ 987 424236).

Accommodation
The well-equipped **albergue** (185 beds, kitchen, open all year) is below the old town; it has pleasant four-person dormitories and a long, sociable dining table.
$ Hostal Santa Cruz, Calle Marcelo Macías 4 (☎ 987 428351)
$$ Hostal San Miguel, Luciana Fernandez 2 (☎ 987 411047)
$$$ Hotel El Castillo, Avenida del Castillo 115 (☎ 987 456227)
$$$$ Hotel Del Temple, Avenida de Portugal 2 (☎ 987 410058)

To leave Ponferrada, walk down the steps from the cathedral plaza. Cross the Río Sil at the Plaza de las Nievas, then turn right at the Plaza San Pedro. Take the first left up Calle Río Urdiales, then turn right on to Avenida Huertas de Sacramento. On your way out of town, there's an attractive sculpture of four traditionally dressed women cooking peppers. Turn right at Avenida Libertad on the edge of town, then turn left past an old electrical power plant. This is the bizarre suburb of **Compostilla**, a North-American-style company town, with evenly spaced blocks, numbered streets and large houses with immaculate front lawns.

Pass through an arch in a building, and a modern, neo-Romanesque church with a statue of the Virgin and Child sitting on a rock in front. You'll soon pass a *cruceiro* (cross) placed here during the 1993 Holy Year and a camino mural on the new *ermita* next to it. In a kilometre or so, walk past the Iglesia de Santa María and into the village of **Columbrianos** (🖳🛒). In front of you are the beautiful mountains of Galicia; the two flat hills to the north contain the remains of Asturi hillforts.

It's just 2km to **Fuentes Nuevas** (✗🖳🛒), and less than that to **Camponaraya** (✗🖳🛒). The second village is a strange mix of dreary modern houses interlaced with lovely old buildings that offer just a taste of the Camponaraya's original architecture. The village's endless exit is made easier by the Co-operativa Viñas del Bierzo, which sells wine by the glass, industrially poured from a huge tap. You can also buy wine by the bottle to spirit you towards Villafranca del Bierzo.

From here, you'll pass, appropriately enough, through vineyards. Most of the

Map 17 (key page 182)

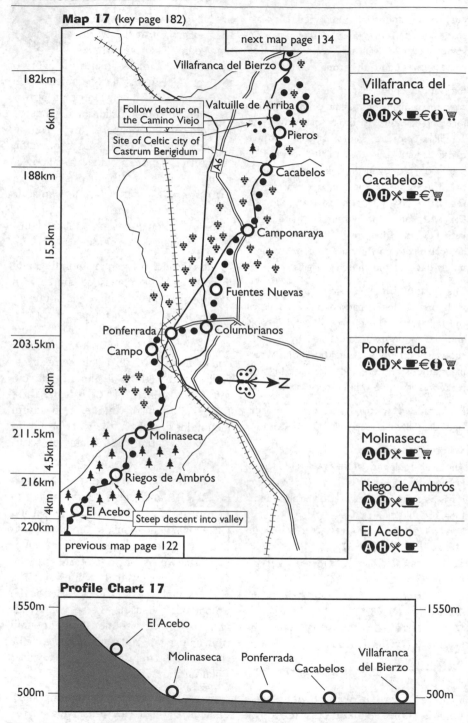

next map page 134

Villafranca del Bierzo

182km

6km

Follow detour on the Camino Viejo

Valtuille de Arriba

Site of Celtic city of Castrum Berigidum

Pieros

A6

188km

Cacabelos

15.5km

Camponaraya

Fuentes Nuevas

Ponferrada

Columbrianos

203.5km

Campo

N

8km

211.5km

Molinaseca

4.5km

216km

Riegos de Ambrós

4km

El Acebo

Steep descent into valley

220km

previous map page 122

Villafranca del Bierzo
ⒶⒽ✗🍴🍺€🛈🛒

Cacabelos
ⒶⒽ✗🍴🍺€🛒

Ponferrada
ⒶⒽ✗🍴🍺€🛈🛒

Molinaseca
ⒶⒽ✗🍴🍺🛒

Riego de Ambrós
ⒶⒽ✗🍴🍺

El Acebo
ⒶⒽ✗🍴🍺

Profile Chart 17

1550m — — 1550m

El Acebo

Molinaseca Ponferrada Villafranca del Bierzo
Cacabelos

500m — — 500m

vines are still grown old-school style with the branches draped along the ground, but modern wire-supported vines, common in La Rioja and Navarra, are starting to surface here. El Bierzo's wine industry is developing fast: there's another wine co-operative in a couple of kilometres, and just before Cacabelos is the new Centro Para Promoción del Vino.

The camino passes through Cacabelos along Calle de los Peregrinos, then crosses the Río Cua to reach the *albergue*.

Cacabelos
Ⓐ Ⓗ ✕ ◼ € 🛒 (188km)

Well known for its wines, Cacabelos is a pretty little town founded by Alfonso IX in the tenth century and rebuilt after a twelfth-century earthquake. The town's archaeological museum has some interesting finds from local excavations and is worth visiting.

At the far end of town, next to the bridge over the Río Cua, there's an old mill that's been beautifully converted into a house, and an antique wooden olive press in front of an excellent *panadería*. On the opposite bank, the eighteenth-century Santuario de la Quinta Angustia is on the site of a former pilgrim hospital; it's notable for a bizarre altar showing the baby Jesus playing cards with San António de Padua. Near the bridge in January 1809, Thomas Plunkett, one of General Sir John Moore's riflemen, shot the commander of Napoleon's pressuring French forces through the head. This accurate display of marksmanship saved the British army from being overrun as it attempted a shambolic winter retreat over the mountains to the safety of its navy on the coast at A Coruña.

Accommodation
Albergue (70 beds, open all year).

$ Pensión El Molino (☎ 987 546829)
$$ Hostal Santa María (☎ 987 549588)
$$ Pensión La Gallega (☎ 987 549355)

Climb out of Cacabelos on the road. At the top of the hill the views across the valley to the mountains are superb. Just to the south is the **Cerro de la Ventosa**, a large circular hill where the Asturian city of Castrum Berigidum once stood. This Celtic metropolis was conquered by the Romans and has given its name to the El Bierzo region. The western side of the defensive wall has been excavated and it's worth climbing the hill for a closer look. From here, there are two ways to Villafranca.

Most people stick to the road, turning right onto a farm track in a few kilometres, but unless you have a thing for tarmac it's far nicer to turn right, following the signs for Camino Viejo. This second route leads you along farm tracks through **Valtuille de Arriba**, a gorgeous village with old-fashioned houses and precarious wooden balconies. Follow farm tracks scented with honeysuckle in late spring, then meet up with the other route about 1km later. Just as you enter Villafranca, head down and right for the municipal *albergue* or keep straight on to reach Albergue Ave Fénix.

Villafranca del Bierzo
Ⓐ Ⓗ ✕ ◼ € ⓘ 🛒 (182km)

As a logical rest stop on the camino before

the pass over O Cebreiro, Villafranca del Bierzo marked the end of the tenth stage of the *Codex Calixtinus*. Villafranca once had eight monasteries and six pilgrim *hospitals*. As its name suggests, it was settled by the Franks, who came here on the orders of King Alfonso VI to guard this strategic trading place on the banks of the Río Burbia and the Río Valcarce.

Life hasn't always been easy here. Plague killed most of the residents in 1589, and floods destroyed the buildings nearest the river in 1715. Less than a century later, the invading French army ransacked the town in 1808 during the **Peninsula War** but was driven out by the British. The townspeople probably wished that the French had stayed, when the British hooligans went on a drunken rampage as they fled from the French army in the winter of 1809. In their search for loot, the British wrecked the castle, robbed the churches and burned their priceless archives. General Sir John Moore eventually stopped the rampage by taking the drastic measure of shooting the ringleaders. More damage was done the following year as the French wrenched back control of the town.

Today, these historic scars are mostly invisible, and Villafranca is one of the loveliest towns in all of Spain, picturesquely set on a river and surrounded by mountains. The industrial revolution passed the town by, so it's not tainted by rampant construction, and the centre of town is a maze of narrow streets and open plazas. The Calle de Agua is lined with splendid mansions, one of which was home to the nineteenth-century novelist Enrique Gil y Carrasco. In spring, there's a poetry festival in the municipal gardens.

On the way into town, next to Albergue Ave Fénix, you pass the beautiful Romanesque **Iglesia de Santiago**, which has a Puerta del Perdón. Just as at other churches along the camino, if you are unable to continue the pilgrimage you can walk through these finely carved doors and receive the same spiritual benefits as if you had made it all the way to Santiago de Compostela.

Try and visit the **Iglesia de San Francisco**, which has a lovely Mudéjar-style ceiling. This church was reputedly founded by St Francis as he made his pilgrimage, and it was heavily damaged when used as barracks in the Napoleonic wars.

At the top of town, the dramatic sixteenth-century **Castillo de los Marqueses de Villafranca** is now the fortified private residence of the Álvarez de Toledo family.

Villafranca has some good restaurants and a lively Tuesday market. The **turismo** is in the town hall (☎ 987 540028).

Accommodation

You can stay at the comfortable **albergue municipal** (78 beds, open all year) or at the eccentric **Ave Fénix** (60 beds, kitchen, open all year), run by Jesús Jato. This impressive man has dedicated his life to helping pilgrims. His first *albergue* burnt down in 1996 and the Ave Fénix, which rose from the ashes, is slowly growing. The house rules are quirky; no getting up before 7am, a separate room for the over-50s, and pilgrims aren't allowed to do any work around the *albergue*. Communal meals are the norm, and on many evenings Jesús leads pilgrims in a *queimada* ritual (page 119).

$ Hostal La Charola, Calle Doctor Aren 19 (☎ 987 540200)
$$ Hostal Casa Méndez, Espíritu Santo 1 (☎ 987 542408)
$$$ Hotel San Francisco, Plaza Generalisimo 6 (☎ 987 540465)
$$$$ Parador de Villafranca de

Bierzo, Avenida Calvo Sotelo 28 (☎ 987 540175)

Walk downhill through Villafranca, following the yellow arrows to the bridge over the Río Burbia. At the end of the bridge, you have two options.

The duller, shorter route follows the old NVI road, no longer as busy or as dangerous as it once was now that the new motorway has taken away most of the traffic, but still an unpleasant walk. At **Pereje** (ⒶⒽ⬛), 4km along the road, there's a basic **albergue** (30 beds, kitchen, open Easter to October), and in another 5km you'll reach **Trabadelo**.

A beautiful but much more strenuous walk takes you over the hill to the right of the road: it's a stunning, heather-lined route with spectacular views. For this option, bear right up Calle Pradela, climbing steeply. The track, lined with heather and intense clusters of white broom, reaches the top of the ridge in a few kilometres. From here, the incredible views make it feel as though you're walking along the roof of the world.

Soon, **Pradela** (⬛) and its vivid green meadows come into view ahead: you'll need to leave the camino to visit the village. The camino descends a little and wanders through chestnut trees, home to red-backed shrikes, goldcrests, bullfinches and cirl buntings. Although you're still nominally in modern Castilla y León, it's clear that you've already crossed culturally into rural, other-worldly Galicia. The track snakes steeply downhill, and after an eerie stretch shaded by high-sided mossy walls, you enter the village of **Trabadelo** (ⒶⒽ✕⬛).

There are no remains of the castle that once guarded the route here, but you can stay at the lovely **albergue** (28 beds, kitchen, open all year) or the soulless **Hostal Nova Ruta** ($$, ☎ 987 566431). In a few kilometres, bear left at the sign for **La Portela** (ⒶⒽ✕⬛), which marks the start of the narrow and attractive Valcarce valley. The valley's enclosed feel led to its Spanish name (valley of the prison). **El Peregrino** ($$, ☎ 987 543197) has rooms and bunk beds, or you can stay at the **Hostal Valcarce** ($$, ☎ 987 543180).

In little more than a kilometre, you'll reach **Ambasmestas** (ⒶⒽ✕⬛), named after the merging of the waters of the Valcarce and Valboa rivers. You can stay at **Albergue das Animas** (20 beds, open Easter to Christmas) or the **Residencial Los Sauces** ($$$, ☎ 987 233768). After less than a kilometre, walk under an impressive, sky-high motorway bridge, pass the Albergue do Brasil and arrive in Vega de Valcarce.

Vega de Valcarce
ⒶⒽ✕⬛🛒 (166km)

Vega de Valcarce's brief moment in the spotlight came when Carlos V stayed the night in 1520 on his way to Santiago. The church here is dedicated to María Magdalena, and the town makes a good stop before tackling the climb up to O Cebreiro.

On the hills above the village are the remains of two ruined castles. It takes about an hour to climb up to Sarracín, on the left hilltop, which was once controlled by the Marqués de Villafranca. Its defensive position offers fantastic views of the entire valley and it's clear why the castle's ninth-century founders would build a fortress here. On the right hand hilltop, Castro de Vega is little more than a pile of rubble.

Accommodation

Albergue municipal (84 beds, kitchen, open April to October)
Albergue do Brasil (46 beds, communal meals, open all year, 1km before centre)
$ Hostal Fernandez (☎ 982 543027)

Leave town on the main road, and you'll soon reach **Ruitelán** (🅐💷), where there are picnic tables and an **albergue** (34 beds, open all year) on the right that serves breakfast and dinner. A cave in the hillside above was said to be the home of San Froilán of Lugo, who became bishop of León in the ninth century.

In another 1km, veer left into **Las Herrerías** (🅗✕💷), passing the **Hotel Paraiso del Bierzo** ($$$, ☎ 987 684138) then crossing a fifteenth-century bridge. Famous in the seventeenth century for its iron forge, Las Herrerías was admired by Domenico Laffi, the sixteenth-century Italian camino chronicler. Today, it's a beautiful little village with the odd bar-café strung out along the camino; one of these contains a restored forge. The original fountain was said to honour Don Suero de Quiñones of the famous jousting tournament in Hospital de Órbigo. Las Herrerías merges into **Hospital** (💷), where there are no visible remains of the former pilgrims' hospice.

Climb uphill out of Las Herrerías, catching occasional glimpses of La Faba high above. In 1km, turn left down a grassy stone track, following a camino sign that directs walkers this way; cyclists should keep to the minor road. The path leads down to the Río Valcarce, then heads steeply uphill towards the hamlet of La Faba.

This steep stretch can be mucky and slippery due to heavy use by local cattle, and you'll have to press tight against the high stone walls if a herd decides to amble past. If you manage to keep your footing, this is an enchanting section of the camino, zig-zagging uphill between stone walls. As you climb, there are dramatic changes in landscape and architecture. It feels like a fast rewind through history, finally settling at some misty, magical period of conical, thatch-roofed *pallozas*, cobbled streets and a new language — *Galega*.

After a couple of kilometres, you'll pass the first house in **La Faba** (🅐💷); look behind you for great views of the Iglesia de San Andrés, rebuilt in the eighteenth century. There's a fountain and a café-bar in La Faba, and an **albergue** (35 beds, open April to October).

The weather is often foggy here and can turn nasty at any time. During a blizzard on these mountains in the early years of the nineteenth century, Sir John Moore's retreating British army mutinied after hundreds of soldiers froze to death, throwing a heavy military chest of gold down a cliff in protest. Sir John was having a hard time of it: his soldiers had already trashed Villafranca and drunk Ponferrada dry, and it was remarkable that he managed to regain order. He almost made it home to Britain, but the unlucky general was shot and killed by the French in A Coruña as he oversaw the embarkation of the British troops.

In 2km, enter **Laguna de Castilla**, then in another kilometre, pass a stone sign marking your entrance into Galicia. From here, you'll reach a road in less than a kilometre. Turn left, neatly avoiding a viewing area clogged with bus tours, then turn right to walk into O Cebreiro; the *albergue* is on the far side of the village.

O Cebreiro

Ⓐ Ⓗ ✗ ▄ ▛ (154.5km)

There are stunning pastoral views from O Cebreiro on the rare occasions that the mist clears enough to see more than three steps ahead. The weather can be truly awful here; summer snowstorms are not unheard of and dense fog is the norm year-round. Although it's pretty in the sunshine, murky mist seems to suit O Cebreiro's architecture perfectly.

The hamlet's round, thatch-roofed **pallozas** are a distinctive form of rural architecture once found across Celtic lands from Africa to Scotland. Their round walls and conical, straw and broom-thatched roofs aerodynamically deflect the strong mountain winds. Chimneys would interfere with the tight weather defences, so smoke escapes through the thatch itself, curing the sausages and hams that hang from the ceiling as it does so. One of these buildings houses the village's small ethnographic museum, which is well worth a look.

The focal point of the village is the modern **Iglesia de Santa María**, rebuilt in the 1960s on top of the ruins of a Romanesque church. It's believed that the Holy Grail from which Christ drank at the Last Supper was hidden here for safe-keeping in the Middle Ages. In the fourteenth century, a local farmer braved a fierce snowstorm to attend Mass at the church. The priest told the man

that it was silly to come all the way just for a bit of bread and wine in such terrible weather, at which point the bread turned into flesh and the wine in the Holy Grail became blood.

The church's statue of the Virgin is said to have tilted her head to get a better look at the miracle, and she's now known as La Virgen del Milagro. Although the grail is no longer here, the remains of the flesh and blood are held in a silver reliquary donated by Queen Isabel.

Outside the church, a bust of Elías Valiña has pride of place. Valiña was a local parish priest who wrote important books on the camino and was a driving force behind its revival during the 1960s and 1970s. He also did much to preserve O Cebreiro's *palloza* architecture, and he's buried in the church graveyard.

O Cebreiro's small **turismo** (☎ 982 367025) has excellent information on accommodation throughout Galicia.

Accommodation

O Cebreiro has sheltered pilgrims from mountain storms for centuries, and there were *hospitals* here from 1072 to 1854. The modern **albergue** (80 beds, kitchen, open all year) is on the far side of the village.

If you'd rather stay in a hotel, it's worth booking ahead, as O Cebreiro can get very busy.
$$ Pensión Pazos (☎ 982 367185)
$$ Hostal San Giraldo de Aurillac (☎ 982 367125)
$$ Casa Carolo (☎ 982 367168)
$$ Hostal Rebollal (☎ 982 367115)

The route down from the mountain is exposed to the elements, but there are striking views of the surrounding mountains and valleys as you descend. In about

Map 18 (key page 182)

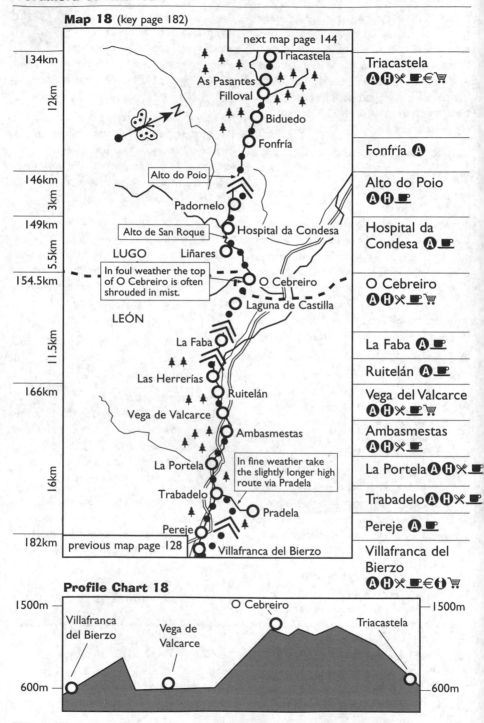

next map page 144

134km — Triacastela

Triacastela
🅐🅗✕🍴🛏€🛒

As Pasantes
Filloval

12km

Biduedo

Fonfría

Fonfría 🅐

146km — Alto do Poio

Alto do Poio
🅐🅗🛏

3km

Padornelo

149km — Alto de San Roque

Hospital da Condesa

Hospital da
Condesa 🅐🛏

5.5km

LUGO   Liñares

154.5km — O Cebreiro

In foul weather the top of O Cebreiro is often shrouded in mist.

O Cebreiro
🅐🅗✕🛏🛒

Laguna de Castilla

LEÓN

11.5km

La Faba

La Faba 🅐🛏

Las Herrerías

Ruitelán 🅐🛏

166km — Ruitelán

Vega del Valcarce
🅐🅗✕🛏🛒

Vega de Valcarce

Ambasmestas

Ambasmestas
🅐🅗✕🛏

16km

La Portela

In fine weather take the slightly longer high route via Pradela

La Portela🅐🅗✕🛏

Trabadelo

Trabadelo🅐🅗✕🛏

Pradela

Pereje 🅐🛏

Pereje

182km — previous map page 128

Villafranca del Bierzo

Villafranca del
Bierzo
🅐🅗✕🛏€ℹ🛒

Profile Chart 18

1500m —   O Cebreiro   — 1500m

Villafranca
del Bierzo   Vega de
                   Valcarce   Triacastela

600m —   — 600m

134

3km, the road arrives at the small hamlet of **Liñares** (🅗💺🛒), set in a windy saddle of the mountains. Liñares' name comes from the local flax fields that supplied the linen for the looms in O Cebreiro's pilgrim hospice. The tiny, lovely twelfth-century village church is dedicated to San Esteban. You can stay at **Casa Rural Jaime** ($, ☎ 982 367166).

Climb up to the **Alto de San Roque**, where an isolated, dramatic statue of a wind-battered pilgrim marks the pass. Watch for harriers and short-toed eagles up high, and look down low for the pimpernel, wild garlic and blue lilies that grow on the local limestone. These wild mountains are also home to wolves: watch closely for their tracks on muddy stretches. Wolves were only part of mediaeval pilgrims' concerns, as attacks by bandits were common along this stretch.

In a couple of kilometres, you come to **Hospital da Condesa** (🅐💺, 149km). Follow the camino through the hamlet, passing the **albergue** (18 beds, kitchen, open spring to autumn). The tiny, beautiful church dates from the twelfth century but was largely rebuilt in 1963.

Pass through **Padornelo** (💺) in 2km, then climb uphill to the **Alto do Poio** (🅐🅗💺, 146km), where a cosy bar has a log fire to warm soggy pilgrims in wet weather. The Hospitaleros de San Juan de Jerusalen once ran the Iglesia de Santa María at this windswept pass; nowadays you can stay at the **albergue** (50 beds, open all year) or the **Hostal-**

Restaurante Santa María do Poio ($$, ☎ 982 367167).

Turn right at the café on to the main tarmac road, then veer right in about 500m to follow a track into **Fonfría** (🅐). The village, whose name means cold spring, is a wonderful collection of farm buildings. In mediaeval times, the Hospital de Santa Catalina offered healthy pilgrims heat, salt, water and a bed with two blankets, while the sick received a bonus of a quarter pound of bread, eggs and butter. Such luxuries are long gone, but there is an **albergue** (38 beds, open all year).

From Fonfría, there's a drop in altitude of 600m to Triacastela. The views as you curve down the ridge are fantastic, and the picture-perfect lush fields and farms are only slightly spoilt by a slate quarry on the valley floor. Walk along a track lined with beech trees, watching out for sparrowhawks hunting for prey in the fields on either side of the camino.

In a couple of kilometres, the camino winds through the small hamlet of **Biduedo** (🅗✖💺), where both **Casa Quiroga** ($, ☎ 982 187299) or **Casa Xato** ($, ☎ 982 187301) are good value. Keep heading downhill through **Filloval** and **As Pasantes** (🅗), where you can stay at **Casa Caloto** ($, ☎ 982 187347), and where there's some great rural architecture. Near the bottom of the mountain, you enter Triacastela; the *albergue* is in a field on your left just before the town.

Regional Map (key page 182)

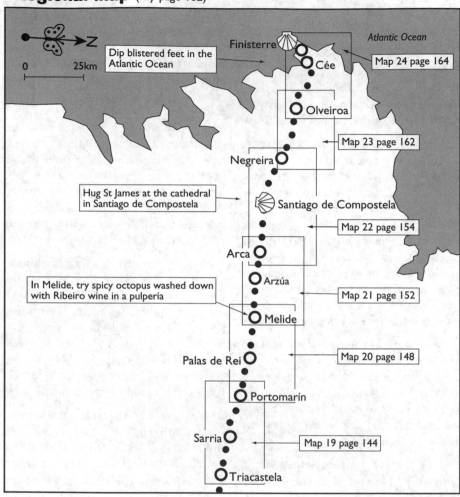

Atlantic Ocean

Finisterre

Dip blistered feet in the Atlantic Ocean

Cée

Map 24 page 164

Olveiroa

Map 23 page 162

Negreira

Hug St James at the cathedral in Santiago de Compostela

Santiago de Compostela

Map 22 page 154

Arca

Arzúa

Map 21 page 152

In Melide, try spicy octopus washed down with Ribeiro wine in a pulpería

Melide

Palas de Rei

Map 20 page 148

Portomarín

Sarria

Map 19 page 144

Triacastela

0   25km

What's the weather like?

	Jan	April	July	Oct
Sun	3hrs	6hrs	8hrs	5hrs
Rainfall	27cm	15cm	3cm	19cm
Maximum Temp	11°C	15°C	22°C	17°C
Minimum Temp	3°C	6°C	12°C	7°C

Average hours of sun, total average rainfall in cm and average temperature in degrees Celsius

Galicia

Triacastela to Finisterre via Santiago

Once you're in Galicia, it's a winding, up-and-down route through tiny farms and one-house hamlets and alongside rain-drenched fields and rivers. The volume of pilgrims reaches a crescendo at Santiago, where you give thanks to St James in a series of historic rituals. But don't stop there: if you follow the old Celtic route to the sea at Finisterre, you'll reach the end of the known world via the solitude of quiet lanes and ancient ways.

 **Walking**

Geography

Soggy storms clip this corner of Iberia as they fly along the Gulf Stream, dumping bucketsful of water almost all year round. In an average year, Galicia gets rain on one day in three.

The foggy Costa da Morte is a jagged mix of cliffs and long estuaries that penetrate deep inland, and the coast is a legendary wrecker of countless ships, blown on to the rocks by storms. This maritime carnage may explain the name Costa da Morte (coast of death), but the coast may also be named for the nightly death of the sun as it sets on Spain's westernmost shore.

The inland landscape is one of rolling hills and steep river valleys eroded by aeons of rainfall. Lush vegetation and mild winters make Galicia stand out from other, more arid parts of Spain, but for those who know the wilder parts of Ireland, the scenery will be very familiar.

Trails

The Galician government has made a huge effort to promote the camino. Concrete bollards line the route every half a kilometre and are engraved with the distance to Santiago and local place names, although some rural folk say that a lot of these names are made up, and many bollards have been vandalized. The government invested heavily in the camino for the 1993 Holy Year and introduced Pelerín, a cartoon mascot for the camino through Galicia.

The camino is much less crowded after Santiago, and the route is well marked and wonderfully scenic.

When to go

The old saying, "Be prepared for rain and pray for sunshine" rings true in Galicia.

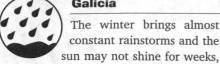
The winter brings almost constant rainstorms and the sun may not shine for weeks, although it's unlikely to snow as the temperature rarely dips below freezing. In spring and autumn the weather is unpredictable, and mists are frequent. Summer brings the most settled good weather but is also the most popular time of year; *albergues* will be stuffed to the gills and the camino can seem like a well-attended sponsored walk.

 # Flora & Fauna

The **oak** forest of Galicia is a national treasure. Its sturdy wood was used to build Spain's mighty naval armada, and by the early sixteenth century, in an attempt to preserve the forest for state use, a royal decree forbade anyone from felling the huge trees without a licence.

Then, in the nineteenth century, **eucalyptus** was brought to Spain under the mistaken belief that it would be good for construction. Eucalyptus can grow by as much as 13m in three years, much faster than the local oak, making it popular as a source of both pulp and firewood. In 1941, Franco introduced the badly misnamed State Forest Heritage Act, under which oak was widely chopped down and eucalyptus was planted in its place to feed the fledgling pulp industry. The non-native species now accounts for almost a third of the forest in Galicia.

When you're out walking, take a look at the undergrowth of oak and eucalyptus woods. In eucalyptus forests, there's limited plant life and very few animals; birds find little food to eat here and the tree's sticky gum can clog up a bird's throat and kill it. In stark contrast, an old oak wood is a multi-layered canopy of green. Oak forests develop slowly, the soil growing rich with decaying leaves and acorns. Ferns, foxgloves, and other small shrubs provide shelter and food for a variety of animals, and the trees themselves are covered in moss and lichen — a miniature ecosystem in their own right. Black woodpeckers nest in the hollows of old trees, while thrushes and wrens hunt for beetles and grubs among the shrubs. The stubby bullfinch with its rosy breast and black cap is often seen darting through thickets.

Galician **farming** practices are less intensive and pesticide-reliant than those in the more productive *meseta*. As a result, meadows burst with wildflowers in spring and early summer, and the local cows use the lush grasses to produce a rich, creamy milk that's turned into a wide variety of cheeses.

Without the region's persistent **rain**, Galicia would be devoid of damp-loving plants like the purple large-flowered butterwort and the pink bog pimpernel. In the hours after a heavy rainstorm, it's common to see green Iberian wall lizards drying themselves on slabs of rock or on walls. Fire salamanders are most easily spotted during heavy rain when they crawl out of damp crevices: look out for them in wet mountain regions.

 # People & Culture

Picaud was uncharacteristically complimentary about the Galicians, who

"are more like our French people in

their customs than any other of the uncultivated races of Spain, but they have the reputation of being violent-tempered and quarrelsome."

Such quarrelsome behaviour would be understandable today, as locals cope with the tide of pilgrims that washes through their province. Galicians can be more reserved than other Spaniards, but the people are some of the kindest you'll meet along the camino.

In the 1991 census, a massive 91% of inhabitants said they were able to speak **Galega**, the region's Portuguese-like language. *Galega* tends to be heard more in rural areas and it's still thought of as an old person's language. After Galicia was granted autonomous government in 1981, the study of the language took off, and modern writers like Manolo Rivas have led to a new interest in *Galega*.

The region has always been poor. The last feudal holding was only abolished in 1973, and the average worker earns about half that of workers in Germany. Since the 1950s, there's been a massive exodus of people from the countryside, initially to South America but nowadays to industrialized cities like A Coruña.

The historic poverty of the region may go some way to explaining why traditional **farming** methods remain popular. As you walk through tiny hamlets it's common to see *palleiros* (haylofts), *pallozas* (straw-covered huts), *bronas* (outdoor ovens for cooking corn bread) and beautiful *hórreos* that dry and store the corn. *Hórreo* designs and materials change from village to village, from simple, sturdy concrete blocks to intricate wood and slate designs that belie their practical function.

Galician **music** is firmly Celtic, and

perhaps nothing shows the links between northern Celtic nations and Galicia better than the *gaita* (Galician bagpipe). There seems to be a type of music for every occasion. The most widespread and well-known are the *Danzas de Espadas* and *Danzas de Arcos*, which are linked to local celebrations, but more specific music includes *Alboradas,* which celebrate the sunrise, *Pasacorredoiras* (parade tunes) and *Pasarruas* (marching music). If you're lucky, you might hear farmers and field workers singing traditional *jotas* (work songs) in the rural areas between Santiago and Finisterre.

Food & Drink

Galician cooking is simple and hearty. Almost every meal begins with traditional **caldo gallego**, a thick soup made from meat, potatoes, greens and beans. *Empanadas* are a square, pie-like dish made with meat, fish or seafood.

Eat **seafood** every chance you get. When in Melide, try *pulpo a la gallega*: steamed octopus is sliced up, sprinkled with paprika, then served on wooden platters to diners eating communally at long wooden tables. Celebrate your arrival in Santiago with a big seafood dinner: much more expensive than a pilgrim *menú*, but well worth the splurge. Another delight is *vieiras de Santiago*, scallops with onions and cured ham.

Those with a sweet tooth will love **torta de Santiago**, a type of almond cake dusted with sugar outlining the shape of the cross of Santiago. You'll see the cake all over Galicia, but particularly in Compostela itself, where restauranteurs tempt customers into their shops and cafés by offering a free sample.

Galicia's trademark downpours make for happy cows, and their milk is often turned into a soft and creamy teat-shaped cheese named *tetilla* (nipple).

Unlike the red wine–producing rest of Spain, Galicia's climate is better suited to whites. **Albariño** is a straw-coloured wine with a distinctive peach flavour that's slowly becoming respected outside Spain. **Ribeiro**, its lesser-known cousin, is young, fresh, cloudy and perfect with seafood. In more traditional bars it's poured straight out of the barrel into wide, shallow clay cups. Ribeiro rarely makes it outside Galicia, and EU bureaucrats insist that the bottled version is clarified, so drink your fill while you're here.

Made from grape skins, **orujo** is a clear firewater that'll put hairs on your chest. *Orujo blanco* comes straight up, *orujo con hierbas* is flavoured with herbs, and *orujo tostada*'s skins have been toasted for an earthier flavour. If you're feeling brave, ask for *orujo casero* (homemade *orujo*): in true moonshine style, you'll find under-the-counter *orujo casero* in unmarked bottles in bakeries and grocers, as well as in bars and cafés.

Tourist Information

Transport

Local buses link larger towns such as Sarria, Melide and Arzúa, but services can be sporadic. It's easy to catch a train from Santiago to almost any large centre in Spain. For more information on getting home from Santiago, see Getting There & Back on page 26. Between three and seven buses a day connect Santiago and Finisterre, in a journey that takes between two and three hours.

Accommodation

The infrastructure of the camino in Galicia is centralized and supremely organized. Huge government investment in the 1993 Holy Year led to a flurry of new *albergues* and extensive upgrading of existing ones. You'll rarely travel more than 10km without bumping into an *albergue*; most have kitchens, and there's always a payphone outside. Sadly, the initial influx of cash hasn't been kept up, so that kitchens and bathrooms may have broken cookers (stoves), toilets or showers. The *albergues* are run by paid wardens rather than volunteer *hospitaleros*; they can be sparsely staffed, but you'll often be able to get in through an unlocked door.

Events and Festivals

On July 25, the **Día de Santiago** and Galicia's national day, Santiago's Plaza do Obradoiro erupts in a sound-and-light display that dates back to the seventeenth century. Galicia parties for twelve months during **Holy Years**, when July 25 falls on a Sunday (2010 and 2021). Holy Year festivities begin with the opening of the Puerta del Perdón on the east side of the cathedral and end when it's firmly shut at midnight on December 31, and sandwiched in between are thousands of concerts, dances, exhibitions and fireworks.

Galicia's other festivals seem to revolve around **food**. Arzúa's cheese festival takes place in March, Ribeiro wine festivals happen all over the province in late April and early May, there's a barnacle festival in Finisterre at the beginning of August, and other seaside towns hold seasonal shellfish and oyster festivals.

Rest Days & Detours

Some 20km north of Portomarín, the city of **Lugo**, on the camino primitivo, is well worth a visit. Its huge, Roman-built slate walls are some of the best preserved in Spain, and four of the city's ancient gates remain. Lugo's monuments include the twelfth-century cathedral, the seventeenth-century Bishop's palace, and the Gothic churches in the Praza de Santo Domingo. If you're getting bored with churches, you can relax in Lugo's tranquil riverside parks or take the waters at the town's Roman baths.

About 15km northeast of Palas de Rei is the underground chapel of **Santa Eulalia de Bóveda**. Built on the site of a Celtic temple and used for a time as a Roman nymphaeum, the splendid fourth-century Visigothic chapel contains a shallow pool that may have been used to submerge the faithful in early baptisms.

From Melide, it's a 6km walk to **San Antolín de Toques**, a lovely site with

an ancient mill and the overgrown remains of an eleventh-century monastery and earlier church. You can turn the detour into a day trip by heading to the well-preserved *castro* of **A Graña**, about 2km away.

If you're not planning on continuing the camino to **Finisterre**, it's well worth visiting the small fishing town on a day trip, if only to dip your toes into the ocean. A tour of the wild Galician coast can also take in important places in Santiago's life. Many pilgrims visit **Padrón**, the landing place of Santiago's stone boat some 20km southwest of Compostela, where the stone pillar to which Santiago's boat was moored is kept beneath the altar in the Iglesia de Santiago. Time your visit to take in lunch and try a plate of *pimientas de Padrón*, deliciously salty, oil-roasted green peppers.

Just up the coast from Finisterre, the Virgin Mary is said to have visited **Muxia** to hear Santiago preach, sailing there in a stone boat, which was clearly the transport of choice in the early first century. At the sanctuary of Nostra Señora de la Barca, you can see various bits of her boat. The hull moves whenever a person free of sin stands underneath it, while the keel is said to cure digestive problems.

Triacastela

(A)(H)✕💺€🍴 (134km)

Triacastela was founded in the ninth century by Count Gatón of El Bierzo after the area's

reconquest from the Moors. Today, the only evidence of the three castles for which Triacastela is named is on the town's coat of arms. The Romanesque Iglesia de Santiago retains some original features, although it was rebuilt in the eighteenth century.

Triacastela has a long camino history: the area once had many pilgrim hospices, and the town marked the end of stage eleven of the *Codex Calixtinus*. When the cathedral in Santiago de Compostela was being built, twelfth-century pilgrims carried local stone from here to the ovens near Castañeda, almost 100km away. The town also had a prison for pilgrim impostors.

Today, Triacastela is a wonderful place to relax after crossing the mountains; numerous bars and restaurants dot the streets and there are several well-stocked shops.

Accommodation

The town's **albergue municipal** (82 beds, open all year) is popular and well run, with comfortable four-bed dormitories. There are also many private *albergues*: **Albergue Aitzenea** (38 beds, kitchen, open all year), **Refugio del Oribio** (27 beds, kitchen, open all year) and **Albergue Berce do Caminho** (36 beds, kitchen, open February to November).

$ **Hostal Fernández** (☎ 982 548148)
$ **Casa Olga** (☎ 982 548134)
$ **Pensión O Novo** (☎ 982 548105)
$ **Pensión Vilasante** (☎ 982 548116)

Walk through Triacastela until you reach a T-junction at the end of town. From here, there are two ways to reach Sarria.

To Sarria via Samos

The route to Samos is an enchanting one, along walled lanes and through gorgeous hamlets. First, though, you have to turn left to walk for 4km along the LU633: if it wasn't for the trucks that whistle past your ears it would be a wonderful down-hill stroll through a heather-clad gorge.

Turn off the road to walk into **San Cristobal**, a tranquil stone-and-slate village where water seems to rush down every street and under every house. Leave the village on a walled track lined with chestnuts and oaks. In Galicia, slate is so plentiful that fields are often divided by huge slate slabs rather than by hedges. Between here and Samos, the route is dotted with tiny villages and hamlets: pass through **Vigo do Real** (🍴), then at **San Martiño do Real**, 4km from San Cristobal, there's a beautifully restored whitewashed church with wonderful frescoes inside.

You'll soon reach **Samos** (🅰🅗✕🍴) via a pretty, high-walled lane. The **Monasterio de Samos** was founded in the sixth century and still preserves some Visigothic stones from its original construction. The influence of the monastery was so great that at its height it controlled some 200 towns, 105 churches and 300 other monasteries. As a seat of learning, the famous library was perhaps without equal until it was tragically destroyed by fire in 1951. The Latin motto on the door reads, "A cloister without a library is like a fort without an armoury." The library's most famous patron was Padre Benito Feijóo, a luminary of the Spanish Enlightenment who wrote on such varied subjects as astronomy, medicine and religion. You can get a tour from one of the monks if you ask nicely.

There's an **albergue** in Samos' monastery (90 beds, open all year), which can be damp and gloomy year-round. You can also stay at **Casa Liceiro** ($$, ☎ 982 546012), **Hostal A Veiga** ($$, ☎ 982 546052) or **Hostal Victoria** ($$, ☎ 982 546022).

Leave Samos on the main road, passing through **Foxos** and **Teiguin**, where there's a recreational area with a fountain and trout fishing in the river. A couple of kilometres outside Samos, turn right along a narrow tarmac road uphill.

From here, the route alternates between narrow roads and tracks, passing through tiny hamlets and farms. Although corn and potatoes are grown in this region, dairy farming is the main occupation of farmers in these valleys. Most of the cows are friesians but you'll also see some *rubia gallega*, a smooth, russet-coloured cow native to Galicia. At **Aguiada** (⟁), meet up with the route via San Xil.

To Sarria via San Xil

If you don't want to visit Samos, turn right at the T-junction in Triacastela to go to Sarria via San Xil. It's a less interesting route but also considerably shorter than the Samos version.

After a couple of kilometres, you arrive at the beautiful hamlet of **A Balsa**, which boasts stunning farmhouses and gorgeous verandas that overhang the road. Pass an *ermita* and climb up along the small valley of the Río Valdeoscuro. As its name, dark valley, suggests, this lovely stretch of the camino is shaded by mature oaks and chestnut trees. Keep your eyes peeled along the forest edge for a glimpse of a pine marten as it hunts voles, rabbits and birds.

The last part of the climb to the village of **San Xil** is steep, but at the top you'll see wave upon wave of rolling Galician hills as you finally leave the Cordillera Cantábrica behind. Within a couple of kilometres, you'll get your first glimpse of Sarria in the Río Celeiro valley up ahead.

The camino slowly descends along a well-worn lane, enclosed by the dry stone walls that are a common sight along the route through Galicia. Notice the grooves in the stone made from the centuries of cartwheels rolling by. Pass through **Montán** with its Iglesia de Santa María, then through **Furela**, **Pintín** and **Calvor** (⟁, 120km), where there's a small **albergue** (22 beds, kitchen, open all year). A few hundred metres after Calvor, reach **Aguiada** (⟁) and meet up with the route via Samos.

Take a roadside track into Sarria. Follow the road through the outskirts of town and arrive at the Ponterribeira, a bridge decorated with modern art sculpture that spans the Río Ouribio. Turn right at the end of the bridge, then turn first left to climb up the Escalinata Mayor steps to the *albergues* on and near Rúa Maior.

Sarria
Ⓐ Ⓗ ✗ ⟁ € (115.5km)

The layout of Sarria's old town is based on its mediaeval plan, although the Celtic castle that once dominated the town's skyline was dismantled in 1860 under the banner of civic progress, so that its stone could be used to pave the town's streets. The Renaissance sculptor Gregorio Hernández, whose work graces many of the churches along the camino, was born in Sarria, while Alfonso IX, the last king of León, died here in 1230.

The camino passes the modern, undistinguished Iglesia de Santa Marina, from where there are fantastic views of the surrounding countryside. Farther along, the **Iglesia de San Salvador** retains some beautiful

Map 19 (key page 182)

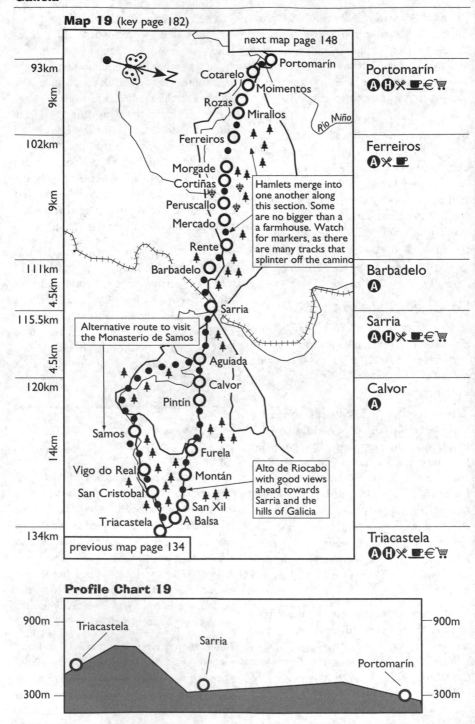

next map page 148

93km

9km

102km

9km

111km

4.5km

115.5km

4.5km

120km

14km

134km

Portomarín
Cotarelo
Moimentos
Rozas
Mirallos
Ferreiros
Morgade
Cortiñas
Peruscallo
Mercado
Rente
Barbadelo
Sarria

Río Miño

Hamlets merge into one another along this section. Some are no bigger than a a farmhouse. Watch for markers, as there are many tracks that splinter off the camino

Alternative route to visit the Monasterio de Samos

Aguiada
Calvor
Pintín
Samos
Furela
Vigo do Real
Montán
San Cristobal
San Xil
Triacastela
A Balsa

Alto de Riocabo with good views ahead towards Sarria and the hills of Galicia

previous map page 134

Portomarín
Ⓐ🅷✕🍽€🛒

Ferreiros
Ⓐ✕🍽

Barbadelo
Ⓐ

Sarria
Ⓐ🅷✕🍽€🛒

Calvor
Ⓐ

Triacastela
Ⓐ🅷✕🍽€🛒

Profile Chart 19

900m — Triacastela

Sarria

Portomarín

900m

300m —

300m

Romanesque decorations. The **Convento de la Magdalena** is home to the Order of Mercedarians (Order of Mercy), who were less violent than contemporaries such as the Templars and Knights of St James and simply sought to free captive Christians from the Moors. Pilgrims leaving Sarria in the early morning may be met by the ghostly figure of a monk standing in a distinctive white wool habit and offering a guided tour of the church and cloister.

There are a few stork nests around town, and these may be the last of the distinctive, untidy landmarks that you'll see on the camino. The newer, lower modern town has little soul and no real centre, but there are some interesting antique shops on its western outskirts.

Accommodation
The **albergue municipal** (40 beds, open all year) is in a tall, narrow house just off Rúa Maior. There are also three private *albergues* on Rúa Maior itself: **Don Álvaro**, **O Durmiñeto** and **Los Blasones**.

$$ Hostal Londres, Calle Calvo Sotelo 13 (☎ 982 532456)
$$ Hostal Roma, Calle Calvo Sotelo 2 (☎ 982 532211)
$$$ Hotel Oca Villa de Sarria, Calle Benigno Quiroga 49 (☎ 982 533873)
$$$ Hotel El Alfonso IX, Rúa do Peregrino 29 (☎ 982 530005)

Follow the old Rúa Maior across the top of Sarria, then turn left just before the Convento de la Magdalena. Cross the Ponte Áspera over the Río Celeiro, then cross the Madrid–A Coruña railway. You'll soon begin to climb out of the valley through a lush, mossy oak wood, a wonderful place to spot black woodpeckers as they drill into trees looking for insects.

The slope begins to flatten out as you walk between fields, and the camino eventually joins the road at **Vilei**. Turn left onto the road and head towards Barbadelo.

Barbadelo (Ⓐ, 111km) was originally part of a large monastery that housed both nuns and monks, a co-habitation arrangement that didn't sit well with the powers at Samos, who staged an ecclesiastical coup in 1009. The church you see today was built soon afterwards and is the only monastery building that remains; it's dominated by a fortified tower, which has strange and fantastical animals carved into the stone blocks.

The slate-roofed stone farmhouses that dot the surrounding patchwork fields look like they should be on the western fringes of Ireland rather than in Spain. More distinctly Iberian are Barbadelos' *hórreos*, rectangular granaries built on stilts that are used to dry corn and keep it out of the reach of rodents. They usually have a cross on top for divine crop protection. Barbadelo's **albergue** (18 beds, kitchen, open all year) is on the right about 500m after the village.

From Barbadelo, walk through **Rente** (Ⓑ), passing the **Casa Nova de Rente** ($, ☎ 982 187854) in about 1km, then pass **Mercado** and **Peruscallo** (✕), where there's a restaurant.

Moss-covered dry stone walls line the route to **Morgade** (⬛), a one-house hamlet where there's a lovely old wooden *hórreo* in front of a dairy shed and an excellent café that sells mouthwatering homemade cakes. Just past the hamlet, the tiny *ermita* on the right has been built into the natural surroundings, using the natural uneven rock as its floor.

Walk through **Ferreiros** (🅐✖🅛, 102km), where there's an **albergue** (22 beds, kitchen, open all year), a café and a fountain, and the first vines since El Bierzo. Turn right at a sign for the Igrexia Romana at **Mirallos** (✖), which you'll soon reach. The church has a lovely Romanesque doorway and the adjacent cemetery is home to large, ornate tombs. There's also a restaurant next door.

The camino passes through a series of tiny hamlets: **Rozas**, **Moimentos**, **Montrás**, **Parrocha** and **Cotarelo**. Barns and farms in these places are fascinating, ad hoc ethnographic museums of antique ploughs, wooden racks and ox-carts gathering dust.

Finally, after some 7km, cross the dammed Río Miño into Portomarín. As you walk over the bridge, lean over the rails into the gloomy waters below to see walled lanes leading out from the submerged old town. Lots of birds call this artificial lake home, and it's common to see kingfishers, cormorants, egrets and herons.

Walk straight up the stairs at the end of bridge. Follow the cobbled street past a fountain, then turn right for the small town centre. The *albergue* is just past the church. To bypass the town, turn left at the foot of the stairs and follow the road.

Portomarín

🅐🅗✖🅛€🖤 (93km)

In 1956, it must have seemed to the people of Portomarín that their lucky charm had let them down. For centuries, locals believed that **La Virgen de las Nieves** protected them from drowning, and they built a shrine to her in the Middle Ages at the centre of the bridge over the Río Miño. Her statue and the town itself were threatened by Franco's plans to construct the Embalse de Belesar, a hydro-electric dam 40km downriver, creating a large lake and condemning the town to a watery grave. Maybe it was the Virgin herself who bent the dictator's ear, for a decision was eventually made to move Portomarín away from the grasp of the rising waters, although it took until 1962 to move the town's monuments to the new site above the west bank of the dammed river. A single span of the old bridge sits at the end of the new bridge, and the Iglesia de Santa María was placed on top to house the talismanic La Virgen de las Nieves.

The modern town somehow retains a lingering atmosphere of displacement and impermanence and is perched uncomfortably and unnaturally high above the Miño.

In Portomarín, all roads lead to the chunky, fortified **Iglesia de San Juan**, built in the thirteenth century by the Knights of St John. The church, which is also known as San Nicolás, has four towers and battlements on top, and it looks more like a castle keep than a place of worship, although its militaristic outline is softened by a magnificent rose window and carved doorway.

Accommodation
Albergue (160 beds, kitchen, open all year)
$ Pensión El Caminante (☎ 982 545176)
$$ Posada del Camino (☎ 982 545081)
$$ Hotel Villajardín (☎ 982 545252)
$$$$ Hotel Posada de Portomarín (☎ 982 545200)

From Portomarín, walk down the main

street, turn left at the main road and then turn right almost immediately, doubling back on yourself to cross a rickety metal footbridge. Turn right at the end of the bridge to head up a dirt track through oak trees. According to Aymeric Picaud's twelfth-century guide, this part of the camino was famous as an open-air brothel. The track shadows the C535 to Gonzar, which you'll reach in about 7km.

There's little more to **Gonzar** (**❹**▪**❧**, 85.5km) than the local dairy farm, and at times the smell from the cowshed can be overpowering. The **albergue** (20 beds, kitchen, open all year) has very strange showers with half-height, Wild West–style swinging doors.

In about 1km, enter **Castromaior** (**❻**▪**❧**▪**❦**), named after the large prehistoric *castro* that once stood north of here across the river. The ruins of a Roman camp have also been discovered on the edge of the village. Pass the small Iglesia de Santa María and the **Pensión Casa Maruja** ($, ☎ 982 189054). An ancient local legend tells of a pig herder girl who left pig snouts at Castromaior for the traditional annual sacrifice. Next day, she returned to find that the snouts had turned into lumps of coal, which she threw away. At the last moment she decided to keep a single lump. Next morning, she awoke to discover that the lump of coal had turned into a gold nugget. The girl rushed back for the rest of the coal, but by the time she arrived the lumps had vanished.

You'll reach **Hospital de la Cruz** (**❧**, 81km) in another 2km and **Ventas de Narón** (**❹❻✕▪❧**) just over 1km later. In 820, a few short years after the discovery of the tomb of Santiago, the Christians gained a bloody victory over the troops of the Emir of Córdoba here. You can stay at the **albergue** (22 beds, kitchen, open all year) or at **Casa Malor** ($).

From here to Palas de Rei, the road has been narrowed to make way for a gravel camino track. Climb out of the village and over the Serra de Ligonde, the watershed of the Río Miño and the Río Ulla, from where there are great views. Several significant Celtic settlements dot the route here, and a number of hamlets just off the camino incorporate the word *castro* (hill fort) into their name: Castro de Ligonde, Castro de Lardeiros, Castro de Gimonde and Castro de San Símon all have significant archaeological remains, and it's worth exploring these prehistoric treasures if you have time.

Walk through **Presbisa**, **Lameiros**, where there's a lovely *cruceiro*, then enter **Ligonde** (**❹**, 77.5km), a hamlet stretching out along the camino for several hundred metres. You can stay at the **albergue** here (20 beds, kitchen, open all year) or wait another 1km until **Airexe** (**❹**, 76km), where there's also another *cruceiro*. Airexe's **albergue** has 18 beds and a kitchen, and is open all year. The *albergues* are coming thick and fast now, and it's just 2km to the next one at **Portos** (**❹**, 74km), which has 20 beds and a kitchen and is open all year. From here, a lane on the right detours in 3km to the Monasterio de San Salvador at Vilar de Donas. The monastery was the official burial place of the *Caballeros de Santiago* (Knights of Santiago), and its fantastic frescoes show the Parable of the Ten Virgins.

Veer right at a fountain into **Lestedo** (**❻✕**), where you can stay and eat at the

Map 20 (key page 182)

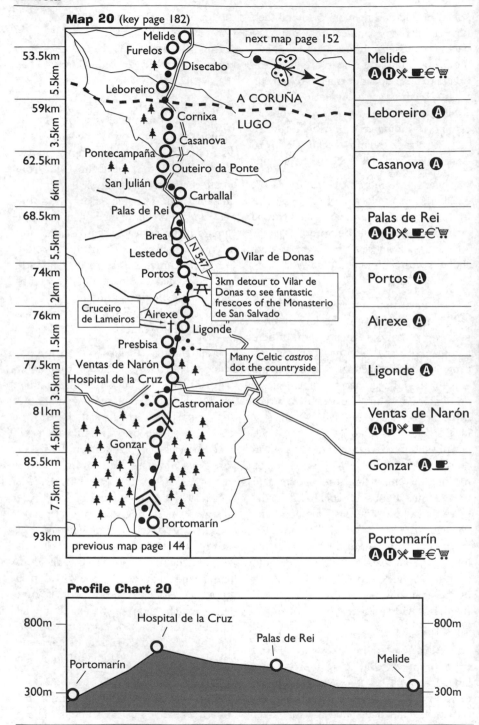

next map page 152

53.5km	**Melide** Ⓐ Ⓗ ✖ ☕ € 🛒
5.5km	
59km	**Leboreiro** Ⓐ
3.5km	
62.5km	**Casanova** Ⓐ
6km	
68.5km	**Palas de Rei** Ⓐ Ⓗ ✖ ☕ € 🛒
5.5km	
74km	**Portos** Ⓐ
2km	
76km	**Airexe** Ⓐ
1.5km	
77.5km	**Ligonde** Ⓐ
3.5km	
81km	**Ventas de Narón** Ⓐ Ⓗ ✖ ☕
4.5km	
85.5km	**Gonzar** Ⓐ ☕
7.5km	
93km	**Portomarín** Ⓐ Ⓗ ✖ ☕ € 🛒

Melide
Furelos
Disecabo
Leboreiro
A CORUÑA
Cornixa
LUGO
Casanova
Pontecampaña
Outeiro da Ponte
San Julián
Carballal
Palas de Rei
Brea
Lestedo
Vilar de Donas
N 547
Portos

3km detour to Vilar de Donas to see fantastic frescoes of the Monasterio de San Salvado

Cruceiro de Lameiros
Airexe
Ligonde
Presbisa

Many Celtic *castros* dot the countryside

Ventas de Narón
Hospital de la Cruz
Castromaior
Gonzar
Portomarín

previous map page 144

Profile Chart 20

800m — Hospital de la Cruz — 800m
Palas de Rei
Portomarín
Melide
300m — — 300m

gorgeous **Rectoral de Lestedo** ($$$, ☎ 982 153435). Pass through the hamlet of **Valos**, then just before the track joins the N547 main road, keep left in **Brea** (✗) along a dirt track between a restaurant and a picnic area.

Climb to the top of **Alto Rosario**, the name of both a hill and the hamlet that you'll soon pass through, picking up a cobbled track at the end of the hamlet. Soon afterwards, turn left onto a dirt lane, arriving at a picnic area and sports field with fantastic views of the valley below; on a clear day, it's possible to see Monte Pico Sacro near Santiago de Compostela from here. You're almost at Palas de Rei now, but there are rooms and food at **La Castaña** ($$).

Wind down into Palas de Rei, passing the modern church, where there's a fountain and a *cruceiro*, then head down some steps into town. The *albergue* is just to the left of the main street, down another flight of steps.

Palas de Rei
Ⓐ Ⓗ ✗ ⬛ € 🛒 (68.5km)

Palas de Rei's origins are murky. No one really knows where the name comes from and it doesn't appear in historical documents until the ninth century, although there's probably been a settlement here for much longer as the surrounding area is jammed with Roman and Celtic remains. What isn't in doubt is that Palas de Rei has always been an important stop on the camino, and marked the end of the twelfth stage in Aymeric Picaud's famous guide. Predictably, Picaud didn't like the town much, thinking it full of harlots who deserved, "not only be excommunicated, but stripped of everything and exposed to public ridicule, after having their noses cut off."

There's not much left from Palas de Rei's twelfth-century heyday, and the **Iglesia de San Tirso**'s Romanesque origins have been mostly obscured by later restorations.

Accommodation
Albergue (60 beds, open all year)
$ Hospedaje Gun Tina (☎ 982 380080)
$$ Pensión Ponterroxán (☎ 982 380132)
$$ Hostal Vilariño (☎ 982 380152)
$$$ Hotel Casa Benilde (☎ 982 380717)

The walk from Palas de Rei is a lovely, winding route on woodland tracks. You're quickly out of town and walking alongside the main road. Pass through **Carballal**, then cross the main road to follow a dirt track through trees. Don't be surprised if you're met by a chorus of frogs, as this section can be damp and swampy.

Soon the camino heads into **San Julián** (San Xulián). The twelfth-century Romanesque **Iglesia de San Julián** is worth a short visit, and the local architecture is very different here, with roofs made from tile rather than slate.

The legend of San Julián, the patron saint of ferrymen, innkeepers and circus performers, reads more like a Greek tragedy than the life of a saint. One day, Julián was out hunting when a deer he killed warned him that he would murder his own parents. To avoid this fate, Julián went into self-imposed exile, but a few years later, Julián's parents discovered his whereabouts and decided to visit. Julián was out at the time, and the parents were tired, so Julián's wife offered them her own bed to rest in. On his return, Julián thought that the people in his bed were his wife and a lover, and flew into a rage, murdering his parents with his sword. Horrified by what happened, Julián and his wife made the pilgrimage to Rome to repent, and set up a hospice for poor travellers and pilgrims. After years of helping people, an angel appeared and granted the couple divine pardon.

In **Outeiro da Ponte**, 1km later, rejoin the paved road and cross a bridge over the Río Pambre. Climb up the other side of the valley through the tiny hamlet of **Pontecampaña**, a lovely walk through oak trees along a stone trail grooved with many years of cart tracks. Rejoin the paved road and turn left into **Casanova** (Ⓐ, 62.5km), where there's an **albergue** (20 beds, kitchen, open all year).

At **Cornixa** (Ⓗ✕💷), a bar and restaurant straddle the camino, and you can stay at the **Casa de los Somozas** (**$$**, ☎ 981 507372).

You'll reach **Leboreiro** (Ⓐ, 59km) in less than a kilometre. The village declined sharply after its heyday in the eleventh to thirteenth centuries, when the **Iglesia de Santa María** was built to house a statue of the Virgin. Villagers following a lovely smell and a glowing light discovered the statue at a local fountain. They placed the Virgin in their church altar, but she miraculously returned to her fountain. For a few days, the villagers returned the statue to the altar, but by the following morning she had always reappeared at the fountain. Eventually, the villagers decided to honour the Virgin by carving a

tympanum and dedicating the church to her. Her ego satisfied, the Virgin stayed put, although some say that she returns to the fountain each night to comb her hair. The Casa de la Enfermería, an old pilgrim hospice, is just opposite the church. Modern pilgrims can stay at the **albergue** (20 beds, kitchen, open all year).

Head downhill to **Disecabo** and cross a humpbacked bridge dedicated to María Magdalena. The countryside is now much drier, with fewer trees and more thorn, broom and heather. Skirt some industrial land, then pass a picnic area with fountains paid for by the modern Knights of Santiago, who have marked the area with a giant cross.

In just over 1km, cross the four-arched mediaeval Ponte Velha into the village of **Furelos**, now merged with the larger town of Melide. The Iglesia de San Juan on the other side of the bridge offers guided tours, sometimes in English. Walk up Melide's main street, turn right at the roundabout, then take the first road to the left. At the edge of town, turn right for the *albergue*, or keep straight on to continue the camino.

Melide
Ⓐ Ⓗ ✕ 💷 € 🛒 (53.5km)

Archaeological evidence shows that people have lived in this area, slap bang in the middle of Galicia, since megalithic builders erected their *dolmens* almost 4000 years ago. The **Museo da Terra de Melide** is a wonderful place to learn more about the region's history and about traditional life, customs and craftsmanship.

Melide's religious monuments, like those of

many towns along the camino, are spread out along the pilgrim road. The **Iglesia de San Pedro** contains some fourteenth-century tombs, but they're overshadowed by the magnificently carved Cruceiro de Melide outside its doors. If it's open, the **Iglesia de Sancti Spiritus**, built with stones from the old castle and once part of a fourteenth-century Franciscan monastery, is worth visiting. Towards the western edge of town, the **Iglesia del Carmen** sits at the foot of a hill that was once the site of a castle and an ancient hill fort.

Don't pass through Melide without visiting a **pulpería**. At Pulpería Ezequiel on Melide's main street, sit at long, wooden benches and sample the house speciality: *pulpo* (octopus). The *pulpo* is sprinkled with Spanish paprika and drizzled with olive oil, then picked up from a rustic wooden platter with toothpicks. Mop up the tasty, spicy juice with hunks of bread, and wash the lot down with characteristically cloudy Ribeiro wine served in ceramic cups. On Sundays all over Galicia, street sellers serve *pulpo* fresh from big copper cauldrons.

Accommodation
Albergue (130 beds, kitchen, open all year)
$ Fonda Xaneiro I San Pedro 2 (☎ 981 505015)
$$ Hostal Carlos Avenida de Lugo 119 (☎ 981 507633)
$$ Hotel Xaneiro II Avenida de la Habana 43 (☎ 981 506140)

From Melide to Arzúa, there's a lot of up-and-down climbing as you traverse this part of Galicia's many small valleys. Less than 1km outside town, pass the twelfth-century Romanesque **Iglesia de Santa María de Melide**, which has some

beautiful frescoes inside. A little farther on, pass through **Carballos**. You're soon walking through eucalyptus trees, interspersed with the odd section of pine or oak. As in much of the rest of Galicia, local farmers are chopping down the native oak forest and planting fast-growing eucalyptus in its stead.

Walk through **Raído** and **A Peroxa**, then turn left to walk through **Boente** (💭), known for its local fountain, the Fonte da Saleta. The route changes to a dirt road once more, becoming a pleasant stroll through rolling countryside.

At **Castañeda** (🕒💭) you can stay at **Casa Milia ($$,** ☎ 981 515241), but there's no trace of the ovens where the stone blocks for Santiago's cathedral were finished. Pity the mediaeval pilgrims who carried the limestone from Triacastela to here! Pass through **Pedrido**, then you'll soon see Arzúa on the hill opposite. At the bottom of yet another valley and just after passing a café, cross the Río Isa as you enter the tiny hamlet of **Ribadiso do Baixo** (🅰💭, 42.5km). Also known to pilgrims as Puente Paradiso, it's a beautiful location with an excellent **albergue** (62 beds, kitchen, open all year) in the restored hospice of San Antón, which dates from the fourteenth century.

Walk uphill to follow a long approach through Arzúa's ugly outskirts into town. The *albergue* is just past the main square.

Arzúa
🅰🕒✕💭€🛒 (39km)

Arzúa is a bustling town, renowned throughout Spain for its smooth, creamy **cheese**. This local gastronomic delight is celebrated

Map 21 (key page 182)

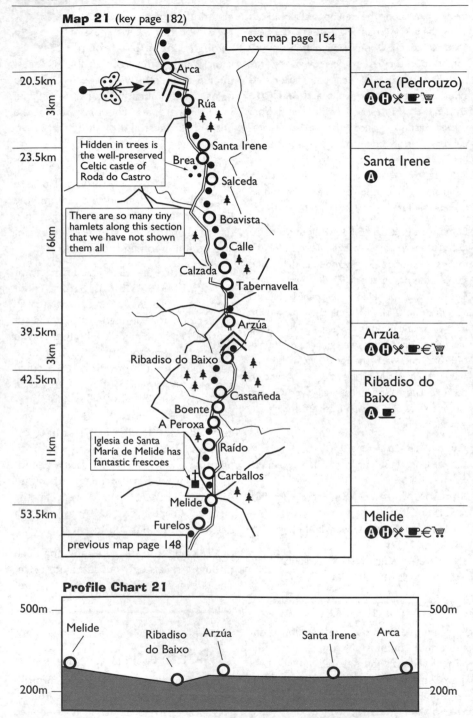

next map page 154

20.5km

3km

Arca

Rúa

Santa Irene

23.5km

Hidden in trees is
the well-preserved
Celtic castle of
Roda do Castro

Brea

Salceda

16km

There are so many tiny
hamlets along this section
that we have not shown
them all

Boavista

Calle

Calzada

Tabernavella

39.5km

Arzúa

3km

Ribadiso do Baixo

42.5km

Castañeda

Boente

A Peroxa

11km

Iglesia de Santa
María de Melide has
fantastic frescoes

Raído

Carballos

Melide

53.5km

Furelos

previous map page 148

Arca (Pedrouzo)
🅐🅗✖🍴🛒

Santa Irene
🅐

Arzúa
🅐🅗✖🍴€🛒

Ribadiso do
Baixo
🅐🍴

Melide
🅐🅗✖🍴€🛒

Profile Chart 21

500m

Melide

Ribadiso
do Baixo

Arzúa

Santa Irene

Arca

500m

200m

200m

with a statue of a cheesemaker in the main square, and if you're lucky enough to be here in March, you can celebrate alongside the locals at the town's annual cheese festival. Traditionally, Arzúa was the last stop before Santiago, although many pilgrims now opt to stop closer to their final destination.

The **Iglesia de Santiago** dates from the 1950s; inside, the saint adopts his war-like Matamoros pose on top of the nineteenth-century *retablo*.

Accommodation
Albergue (46 beds, kitchen, open all year)
$$ **Pensión Teodora** (☎ 981 500083)
$$ **Hostal Mesón do Peregrino** (☎ 981 500830)
$$$ **Hotel Suiza** (☎ 981 500862)

The valleys are gentler from Arzúa onwards, making the final approach into Santiago a lovely walk. Camino legend tells of a local woman baking bread, who was asked to provide food for a pilgrim. The woman denied that she had any food, and the pilgrim cursed, "I hope that your bread turns to stone!" Sure enough, when the woman returned to her oven, she found a loaf of stone.

The camino passes through the tiny hamlets of **Preguntoño**, **Cortobe**, **Tabernavella** and **Calzada**. At **Calle** (■), some 7km from Arzúa, walk past a fountain and down a wide stone slab path, then walk under an *hórreo* that attractively straddles the camino. There are two cafés in this tiny village, and great competition between the two for passing pilgrim trade.

After **Boavista**, which you'll reach in 1.5km, the camino heads through farmland, criss-crossing the C547 and passing

Alto and **Salceda** (■), where there's a bar. Walk through **Xen** and **Ras**, then carry on into **Brea** (H), where you can stay at the **Hospedaje O Meson** ($$, ☎ 981 511040).

There's a fountain and picnic area at the **Alto de Santa Irene** (✕■). At the top of a nearby hill is the the Roda do Castro, a Celtic hill fort, with circular defensive walls that are three metres thick in places. There are two short routes to **Santa Irene** (A, 23.5km). Either stay on the left-hand side of the road and follow the track to reach the **Albergue de Santa Irene** (15 beds, open all year), or cross the road for the **Albergue Santa Irene de la Xunta de Galicia** (36 beds, kitchen, open all year). The eighteenth-century chapel is dedicated to the town's namesake, a beautiful young Portuguese nun who died in 653 defending her vow of chastity in the ancient town of Scalabris.

The camino soon approaches **Rúa** (H✕■), a row of houses prettified with flowerpots; turn right just before the houses for the **Hotel O Pino** ($$, ☎ 981 511148), or keep straight on for the **Casa do Acivro** ($$, ☎ 981 511316) and the **Casa Calvo** ($$, ☎ 981 814401). In another 1km, you'll reach **Arca** (Pedrouzo) (A H✕■🍽). Turn left for the *albergue* or cross the road to continue the camino towards Santiago. The **albergue** (120 beds, kitchen, open all year) is next door to a supermarket. There are also rooms at the **Restaurante Compás** ($$, ☎ 981 511309).

The route from Arca heads through forest and farmland, although brash new houses spring up as you near Santiago.

Map 22 (key page 182)

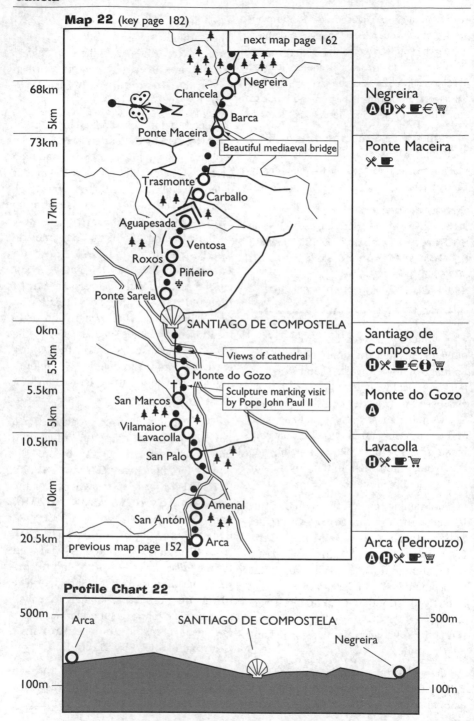

next map page 162

68km
5km
73km
17km

Chancela
Negreira
Barca
Ponte Maceira

Beautiful mediaeval bridge

Trasmonte
Carballo

Aguapesada
Ventosa
Roxos
Piñeiro
Ponte Sarela

0km
5.5km

SANTIAGO DE COMPOSTELA

Views of cathedral

5.5km
5km
10.5km

Monte do Gozo

Sculpture marking visit
by Pope John Paul II

San Marcos
Vilamaior
Lavacolla
San Palo

10km
20.5km

San Antón
Amenal
Arca

previous map page 152

Negreira
Ⓐ Ⓗ ✕ ⏛ € 🛒

Ponte Maceira
✕ ⏛

Santiago de Compostela
Ⓗ ✕ ⏛ € ⓘ 🛒

Monte do Gozo
Ⓐ

Lavacolla
Ⓗ ✕ ⏛ 🛒

Arca (Pedrouzo)
Ⓐ Ⓗ ✕ ⏛ 🛒

Profile Chart 22

500m
Arca
SANTIAGO DE COMPOSTELA
500m
Negreira
100m
100m

Pass through **San Antón** and **Amenal**, then climb uphill through a mostly eucalyptus forest. After about 2km you come to the main road at a large roundabout; turn left and follow the road past the airport. There's a large stone here, indicating that you've arrived in the district of Santiago, proof that you've just about made it. Head downhill past the end of the airport runway, which can be quite dramatic when planes land or take off.

Walk into **San Palo** (✖), where there's a restored church and a restaurant. Larger groups of pilgrims may want to rent the three-bedroom **Casa Porta de Santiago** ($$$$, ☎ 902 889761). Otherwise, stay on the minor road for the 2km to Lavacolla.

Lavacolla

Ⓗ✖⊒⊒☷ (10.5km)

In the Middle Ages, Lavacolla was a ceremonial stop for pilgrims who would clean themselves up here before heading into Santiago. Although today's pilgrims may seem smelly, in the Middle Ages the whiff was much worse, as Christians hardly ever washed, and it was common to mock Jews and Muslims who were more concerned with personal hygiene and bathed regularly. Revoltingly, this may have been the pilgrims' first wash since they began the camino.

Pilgrims would wash themselves in the small river at Lavacolla, called Lavamentula in the *Codex Calixtinus*, paying particular attention to their private parts: *mentula* means phallus, and *colla* means scrotum. Should you wish to avail yourself of Lavacolla's facilities, the river is on the other side of the village.

Accommodation
$$ Hostal San Paio (☎ 981 888221)
$$ Hotel Garcas (☎ 981 888225)

If you're in a group and hung up on pilgrim traditions, start running. The first one to reach Monte do Gozo and the view of Santiago cathedral, more than 5km away, will be declared king, a custom that seems to undo all the good work of the hosedown at Lavacolla.

The camino skirts Lavacolla's bars and passes close to the **Iglesia de Benaval**. The church, together with the Cruz de Benaval that stands in front of it, is named after the plaintive cry of a local rebel. Juán Pourón, who led an early fourteenth-century uprising, cried out to the Virgen de Belén, *Ven e valme* (come and save me), as he was sentenced to be hung for his crimes. The Virgin catapulted him to heaven instantly, denying local officials the pleasure of a hanging.

Once past the church, cross the main road and head down to the river, stopping here if you're in need of a wash. Climb uphill to **Vilamaior**, pass the militaristic San Marcos campground (⊒) and turn right at a TV station. Climb a short rise, from where you can make out the crazy hilltop sculpture at the top of Monte do Gozo. Turn right and then walk through the hamlet of **San Marcos** (⊒☷) and reach the Monte do Gozo in less than a kilometre.

The **Monte do Gozo** (Ⓐ, 5.5km) is the Mount of Joy of camino tradition, from where pilgrims got their first, rapturous view of Santiago's cathedral spires.

Santiago

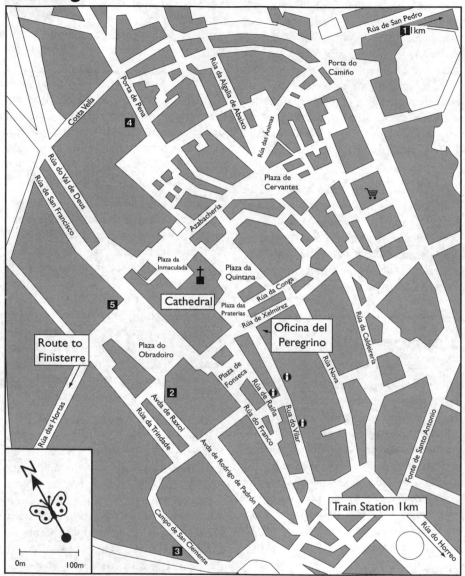

Rúa de San Pedro

1 km

Porta do Camiño

Costa Vella

Porta de Pena

Rúa da Algalia de Abaixo

Rúa do Val de Deus

Rúa de San Francisco

Rúa das Ánimas

Plaza de Cervantes

Azabachería

4

Plaza da Inmaculada

Plaza da Quintana

Rúa da Conga

Cathedral

Plaza das Praterías

Rúa de Xelmírez

5

Oficina del Peregrino

Rúa da Caldeirería

Route to Finisterre

Plaza do Obradoiro

Plaza de Fonseca

Rúa Nova

Rúa das Hortas

Avda de Raxoi

Rúa da Trindade

2

Rúa de Raíña

Rúa do Franco

Rúa do Vilar

Avda de Rodrigo de Padrón

Fonte de Santo Antonio

Campo de San Clemente

3

Train Station 1km

Rúa do Horreo

N

0m   100m

Accommodation

1 Albergue Seminario Mayor

2 Hostal La Estela

3 Hostal Alameda

4 Costa Vella

5 Hostal de los Reyes Católicos

Today, trees and suburbs block the view, and your eyes are drawn instead to the sculpture erected to celebrate Pope John Paul II's 1993 Holy Year visit. A few hundred metres later, the **albergue** (500 beds, kitchen, open all year), also part of 1993's building frenzy, does much to relieve the pressure on accommodation in Santiago during peak times. It's also soul-crushingly awful, and looks as if it was designed by a Butlins architect going through a bad bout of depression.

It's about 5km from Monte do Gozo to the centre of Santiago, but the route is well marked with signposts high above the sidewalk. Opposite the **Capilla de San Lázaro** (❹), which stands on the site of a twelfth-century lepers' hospital, there's an **albergue** (80 beds, open all year). Follow the Calle de los Concheiros through modern suburbs for a couple of kilometres, passing the **Albergue Acuário** (50 beds, open all year) then turn left to walk down Rúa de San Pedro.

Enter Santiago proper through the Porta do Camino, the historic entry point into the old city, and one of seven gates through the former city walls. Walk down Rúa das Casas Reais and the Rúa das Animas to the small Plaza de Cervantes, then head right up Rúa da Azabachería, and cross over the Plaza de la Inmaculada. Pass under the Arco del Obispo and arrive at the Plaza de Obradoiro and your destination, the cathedral at Santiago de Compostela.

Santiago de Compostela

❶✕◩€❶🍴 (0km)

It's worth planning to spend at least two days in Santiago de Compostela. The city, a UNESCO World Heritage site, is one of the most beautiful in Europe, and the mostly pedestrianized old centre is a maze of narrow cobbled streets and plazas that make wandering around Santiago a dream-like, random experience. The religious zeal of the pilgrimage is tempered by a thriving university whose students drive a wicked nightlife.

The first thing most pilgrims do on arrival in Santiago is visit the **cathedral**, give Santiago a hug and get their *compostela*. Mediaeval pilgrims would spend their first night in vigil at the cathedral and, if it was open, they would gather in front of the high altar, jostling for the best spot. This could get nasty, and in 1207 the cathedral had to be cleansed and reconsecrated because things had got so violently out of hand.

The original church was built by Alfonso II to house Santiago's tomb. Alfonso III the Greater built an even bigger church on the same spot in 899, but this was destroyed by Almanzor's Moorish army in 997. Starting from scratch, construction of the present building began in 1075 and was completed in 1211. Skilled craftsmen came to Galicia from all over Europe, and hunks of limestone were hefted from Triacastela to Castañeda, where they were formed into the cathedral's stone blocks.

The cathedral is so massive and so dominates Santiago that its doors open out on to three separate city squares. The most dramatic entrance leads from the huge Plaza de Obradoiro, up the imposing double staircase to the Baroque **Obradoiro Façade**. Before you climb the stairs, walk backwards to the far side of the square so that you can take in the whole, glorious façade. For an even better view, come to the square on a clear night, face away from the façade, then lie down on the square's cobbles and look up at the cathedral.

As you enter from this side, you'll suddenly reach the jaw-dropping **Pórtico de la Gloria**, built in 1168 by the Maestro Mateo, and the main entrance into the cathedral before the outer façade was built. Art historians suggest that this doorway inspired the movement from Romanesque to Gothic architecture across Europe. The *pórtico* is jammed with Christian symbolism and, like most things in the cathedral, it's worth visiting more than once. The middle pillar of the Pórtico de la Gloria depicts the Tree of Jesse, Santiago and the Virgin.

Over the years, a ritual for arriving pilgrims has developed. First, touch your right hand in the middle of the central column of the **Tree of Jesse** to give thanks for your safe arrival. Centuries of devoted hands have worn five finger grooves deep into the marble pillar, a humbling reminder of the tradition you're following. Around the back of the pillar is a small bust of **Maestro Mateo**, the architect of the Pórtico de la Gloria. Butting his head three times is said to impart some of his considerable intelligence to you.

Proceed up to the high altar. On top of it sits Santiago Matamoros shouldered by massive gold angels. On the right-hand side as you look at the altar you'll find a narrow set of stairs that lead behind the figure of **Santiago Peregrino**. Climb up into the shrine and embrace the thirteenth-century, jewelled statue of St James from behind. The gold crown that pilgrims could place on their heads has now sadly disappeared, along with the pilgrim tradition of placing their own hats on Santiago's head.

Next, head down into the **crypt** to see the casket that's said to contain the bones of the saint and two of his disciples, Theodore and Athanasius. The tomb of Santiago was first discovered in the ninth century, enclosed in a stone mausoleum on this ancient necropolis. Santiago's bones were hidden several times over the centuries to keep them away from thieves and kings who wanted the relics for themselves. The bones were so well hidden that their exact location was forgotten, but pilgrims continued to venerate an urn on the altar that was believed to hold the saint's bones. Excavations in the late nineteenth century unearthed some bones, said to be those of Santiago when the discoverer went temporarily blind. Pope Leo XIII verified their validity a few years later, and the remains now rest in a silver coffin below the altar.

Every day at noon, there's a pilgrims' Mass. The ceremony often culminates in the swinging of the **botafumeiro** (smoke belcher), a massive silver incense burner said to be the largest in the Catholic world. It takes up to eight men in a team called a *tiraboleiros* to tie the knots and get the massive silver apparatus swinging across the cathedral. This *botafumeiro* dates from 1851, after the original was stolen by Napoleon's troops when they looted the cathedral. During Mass, the best place to sit is on either side of the main altar, so that the *botafumeiro* seems to skim the top of your head before it swings back to the roof of the cathedral.

If you're lucky enough to arrive in Santiago during a Holy Year, when the Día de Santiago, July 25, falls on a Sunday (2010, 2021), you can enter the cathedral through the **Puerta del Perdón**. The door is opened on the eve of a Holy Year and firmly closed on December 31.

To receive your **compostela**, final proof that you've completed the pilgrimage, present your stamped pilgrim's passport at the Oficina del Peregrino on the second floor of the Casa del Deán, just off Plaza Platerías on the south side of the cathedral. The friendly but busy staff will record your nationality and your place of departure, to be read out at the next day's pilgrims' Mass. If your motivations for the pilgrimage aren't religious or spiritual, you'll get a colourful alternative certificate instead of the traditional *compostela*. The staff also acts as a quasi-tourist office, pointing pilgrims in the direction of accommodation and transport.

Dominating the northern side of the **Plaza de Obradoiro** and now a grand five-star hotel, the Hostal de los Reyes Católicos was originally built on the orders of Fernando and Isabel to house pilgrims and provide them with medical treatment. As part of its continuing obligation to pilgrims, the *parador* provides free meals to the first ten pilgrims to arrive at 9am, 12pm and 7pm. You'll eat what the restaurant staff eat, washed down with a bottle or two of wine. Arrive early as there's almost always a crowd of hungry pilgrims wanting to eat for free. To line up for your free meal, face the *parador* and turn left to walk along the front of the building to the underground parking garage and present the doorman with a copy of your *compostela*.

There's much more to see in Santiago. The market is great for picking up picnic supplies or ogling the strange fish. There are lots of trinket shops hoping to lure money from your wallet, and you can buy anything from tacky key chains decorated with a *flecha amarilla* (yellow arrow), to a life-size replica of the *botafumeiro*.

There are three **turismos** in Santiago: the municipal, the camino and the regional ones are all on Rúa do Vilar.

Accommodation

Pilgrims can stay at the **Albergue Seminario Menor**, just outside town (60 beds, open all year). For the *albergues* on the camino just before Santiago, see the descriptions in the text.

$ Hostal La Estela, Raxoi 1 (☎ 981 582796)
$$ Hostal Alameda, Rúa do San Clemente 32 (☎ 981 588100)
$$$ Costa Vella, Calle Puerta da Pena 17 (☎ 981 569530)
$$$$ Hostal de los Reyes Católicos, Plaza de Obradoiro (☎ 981 582200)

Although most pilgrims end their journey at Santiago, it's well worth lacing up your boots and continuing to the ocean.

The camino to Finisterre predates the mediaeval pilgrimage by at least a millennium. Celts and other ancient peoples travelled to the solar temple of Ara Solis, on the tip of Cabo Finisterre, to worship the sun, or simply walked as far west as

they could without getting their feet wet.

Romans thought that the westernmost tip of Spain, Finis Terrae, was the end of the world, and would watch with concern as the sea engulfed the sun each night, hoping that it would rise again the next morning. In fact, a quick glance at a map will show that bits of Portugal stick out further into the Atlantic than Finisterre.

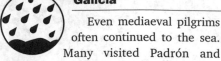

Even mediaeval pilgrims often continued to the sea. Many visited Padrón and Muxía, places connected with Santiago's miraculous arrival in Spain, but churches dedicated to the saint and pilgrim hospices also lined the route to Finisterre.

The easy-to-follow *Camino de Fisterra* is much quieter than the *camino francés* before Santiago. The locals along the path aren't overly burdened by throngs of pilgrims and are often genuinely pleased to see you. Dogs are happy to see you too, but some can be vicious, so take care. If you're returning to Santiago, consider leaving some equipment at your hotel and travelling light to Finisterre.

Stand in the Plaza do Obradoiro facing the *parador*, and turn left to walk down Rúa das Hortas. In about 200m, cross a road to walk along Rúa do Cruceiro do Gaio, which changes its name, first to Rúa do Pozo de Bar and then to Rúa de San Lorenzo. Occasional faded yellow arrows are painted on the road but, apart from these, there are no signs until you reach a park in a few hundred metres. Turn right at a concrete bollard here, the first of many on a mostly well-marked trail, to head through the small park, then turn left at the end of park and walk down Costa do Cano. Cross a stone bridge at **Ponte Sarela**, turn left to walk down a dirt track, then at a fork in 50m, take the left-hand (lower) track, which soon narrows to a path.

You're soon in the countryside, and the rapid exit from Santiago is a stark contrast to your arrival in the city. Walk uphill on a trail lined with foxgloves, ferns and blackberries, turning around for great views of Santiago behind you. In little more than 1km, you'll reach **Piñeiro**,

where the traditional architecture is overwhelmed by big, modern houses as Santiago's commuter belt stretches westwards.

Leave Piñeiro on a narrow tarmac road. It's a lovely, pastoral scene, with great views back towards the village of meadows, stone houses and *hórreos*. You'll reach **Vilariñas** in about 2km, then enter **Roxos** (▆✕) in another 2km, where there's a restaurant/bar called Meson Alto do Vento.

Turn right at the restaurant, then walk downhill on the road through **Ventosa** (▆✕). The café here is usually open earlier than the one in Roxos. Turn right down a narrow tarmac road and keep heading downhill into **Aguapesada** (✕🛒), a village of pretty stone houses with small square windows. At the bottom of the valley, turn left down a paved stone street next to a lovely, single-arched mediaeval bridge that's been recently restored. Catch your breath here, as it's a very steep, 2km-long climb to **Carballo**, scenically set amongst fields and trees, and dotted with the region's traditional red-roofed stone houses. There are lots of songbirds here, too, and gorgeous views across another beautiful valley of red-topped houses. You'll soon reach **Trasmonte** (▆), which boasts two tiny bars.

Walk downhill through **Reino** and **Burgueiros**, a wealthy hamlet with lots of big new houses, and arrive at **Ponte Maceira** (✕▆, 73km) in less than 2km. The gorgeous village is idyllically set in a brilliant green valley next to the wide Río Tambre. The bridge after which Ponte Maceira is named elegantly spans the river; from its centre you may see a heron calmly standing at the edge of the river, or a kingfisher darting just above the water. Construction of the bridge began at the end of the fourteenth century, though much of what you see today dates from a sympathetic eighteenth-century restoration.

Turn right to cross the river, then turn left at the end of the bridge. On the other side of the river you'll see the Capilla de San Blas and a mediaeval *pazo*, a grand Galician country house, surrounded by stately gardens. Walk past a *cruceiro* on your left, gruesomely decorated with a carved skull and crossbones at its base. Follow the lovely valley for a kilometre or so, passing under a road bridge and the "new" nineteenth-century bridge that leads to Ponte Maceira Nova.

Walk through **Barca** and **Chancela**, then turn left at the main road to enter Negreira. Pass some apartment buildings and a statue of a pilgrim on the main road into town. The *albergue* is just outside town; to reach it, turn left a few hundred metres after the statue down the Rúa de San Mauro. In a few hundred metres, pass under the stone arch that links Pazo de Cotón with Capela de San Mauro. Cross a bridge over the Río Barcala, and turn left 100m later up a narrow tarmac road. You'll reach the *albergue* in less than 1km.

Negreira

Ⓐ Ⓗ ✕ ⌷ € ☕ (68km)

Negreira is a modern town with decadent pastry shops and good seafood restaurants. The town's notable monument is the fortified, mediaeval Pazo del Cotón. Its solid grey exterior was restored in the seventeenth century, and it's joined to the Capilla de San Mauro by an enclosed, arched walkway.

The modern **albergue** (16 beds, kitchen, open all year) has the twin luxuries of single beds and modern, sex-segregated bathrooms. There are extra mattresses for summer overflow.

$$ Hostal Residencial Tamara (☎ 981 885201)

$$ Hostal-Restaurante La Mezquita (☎ 981 885128)

The route from Negreira to Olveiroa passes through a mix of forest and farms. There's almost nowhere to buy supplies, so make sure you stock up on lunch and dinner provisions before leaving Negreira.

The beginning is especially lovely, heading along an old trail, with fantastic views across multiple valleys. Pass through **Zas** and **Rapote** then follow a lovely stretch of oak forest with ferns, ivy and big black slugs to **Peña** (⌷, 60km). You'll need to pop up to the main road to visit the village bar; otherwise carry on through the village past a church and a *cruceiro*. Join a road and keep straight on through **Porto Camiño**, then turn right to walk along tracks and roads to **Vilaserio** (Ⓐ⌷, 56km). The village bar, which also has limited supplies, is the last refreshment for 8km. You can sleep on mattresses at the village school, which acts as Vilaserio's makeshift *albergue*.

Follow the road to **Cornado**, then follow mostly farm tracks to **Maroñas**. Notice the different style of *hórreos* in the village: Maroñas' granaries are made entirely of stone boulders, as the rain-drenched Galician climate rots wood quickly, and stone is plentiful locally. Walk through the village, then turn left at a T-junction 1km later to head into **Santa**

Map 23 (key page 182)

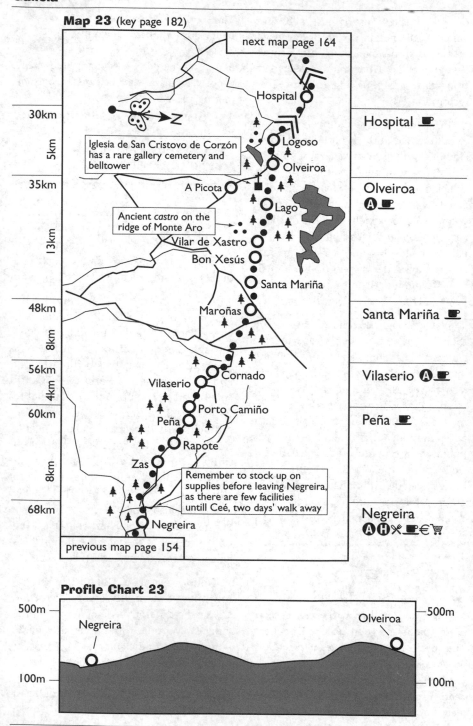

next map page 164

Hospital

30km

5km

Iglesia de San Cristovo de Corzón
has a rare gallery cemetery and
belltower

Logoso

Olveiroa

35km

A Picota

Lago

13km

Ancient *castro* on the
ridge of Monte Aro

Vilar de Xastro

Bon Xesús

Santa Mariña

48km

8km

Maroñas

56km

4km

Cornado

Vilaserio

60km

Porto Camiño

Peña

8km

Rapote

Zas

Remember to stock up on
supplies before leaving Negreira,
as there are few facilities
untill Ceé, two days' walk away

68km

Negreira

previous map page 154

Hospital 🍺

Olveiroa
Ⓐ🍺

Santa Mariña 🍺

Vilaserio Ⓐ🍺

Peña 🍺

Negreira
Ⓐ🏠✕🍺€🛒

Profile Chart 23

500m

Negreira

Olveiroa

500m

100m

100m

Mariña (🍴, 48km). Turn left at the main road, passing two bars on the right.

Keep straight on the road for about 500m, then turn right up a paved road into the hamlets of **Bon Xesús** and **Vilar de Xastro**, skirting **Monte Aro**, where there are some remains of an ancient *castro*. On the other side of the hill, there are fantastic views of the surrounding countryside and the Embalse de Fervenza, and there are many *rubias gallega*, Galicia's typical rust-red cows, in the fields. Walk downhill into **Lago**, then turn right next to a bus shelter at **Abeleiroas**. There are fabulous views of modern windmills up ahead. From here, you can detour to **A Picota** (🏠🍴), almost 4km away, where there are good shops and the **Casa Jurjo** (**$$$**, ☎ 981 852015).

Otherwise, continue along the paved road lined with gorse and pine trees. After a couple of kilometres, you arrive at the unusual Iglesia de San Cristovo de Corzón. The church is completely detached from its belltower and the arched cemetery looks like a gallery of graves around the church; the graveyard itself contains some splendid-looking crosses. Turn left just after the church, then turn right at the main road to cross the much-restored sixteenth-century bridge over the Río Xallas, where locals fought Napoleon's troops during the Peninsula War. In 2km, you'll reach Olveiroa; turn left, then right for the *albergue*.

Olveiroa (🅰🍴, 35km) is a tiny village with stunning examples of rural architecture. Its houses are made of thick stone walls, village *hórreos* are made of stone and are precariously balanced on mushroom-shaped legs; the village's *cruceiro* is a lovely one. The **albergue** (35 beds, kitchen, open all year) has separate, beautifully restored stone buildings for sleeping, eating and relaxing, with farm animals right next door. The *hospitalera* cooks a wonderful meal, and pilgrims chip in with bread, cheese and whatever else they have, then sit at a communal table in front of a roaring fire. The village bar sells *bocadillos* and bottles of wine.

To leave Olveiroa, turn left next to the village *lavadero* (wash house) to walk over a concrete bridge just before the main road. Head uphill, looking out for a hill fort on your left. There are great views of the river in the gorge below, and of the hills and windmills that surround you. Descend to the river, and cross it via a concrete bridge. Follow a dirt track into **Logoso**, then just over 1km later, reach **Hospital** (🍴, 30km), which is dominated by a massive carbide factory. The bar on the road serves great *bocadillos*, the last food for 14km.

A few hundred metres later, the camino splits. The right-hand turn takes you to Muxia, a popular pilgrim destination just north of Finisterre. Turn left to continue on your way to Finisterre, walking past the carbide factory. Soon after you leave its belching fumes behind, turn right down a dirt track. Follow the track through moorland, easy on the feet after yesterday's paved roads. If the skies are clear, you can see Cabo Finisterre and if the wind is in the right direction, you'll be able to smell the salt air.

Reach the **Santuario de Nosa Señora das Neves** in about 5km. Near the restored *santuario*, there's a *fonte*

Map 24 (key page 182)

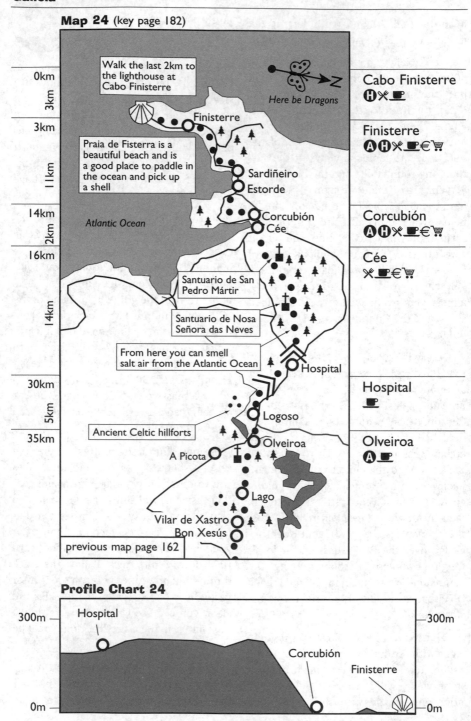

Walk the last 2km to the lighthouse at Cabo Finisterre

Here be Dragons

Cabo Finisterre

Finisterre

Praia de Fisterra is a beautiful beach and is a good place to paddle in the ocean and pick up a shell

Sardiñeiro

Estorde

Atlantic Ocean

Corcubión

Cée

Finisterre

Corcubión

Cée

Santuario de San Pedro Mártir

Santuario de Nosa Señora das Neves

From here you can smell salt air from the Atlantic Ocean

Hospital

Hospital

Logoso

Olveiroa

Ancient Celtic hillforts

A Picota

Olveiroa

Lago

Vilar de Xastro
Bon Xesús

previous map page 162

0km
3km
3km
11km
14km
2km
16km
14km
30km
5km
35km

Profile Chart 24

300m — Hospital

Corcubión

Finisterre

0m

300m

0m

santa (holy fountain) said to cure all manner of ailments. Each September 8, local people arrive here for a *romería* (pilgrimage). There's a *cruceiro* in the field below.

From here, it's mostly uphill to the **Santuario de San Pedro Mártir**, whose *fonte santa* is thought to heal verrucas, rheumatism and, happily for tired pilgrims, sore feet. Keep straight on, heading steadily downhill. The wind rushes through the sparse eucalyptus trees here; a wonderfully haunting sound when it's fine, but a bit miserable in rough weather. The track gets steeper as you descend into Cée, and even on a cloudy day you should be able to see the sea by now.

Walk into **Cée** (✗ ♨ € ☕, 16km), turning right onto the main road. Turn left down a side street 500m later, then walk down a flight of steps and turn right to follow a street to the main square. Yellow arrows can be hard to see on this stretch. Turn left to follow the waterfront road, then walk past the hospital and into Corcubión, now merged into Cée. Yellow arrows direct you right almost immediately; ignore these if you want to buy provisions in Corcubión.

Corcubión (Ⓐ Ⓗ ✗ ♨ € ☕, 14km) has some lovely manor houses, emblazoned with maritime-motif crests. There's a range of accommodation, including **La Cirena** ($, ☎ 981 745036), **Las Hortensias** ($$$, ☎ 981 746125) and **El Hórreo** ($$$, ☎ 981 745500). The *albergue* is about 1km out of town. To get there, turn right just before a church, then keep left at a fork. Walk through the Plaza de Castelao towards the Iglesia de San Marcos, a thirteenth-century church with neo-Gothic towers and a fifteenth-century sculpture of the church's patron Saint. At the church door, take a sharp right up some steps, and follow the street to a small square called Campo de Rollo. Cross straight over to a tiny, high-walled lane, and follow its overgrown route uphill.

Turn left once you meet another lane at the top of the hill, then turn right soon afterwards. Cross the main road and reach the **albergue** (20 beds, kitchen, open all year), which doesn't open until 4pm. Follow a track, then rejoin the road and head into Estorde.

In about 500m, you'll arrive at the main road again. Turn left here, then turn right at a bend about 300m later, veering right soon afterwards onto a track. In a kilometre or so, turn right on rejoining the main road and follow it into the village of **Estorde** (Ⓗ ✗ ♨), where you can stay at the **Playa de Estorde** ($$$, ☎ 981 745585). Keep on the busy main road to **Sardiñeiro** (Ⓗ ✗ ♨ ☕), where the **Restaurante Nicola** ($$, ☎ 981 743741) has rooms.

Just 50m after the beach, turn right down a narrow road, then turn immediately left down a small lane; climb slowly along the old Rúa da Finisterra. The camino heads through a beautiful pine forest, then crosses the road to head down a gully towards a tiny, dramatic cove, before climbing up the other side to meet the main road once more. Take the next left along a paved road down to the beach at Finisterre.

To get to Finisterre, either stroll along the beach to collect your scallop shell and splash about in the sea, or walk along a broad boardwalk into town. Look out for a marker with a downward-pointing scallop shell here, showing that your journey is almost at an end. Finisterre's *albergue* is just past the port.

Finisterre

Ⓐ Ⓗ ✕ ▆ € 🛒 (3km)

Finisterre is a working port with all the services of a small town. A fifteenth-century *cruceiro* stands in front of the twelfth-century Romanesque-Gothic **Iglesia de Santa María de Areas**. Domenico Laffi, the Italian camino chronicler, visited the church in the seventeenth century; the chapel next door was once a pilgrim hospice.

Finisterre shows few other signs of its camino past. Its character comes more from the sea, and it's fascinating to wander around the port, watching the primary-coloured fishing boats in the bay or chatting with fishermen as they mend gnarled nets. The town has a couple of great fish restaurants if you fancy a night on the town, and a cluster of down-at-heel bars and cafés if you hanker after something earthier.

Pilgrims who walk or cycle from Santiago to Finisterre are entitled to a *fisterrana*, a certificate of completion of the pilgrimage; you can get yours from the *hospitalera* at the *albergue*.

Accommodation
Finisterre's **albergue** (40 beds, kitchen, open all year) doesn't open until 7pm.
$ Hostal Cabo Finisterre (☎ 981 740000)
$ Hostal Rivas (☎ 981 740027)
$$ Hotel Finisterre (☎ 981 740000)
$$ Hotel O Semáforo (☎ 981 725869)

From Finisterre, it's a short walk to the end of the world. To continue to the *faro*

(lighthouse), walk past the *albergue*, turn right in a couple of hundred metres at Plaza Ara Solis, then turn left 50m later past the Capella de Nossa Senhora del Buensuccesso. Turn left when you reach the main road, and follow it all the way to Cabo Finisterre, just over 2km away, watching out for cars as there's no shoulder. There are great views out to sea when the sun's out, but the walk is also murkily marvellous in bad weather.

You'll soon reach **Cabo Finisterre** (Ⓗ ✕ ▆, 0km), the end of the world perched on a rocky headland. The Celts believed that the surrounding ocean was the Sea of Tenesbrosum, home to monsters and the gateway to paradise. The Romans were convinced that Finis Terrae was the end of the world, where the sun was engulfed by the sea each night.

There are great views from the **Vista Monte do Facho**, high above the lighthouse. The *menhir* that once stood here was the scene of Celtic fertility rites, and couples copulated against the rock to increase their chances of conception before prudish church officials tore down the *menhir* in the eighteenth century.

There's no trace of Ara Solis, the temple that drew sun-worshipping Iron Age pilgrims: you'll have to make do with the solid, whitewashed *faro* (lighthouse), a hotel-restaurant, and a couple of pilgrim highlights. Below the lighthouse there's a small sculpture of a pair of walking boots, where profligate pilgrims traditionally burn their shoes to celebrate their arrival at the cape. Nearby, a concrete post with a downward pointing scallop shell marks the end of the camino, a familiar and fittingly poignant symbol of your journey's end.

Reference

❓ Pilgrim Associations

Pilgrim associations are great places to get advice and to pick up a *credencial* (pilgrim passport) before you go.

The **Confraternity of Saint James** (☎ 020 7928 9988; www.csj.org.uk) is the most well-established and -respected English-language pilgrims' association. It promotes and conducts research into the camino, publishes a newsletter, maintains a library, organizes meetings and runs two *albergues*.

American Pilgrims on the Camino (www.americanpilgrims.com) publish a newsletter and run a list-serv. In Canada, **The Little Company of Pilgrims** (www.santiago.ca) publish a newsletter and offer helpful advice.

Irish pilgrims can get useful information from the **Irish Society of the Friends of St James**. The web site (www.stjamesirl.com) includes an electronic notice board for announcements.

The **Confraternity of Saint James of South Africa** has a useful web site (www.geocities.com/marievanus) with helpful tips and information on getting to the camino from South Africa.

❓ Further Reading

This is a selection of our favourite books on the Camino de Santiago and about Spain in general.

General

David Gitlitz and Linda Kay Davidson's *The Pilgrimage Road to Santiago: The Complete Cultural Handbook* (St Martin's Griffin, 2000) is a hefty, detailed description of all the churches, monasteries and other monuments you'll pass along the camino. Nancy Frey's *Pilgrim Stories: On and Off the Road to Santiago* (University of California Press, 1998) looks at pilgrims and the pilgrimage in a refreshing, accessible and thoughtful way; its fascinating insights into pilgrims' motivations make it one of the best books on the camino.

Pilgrim Accounts

The Confraternity of St James publish *The Pilgrim's Guide: A 12th Century Guide for the Pilgrim to St James of Compostella* (1992), a translation of Aymeric Picaud's *Codex Calixtinus*, a fascinatingly misanthropic account that was one of the world's first travel guides. James Hall's translation of Domenico Laffi's seventeenth-century account is out-of-print and difficult to find, but Edwin Mullins' classic 1970s *The Pilgrimage to Santiago* has been re-issued by Interlink (2001).

Personal accounts of the camino almost inevitably reveal more about the writer than the walk itself. The most popular voyages of self-discovery are Shirley Maclaine's *The Camino: A Journey of the Spirit* (Pocket Books, 2001) and Paulo Coelho's *The Pilgrimage: A Contemporary Quest for Ancient Wisdom* (HarperCollins, 1995). The best of the more modern and less reverent accounts is Tim Moore's *Spanish Steps: One Man and His Ass on the Road to Santiago* (Random House, 2005).

Flora & Fauna

Once in Spain, naturalists should look out for *Camino de Santiago: Guía de la Naturaleza* (Edilesa, 1999), so well-organized and -illustrated that even non-Spanish speakers can use it. Both *Wild Spain* (Interlink, 2000) and *Where to Watch Birds in North & East Spain* (A&C Black, 1999) contain good general information, although there's not much specific detail on places along the camino.

People & Culture

For the best background on Spain, read John Hooper's book, *The New Spaniards* (Penguin, 1995), an erudite account of Spanish life and culture by a British journalist. Mark Kulanksy's *The Basque History*

of the World (Penguin, 2001) is an opinionated, eclectic read, while Raymond Carr has collected expert historians' accounts in *Spain: A History* (Oxford University Press, 2000).

Food & Drink

If you're itching to try some Spanish cooking before you leave, Penelope Casas' *Delicioso: The Regional Cooking of Spain* (Knopf, 1996) will have you drooling.

Literature

Manolo Rivas, who writes in his native *Galega*, has done more than any other modern writer to revive Galician literature; his works, including *The Carpenter's Pencil*, have been widely translated. Julián Rios' *Loves That Bind* (Vintage, 1999) is a prize-winning novel from an up-and-coming Galician writer. Born in Galicia but writing in Spanish, Nobel prize winner Camilo José Cela's works include *Boxwood* (New Directions, 2002) and *Mazurka for Two Dead Men* (New Directions, 1994).

Bernardo Atxaga is the Basque country's best modern writer; his most famous book is the dense, challenging *Obabakoak* (Vintage, 1994), but he's also written more accessible thrillers such as *The Lone Man* (Harvill Press, 1996).

Ernest Hemingway's *The Sun Also Rises* (Vintage, 2000) provides an interesting look at Pamplona and Navarra from the perspective of an American Spanophile.

? Language

Castellano (Spanish)

yes	*sí*	please	*por favor*
no	*no*	thank you	*gracias*
hello	*hola* [*h* is silent]	good morning	*buenos días*
goodbye	*adios*	good afternoon	*buenas tardes*

Do you speak English/Spanish?	*¿Habla inglés/castellano?*
I don't speak Spanish	*No hablo castellano*
I (don't) understand	*(No) entiendo*
How much?	*¿Cuanto cuesta?*
Where is ...?	*¿Donde está ...?*
I'd like ...	*Quería ...*
What time does the ... open?	*¿A que hora se abre ...?*
Are there any rooms?	*¿Hay habitaciones?*

Useful walking phrases

What will the weather be like today?	*¿Qué tiempo hay hoy?*
How do I get to ...?	*¿Cómo se va a ....?*
What is this village called?	*¿Cómo se llama este pueblo?*
How many kilometres to ...?	*¿Cuantos kilómetros hay hasta ...?*
Where does this road/path lead?	*¿A dónde se va esta carretera/este sendero?*

More useful walking phrases

I'm lost	*estoy perdido*	(it's) cold	(*hace*) *frío*
Let's go!	*¡Vamos!*	(I'm) hot	(*tengo*) *calor*
right	*derecha*	rain	*lluvia*
left	*izquierdo/a*	snow	*nieve*
straight on	*todo recto*	cloudy	*nubloso*
near	*cerca*	fog	*niebla*
far	*lejos*	wind	*viento*
open	*abierto*	stormy	*tempestuoso*
closed	*cerrado*	sun	*sol*

Days, months & seasons

today	*hoy*	January	*enero*
tonight	*esta noche*	February	*febrero*
tomorrow	*mañana*	March	*marzo*
yesterday	*ayer*	April	*abril*
last night	*anoche*	May	*mayo*
weekend	*fin de semana*	June	*junio*
		July	*julio*
Monday	*lunes*	August	*agosto*
Tuesday	*martes*	September	*septiembre*
Wednesday	*miércoles*	October	*octubre*
Thursday	*jueves*	November	*noviembre*
Friday	*viernes*	December	*diciembre*
Saturday	*sábado*		
Sunday	*domingo*		
spring	*primavera*	autumn/fall	*otoño*
summer	*verano*	winter	*invierno*

Numbers

1	uno/una	17	diecisiete
2	dos	18	dieciocho
3	tres	19	diecinueve
4	cuatro	20	veinte
5	cinco	21	veinte y uno
6	seis	30	treinta
7	siete	40	cuarenta
8	ocho	50	cincuenta
9	nueve	60	sesenta
10	diez	70	setenta
11	once	80	ochenta
12	doce	90	noventa
13	trece	100	cien
14	catorce	200	doscientos
15	quince	300	trescientos
16	dieciséis	1000	mil

Euskara (Basque)

yes	bai	please	arren
no	ez	thank you	eskerrik
hello	kaixo	good morning	egun on
goodbye	agur	good afternoon	arratsalde on

Galega (Galician)

yes	sí	please	por favor
no	non	thank you	gracias
hello	hola	good morning	bos días
goodbye	adeus	good afternoon	boas tardes

Camino Log

Keep track of where you are, where you've been and where you're going.....

date	start/end	km	thoughts

date	start/end	km	thoughts

 **Index**

major places in **bold** type

Index

Map key

• • • • • •	camino	O	town or village
═══════	main road	♠	wood or forest
──────	other road	✗	windmill
++++++++++	railway	⚘	vineyard
── ── ──	international border	》	steep climb
──────	river	†	*cruceiro* (stone crucifix)
⬭	lake or sea	⊤	church
	map orientation	冊	picnic area
		∴	historical site

Text symbols

🅐	*albergue*	€	bank or cashpoint
🅗	hotel	ⓘ	*turismo* (tourist office)
✗	restaurant	🛒	shop
☕	café-bar	☎	phone number

Hotel prices

$	up to €35	$$$	€50–€75
$$	€35–€50	$$$$	more than €75